# A TREASURY OF LINCOLN QUOTATIONS

# A TREASURY OF
# Lincoln Quotations

### COMPILED AND EDITED BY
## FRED KERNER

*Lincoln, Abraham*

DOUBLEDAY & COMPANY, INC.
*Garden City, New York*
1965

Library of Congress Catalog Card Number 65-13990
Copyright © 1965 by Fred Kerner
All Rights Reserved
Printed in the United States of America
First Edition

*For*
*Jon, David and Diane*

# PREFACE

Little more can be said about Abraham Lincoln than has already been said. But his own words will continue to speak for him—often more eloquently than those used by many of his interpreters. His words, which bare the innermost thoughts and conflicts of the man, are all the more remarkable in that they frequently pertain as much today as they did more than a century ago.

And yet Lincoln, so often quoted, is just as often misquoted. If ever a book were to be written on the use of misquotation, the longest chapter might well be devoted to him. In large part, unfortunately, the misquotations arise from the fact that many of his speeches were impromptu, so that his exact words were lost to eternity.

Even contemporary newspaper accounts of his major speeches vary at times—due to the natural foibles and weaknesses of other humans whose task it was to record those words. Misquotation arises, too, through removal from context of a statement by quoters seeking to prove a particular point of view. Too often misquotations are repeated and the reiteration tends to give them credence.

It is a pity that such misinformation gets continued currency. But that pitfall is sometimes difficult to avoid, for the path of Lincolnalia is strewn with forgeries and frauds. And the list of apocrypha grows with each passing year, a fact that is especially pitiful since there is such a mother lode to be mined in Lincoln's authenticated works.

This book includes only the words of Lincoln, words proven

authentic by modern scholarship, words written in Lincoln's own hand, or spoken by him and verified by him in written versions, or newspaper accounts of speeches which Lincoln edited for his own safekeeping.

Many of the epigrams, which have delighted generations of Americans since Lincoln's death, but which have not been traced to the pen or tongue of the man himself, have not been included here. This, despite the fact that some of these "Lincoln clichés" have found such a permanence that they have been engraved over the portals of public buildings.

Research shows, however, that many of these statements were made by friends, or others, seeking to underscore a point of view. Sometimes they were even quotations used by Lincoln from the words of others and then casually attributed to him.

I have been most grateful for the incredibly massive amount of work done by the Abraham Lincoln Association and for the publishing acumen of Rutgers University Press, which brought into print the nine-volume result of that labor, *The Collected Works of Abraham Lincoln.*

Roy P. Basler, editor of *The Collected Works,* and his staff spent many years pinning down the authenticity of documents attributed to Lincoln, and they devoted a great deal of time to determining the correct wording where published variations existed.

The quotations herein are based on the language, where in dispute, determined by the editors of *The Collected Works.* But for the purposes of this treasury, spelling and typographical errors have been corrected, punctuation has been modernized (except in several childhood items, some verse and the two versions of the Gettysburg Address), and occasional word insertions have been made where original documents were damaged. The use of italics—to represent underlining—is exactly as written by Lincoln. Words printed all in capital letters follow style used in printed accounts of various speeches.

Occasionally a quotation comes from a fragment of a document. Where this occurs, and the same material can be found in a later, complete document, attribution is given to the fragment as being the earliest known use of material. Some fragments and other documents with no traceable dates are clearly indicated.

Approximate or probable dates are indicated with question marks. Here again, doubts were resolved by relying on the painstaking work of the editors of *The Collected Works*, who tracked down every possible piece of evidence to place each document as close to its date of writing as possible.

The index is designed to aid the user of this volume in finding quotations on the basis of a familiar phrase for which the topical arrangement of the book itself fails to provide a clue.

I am most grateful to Paul M. Angle, secretary and director of the Chicago Historical Society, for his encouragement and assistance. I also want to acknowledge the assistance of my patient wife, Sally, for aid in research, editing and compilation; Francesca Tillona for assistance in research; and Maureen Meloy for the giant task of typing the final manuscript. My thanks also are due to Kenneth McCormick, my editor, whose encouragement and patience were invaluable.

*Fred Kerner*

# INTRODUCTION

To many Americans, the words of Abraham Lincoln appear to have the force of law. The speaker who can support his argument with an apt quotation from the Civil War President has gone far toward proving his case. The unwary will not suspect that the quotation may have been ripped from its context, or that Lincoln said something quite different on another occasion, or that he may never have said or written what is attributed to him. Some of the best known "Lincoln" quotations are either perversions of genuine statements or sheer fabrications.

Nevertheless, the quoting of Lincoln will continue. That is why a book exemplifying the standards Mr. Kerner has set himself is so valuable. Many of the passages he has selected are long enough to prevent the distortion that often results from the use of only a phrase. He has covered the whole range of Lincoln's works so that the reader may see for himself how an attitude changed. (The entries under "Negroes" are a case in point.) Best of all, Mr. Kerner has excluded everything not fully authenticated. The user who looks in vain for the famous aphorism, "You can fool some of the people all of the time, and all of the people some of the time, but you cannot fool all of the people all of the time," need not accuse the compiler of incompetence: the fact is that Lincoln's authorship simply cannot be proved. And so with many others that pass current.

I know of no other book of Lincoln quotations so complete, so well arranged and indexed, and so rigorously honest.

*Paul M. Angle*
CHICAGO HISTORICAL SOCIETY

"[The Declaration of Independence] gave promise . . . that *all* should have an equal chance. . . . But if this country cannot be saved without giving up that principle—I was about to say I would rather be assassinated on this spot than to surrender it."

ABRAHAM LINCOLN
FEBRUARY 22, 1861

# A TREASURY OF LINCOLN QUOTATIONS

## Abolition

The promulgation of abolition doctrines tends rather to increase than to abate its [slavery's] evils.

PROTEST IN ILLINOIS LEGISLATURE
MARCH 3, 1837

Those who would shiver into fragments the Union of these states, tear to tatters its now venerated Constitution and even burn the last copy of the Bible rather than slavery should continue a single hour, together with all their more halting sympathizers, have received and are receiving their just execration.

EULOGY ON HENRY CLAY
JULY 6, 1852

I know of no word in the language that has been used so much as that one "abolitionist." Having no definition, it has no meaning unless taken as designating a person who is abolishing something.

SPEECH AT KALAMAZOO, MICHIGAN
AUGUST 27, 1856

I cannot but regard it as possible that the higher object of this contest may not be completely attained within the term of my natural life. But I cannot doubt either that it will come in due time. Even in this view, I am proud in my passing speck of time to contribute an humble mite to that glorious consummation which my own poor eyes may not last to see.

FRAGMENT ON THE STRUGGLE AGAINST SLAVERY
JULY 1858 (?)

## Absenteeism

Nothing is operating so ruinously upon us everywhere as "absenteeism." It positively will not do for me to grant leaves of absence in cases not sufficient to procure them under the regular rules.

LETTER TO THOMAS J. HENDERSON
DECEMBER 20, 1862

## Accusation

There is . . . one lesson in morals which he might, not without profit, learn from me—and that is never to add the weight of his character to a charge against a fellow man, without *knowing* it to be true. It is an established maxim in morals that he who makes an assertion without knowing whether it is true or false is guilty of falsehood; and the accidental truth of the assertion does not justify or excuse him.

LETTER TO ALLEN N. FORD
AUGUST 11, 1846

Ready we are all to cry out and ascribe motives when our own toes are pinched.

LETTER TO WILLIAM S. ROSECRANS
MARCH 17, 1863

## Advancement

There may sometimes be ungenerous attempts to keep a young man down; and they will succeed, too, if he allows his mind to be diverted from its true channel to brood over the attempted injury.

LETTER TO WILLIAM H. HERNDON
JULY 10, 1848

The way for a young man to rise is to improve himself every way he can, never suspecting that anybody wishes to hinder him.

LETTER TO WILLIAM H. HERNDON
JULY 10, 1848

## Aggressiveness

Your suggestions as to placing one's self on the offensive, rather than the *defensive*, are certainly correct.

LETTER TO JOHN MATHERS
JULY 20, 1858

## Alexander II of Russia

The great sovereign whose personal and hereditary friendship for the United States so much endears him to Americans.

LETTER TO SIMON CAMERON
JANUARY 11, 1862

## Aliens

Incidents occurring in the progress of our civil war have forced upon my attention the uncertain state of international questions, touching the rights of foreigners in this country and of United States citizens abroad. In regard to some governments these rights are at least partially defined by treaties. In no instance, however, is it expressly stipulated that in the event of civil war a foreigner residing in this country, within the lines of the insurgents, is to be exempted from the rule which classes him as a belligerent in whose behalf the government of his country cannot expect any privileges or immunities distinct from that character. I regret to say, however, that such claims have been put forward and, in some instances, in behalf of foreigners who have lived in the United States the better part of their lives. There is reason to believe that many persons born in foreign countries who have declared their intention to become citizens, or who have been fully naturalized, have evaded the military duty required of them by denying the fact. . . . There is also reason to believe that foreigners frequently become citizens of the United States for the sole purpose of evading duties imposed by the laws of their native countries, to which, on becoming naturalized here, they at once repair, and though never returning to the United States, they still claim the interposition of this government as citizens. . . . It might be advisable to fix a limit beyond which no citizen of the United States residing abroad may claim the interposition of his government.

ANNUAL MESSAGE TO CONGRESS
DECEMBER 8, 1863

The right of suffrage has often been assumed and exercised by aliens under pretenses of naturalization, which they have disavowed when drafted into the military service. I submit the expediency of such an amendment of the law as will make the fact of voting an estoppel against any plea of exemption from military service, or other civil obligation, on the ground of alienage.

ANNUAL MESSAGE TO CONGRESS
DECEMBER 8, 1863

## Altruism

I hold that while man exists it is his duty to improve not only his own condition, but to assist in ameliorating mankind; and therefore, without entering upon the details of the question, I will simply say that I am for those means which give the greatest good to the greatest number.

SPEECH AT CINCINNATI, OHIO
FEBRUARY 12, 1861

It is a cheering thought throughout life that something can be done to ameliorate the condition of those who have been subject to the hard usage of the world.

SPEECH ON COLONIZATION TO A DEPUTATION OF NEGROES
AUGUST 14, 1862

## Ambition

Every man is said to have his peculiar ambition. Whether it be true or not, I can say for one that I have no other so great as that of being truly esteemed of my fellow men by rendering myself worthy of their esteem.

COMMUNICATION TO THE PEOPLE OF
SANGAMON COUNTY, ILLINOIS
MARCH 9, 1832

If you should hear anyone say that Lincoln don't want to go to Congress, I wish you, as a personal friend of mine, would tell him you have reason to believe he is mistaken.

LETTER TO RICHARD S. THOMAS
FEBRUARY 14, 1843

In this troublesome world, we are never quite satisfied.

LETTER TO MARY TODD LINCOLN
APRIL 16, 1848

With *me*, the race of ambition has been a failure—a flat failure.

FRAGMENT ON STEPHEN A. DOUGLAS
DECEMBER 1856

I do not claim . . . to be unselfish, I do not pretend that I would not like to go to the United States Senate, I make no such hypocritical pretense.

SPEECH AT CHICAGO, ILLINOIS
JULY 10, 1858

Ambition has been ascribed to me. God knows how sincerely I prayed from the first that this field of ambition might not be opened. I claim no insensibility to political honors; but today could the Missouri restriction be restored and the whole slavery question replaced on the old ground of "toleration" by *necessity* where it exists, with unyielding hostility to the spread of it, on principle, I would in consideration gladly agree that Judge Douglas should never be *out* and I never *in* an office so long as we both or either live.

SPEECH AT SPRINGFIELD, ILLINOIS
OCTOBER 30, 1858

## America

We find ourselves in the peaceful possession of the fairest portion of the earth as regards extent of territory, fertility of soil, and salubrity of climate.

SPEECH TO YOUNG MEN'S LYCEUM,
SPRINGFIELD, ILLINOIS
JANUARY 27, 1838

All the armies of Europe, Asia and Africa combined, with all the treasure of the earth (our own excepted) in their military chest, with a Bonaparte for a commander, could not by force take a drink from the Ohio, or make a track on the Blue Ridge, in a trial of a thousand years.

SPEECH TO YOUNG MEN'S LYCEUM,
SPRINGFIELD, ILLINOIS
JANUARY 27, 1838

## American Revolution

Of our political revolution of '76, we all are justly proud. It has given us a degree of political freedom, far exceeding that of any other of the nations of the earth. In it the world has found a solution of that long-mooted problem as to the capability of man to govern himself. In it was the germ which has vegetated and still is to grow and expand into the universal liberty of mankind.

SPEECH TO WASHINGTON TEMPERANCE SOCIETY,
SPRINGFIELD, ILLINOIS
FEBRUARY 22, 1842

It breathed forth famine, swam in blood and rode on fire; and long, long after, the orphan's cry and the widow's wail continued to break the sad silence that ensued. These were the price, the inevitable price, paid for the blessings it bought.

SPEECH TO WASHINGTON TEMPERANCE SOCIETY,
SPRINGFIELD, ILLINOIS
FEBRUARY 22, 1842

## Amnesty

The restoration of the rebel states to the Union . . . must be sealed by general amnesty.

LETTER TO JAMES S. WADSWORTH
JANUARY 1864 (?)

## Ancestry

A direct descendant of one who was never a father.

MEMORANDUM ON APPOINTMENT OF EDGAR HARRIOTT*
FEBRUARY 17, 1863

## Anglo-American Relations

The people of the United States are kindred of the people of Great Britain. With all our distinct national interests, objects and

* Harriott claimed to be a "direct descendant" of John Randolph of Roanoke. Randolph had no descendants, however, having been impotent.

aspirations, we are conscious that our moral strength is largely derived from that relationship, and we think we do not deceive ourselves when we suppose that, by constantly cherishing cordial friendship and sympathy with the other branches of the family to which we belong, we impart to them not less strength than we derive from the same connection.

COMMUNICATION TO QUEEN VICTORIA
FEBRUARY 1, 1862

## Appointments

I dislike to make changes in office so long as they can be avoided. It multiplies my trouble and harassment immensely. I dislike to make two appointments when one will do.

LETTER TO WILLIAM JAYNE
FEBRUARY 26, 1864

You howled when [Benjamin F.] Butler went to New Orleans. Others howled when he was removed from that command. Somebody has been howling ever since at his assignment to military command. How long will it be before you, who are howling for his assignment to rule Kentucky, will be howling to me to remove him?

REPLY TO A DELEGATION OF KENTUCKIANS
JANUARY 2, 1865

## Argument

If a man will stand up and assert, and repeat, and re-assert that two and two do not make four, I know nothing in the power of argument that can stop him.

SPEECH AT PEORIA, ILLINOIS
OCTOBER 16, 1854

## Armed Neutrality

"Armed neutrality"—that is, an arming of those states to prevent the Union forces passing one way, or the disunion the other, over their soil— . . . would be disunion completed. . . . It would do for the disunionists that which, of all things, they most desire—feed them well and give them disunion without a struggle of their own. It recognizes no fidelity to the Constitution, no obligation to maintain the Union; and while very many who have favored it are doubtless loyal citizens, it is, nevertheless, treason in effect.

MESSAGE TO CONGRESS IN SPECIAL SESSION
JULY 4, 1861

## Army

Should the [Mexican] war go on, I think volunteers, with the right of electing their own officers, will be voted, but that no more regulars will be voted.

LETTER TO ANDREW MCCALLEN
FEBRUARY 4, 1848

If possible, take the six regiments now offered by Massachusetts. By their peculiar talent for taking care of themselves, they will give us less trouble in supplying them than will most other troops.

LETTER TO SIMON CAMERON
MAY 16, 1861

Say to them as has been said to some others—"Present your regiment in working form, and it will be received."

LETTER TO SIMON CAMERON
JUNE 11, 1861

For your kind expressions I am extremely grateful; but, on the other hand, I assure you that the nation is more indebted to you and such as you than to me. It is upon the brave hearts and strong arms of the people of the country that our reliance has been placed in support of free government and free institutions. For the part that you and the brave army of which you are a part have, under Providence, performed in this great struggle, I tender more thanks—greatest thanks that can possibly be due. . . . The thanks of the nation will follow you, and may God's blessing rest upon you now and forever. I hope that upon your return to your homes you will find your friends and loved ones well and happy.

> SPEECH TO THE TWELFTH INDIANA REGIMENT
> MAY 13, 1862

With us every soldier is a man of character and must be treated with more consideration than is customary in Europe.

> LETTER TO AGÉNOR-ETIENNE DE GASPARIN
> AUGUST 4, 1862

The army, like the nation, has become demoralized by the idea that the war is to be ended, the nation united, and peace restored by *strategy* and not by hard desperate fighting.

> MEMORANDUM ON FURLOUGHS
> NOVEMBER 1862

I much fear that the spirit, which you have aided to infuse into the army, of criticizing their commander and withholding confidence from him will now turn upon you. I shall assist you as far as I can to put it down. Neither you nor Napoleon, if he were alive again, could get any good out of an army while such a spirit prevails in it.

> LETTER TO JOSEPH HOOKER
> JANUARY 26, 1863

There is powerful temptation in money; and it was and is believed that nothing can prevent the paymasters speculating upon the soldiers, but a system by which each is to pay certain regiments so soon after he has notice that he is to pay those particular regiments that he has no time or opportunity to lay plans for speculating on them.

LETTER TO WILLIAM S. ROSECRANS
MARCH 17, 1863

We are contending with an enemy who, as I understand, drives every able-bodied man he can reach into his ranks very much as a butcher drives bullocks into a slaughter-pen. No time is wasted, no argument is used. This produces an army which will soon turn upon our now victorious soldiers already in the field, if they shall not be sustained by recruits as they should be. It produces an army with a rapidity not to be matched on our side, if we first waste time to re-experiment with the volunteer system.

LETTER TO HORATIO SEYMOUR
AUGUST 7, 1863

The strength of the rebellion is its military—its army.

LETTER TO JAMES C. CONKLING
AUGUST 26, 1863

Honor to the soldier and sailor everywhere, who bravely bears his country's cause. Honor also to the citizen who cares for his brother in the field and serves as he best can the same cause— honor to him, only less than to him who braves, for the common good, the storms of heaven and the storms of battle.

LETTER TO GEORGE OPDYKE AND OTHERS
DECEMBER 2, 1863

The pay of the army and navy have been met and fully satisfied. No considerable body of troops, it is believed, were ever more amply provided and more liberally and punctually paid; and it may be added that by no people were the burdens incident to a great war ever more cheerfully borne.

ANNUAL MESSAGE TO CONGRESS
DECEMBER 8, 1863

This extraordinary war in which we are engaged falls heavily upon all classes of people, but the most heavily upon the soldier. For it has been said, all that a man hath will he give for his life; and while all contribute of their substance the soldier puts his life at stake, and often yields it up in his country's cause. The highest merit, then, is due to the soldier.

REMARKS AT SANITARY FAIR, WASHINGTON, D.C.
MARCH 18, 1864

While it is melancholy to reflect that the war has filled so many graves and carried mourning to so many hearts, it is some relief to know that, compared with the surviving, the fallen have been so few. While corps and divisions and brigades and regiments have formed and fought and dwindled and gone out of existence, a great majority of the men who composed them are still living.

ANNUAL MESSAGE TO CONGRESS
DECEMBER 6, 1864

## Army Officers

He who does *something* at the head of one regiment will eclipse him who does *nothing* at the head of a hundred.

LETTER TO DAVID HUNTER
DECEMBER 31, 1861

I fully appreciate Gen. [John] Pope's splendid achievements with their invaluable results; but you must know that Major Generalships in the Regular Army are not as plenty as blackberries.

LETTER TO RICHARD YATES AND WILLIAM BUTLER
APRIL 10, 1862

In considering military merit, it seems to me the world has abundant evidence that I discard politics.

LETTER TO WILLIAM R. MORRISON
NOVEMBER 5, 1862

Many Republicans were appointed [to military commands]; and I mean no disparagement to them when I say that I do not see that their superiority of success has been so marked as to throw great suspicion on the good faith of those who are not Republicans.

LETTER TO CARL SCHURZ
NOVEMBER 10, 1862

I had been brought to fear that there was a class of officers in the army—not very inconsiderable in numbers—who were playing a game to not beat the enemy when they could, on some peculiar notion as to the proper way of saving the Union; and when you were proved to me, in your own presence, to have avowed yourself in favor of that "game" and did not attempt to controvert the proof, I dismissed you as an example and a warning to that supposed class. I bear you no ill will; and I regret that I could not have the example without wounding you personally.

LETTER TO JOHN J. KEY
NOVEMBER 24, 1862

I believe you to be a brave and skillful soldier, which, of course, I like. I also believe you do not mix politics with your profession, in which you are right. You have confidence in yourself, which is a valuable if not an indispensable quality. You are ambitious, which, within reasonable bounds, does good rather than harm.

LETTER TO JOSEPH HOOKER
JANUARY 26, 1863

Truth to speak, I do not appreciate this matter of rank on paper as you officers do. The world will not forget that you fought the battle of "Stone River," and it will never care a fig whether you rank Gen. Grant on paper or he so ranks you.

LETTER TO WILLIAM S. ROSECRANS
MARCH 17, 1863

My belief is that the permanent estimate of what a general does in the field is fixed by the "cloud of witnesses" who have been with him in the field; and that, relying on these, he who has the right needs not to fear.

LETTER TO JOHN A. MCCLERNAND
AUGUST 12, 1863

The Government cannot make men; and it is very easy, when a man has been given the highest commission, for him to turn on those who gave it and vilify them for not giving him a command according to his rank.

LETTER TO JAMES G. BLUNT
AUGUST 18, 1863

A lady called as the wife of John S. Struthers, a Captain . . . and urges that he may be allowed to resign. . . . I would be for accepting it on the general principle that we are rapidly getting an over-proportion of officers.

LETTER TO EDWIN M. STANTON
SEPTEMBER 17, 1863

The application filed by you in behalf of Samuel K. Boyd to be a Captain in the Regular Army has been received and referred to the War Department. You may not be aware that the application is directly in the teeth of the rule which we have felt constrained to adopt. Suppose your relative were now a First Lieut. in the Regular Army and the Captaincy directly above him were vacant, he would be entitled to be promoted to that vacancy. But suppose I should say to him, "Stand back, sir; I want that place for outsider." What would you and he think of it? And yet that is precisely the way you now ask me to treat some other Lieutenant. I suppose you have not thought of this.

LETTER TO WORTHINGTON G. SNETHEN
DECEMBER 16, 1863

Speaking in the North and fighting in the South at the same time are not possible.

LETTER TO CARL SCHURZ
MARCH 23, 1864

How difficult it is to find a *place* for an officer of . . . high rank when there is no place seeking *him.*

LETTER TO ANDREW JOHNSON
JULY 27, 1864

## Art

The picture (I know not the artistic designation) was duly and thankfully received. I consider it a very excellent one; though, truth to say, I am a very indifferent judge.

LETTER TO THOMAS DONEY
JULY 30, 1860

I cannot pretend to be a judge in such matters.

LETTER TO JOHN ROGERS
JUNE 13, 1864

Your picture [of me] is, in the main, very good. From a line across immediately above the eyebrows downward, it appears to me perfect. Above such line I think it is not so good—that is, while it gives perhaps a better forehead, it is not quite true to the original. If you were present I could tell you wherein, but I cannot well do so on paper.

LETTER TO ELIJAH C. MIDDLETON
DECEMBER 30, 1864

## Assassination

Something in that Declaration [of Independence] giving liberty . . . gave promise that in due time the weights should be lifted from the shoulders of all men, and that *all* should have an equal chance. . . . Can this country be saved on that basis? If it can, I will consider myself one of the happiest men in the world if I can help to save it. If it can't be saved upon that principle, it will be truly awful. But if this country cannot be saved without giving up that principle—I was about to say I would rather be assassinated on this spot than to surrender it.

SPEECH AT PHILADELPHIA, PENNSYLVANIA
FEBRUARY 22, 1861

## Autographs

If you collect the signatures of all persons who are no less distinguished than I, you will have a very undistinguishing mass of names.

LETTER TO C. U. SCHLATER
JANUARY 5, 1849

It is represented to me that my autograph appended to this note may somewhat augment, through the means you are so patriotically employing, the contributions for the benefit of our gallant and suffering soldiers, and for such an object I am glad to give it.

LETTER TO THE NEW ENGLAND KITCHEN, BROOKLYN
SANITARY FAIR, BROOKLYN, NEW YORK
MARCH 2, 1864

## Banking

We do not pretend that a National Bank can establish and maintain a sound and uniform state of currency in the country in *spite* of the National Government; but we do say that it has established and maintained such a currency, and can do so again, by the *aid* of that Government; and we further say that no duty is more imperative on that Government than the duty it owes the people of furnishing them a sound and uniform currency.

SPEECH ON THE SUB-TREASURY
DECEMBER 26, 1839

## Betrayal

I am willing to pledge myself in black and white to cut my own throat from ear to ear if, when I meet you, you shall *seriously* say that you believe me capable of betraying my friends for any price.

LETTER TO WILLIAM BUTLER
JANUARY 26, 1839

## Bible

The Bible says somewhere that we are desperately selfish. I think we would have discovered that fact without the Bible.

SEVENTH DEBATE WITH STEPHEN A. DOUGLAS,
ALTON, ILLINOIS
OCTOBER 15, 1858

All the good the Saviour gave to the world was communicated through this book. But for it we could not know right from wrong. All things most desirable for man's welfare, here and hereafter, are to be found portrayed in it.

REPLY TO LOYAL NEGROES OF BALTIMORE
UPON PRESENTATION OF A BIBLE
SEPTEMBER 7, 1864

## Biography

As a matter, *wholly my own*, I would authorize no biography without *time* and *opportunity* to carefully examine and consider every word of it.

LETTER TO SAMUEL GALLOWAY
JUNE 19, 1860

## Bombast

As bombastic and hollow as Napoleon's bulletins sent back from his campaign in Russia.

LETTER TO GUSTAVE P. KOERNER
JULY 15, 1858


## Brotherhood

Let us neither express, nor cherish, any harsh feeling towards any citizen who, by his vote, has differed with us. Let us at all times remember that all Americans are brothers of a common country and should dwell together in the bonds of fraternal feeling.

REMARKS AT SPRINGFIELD, ILLINOIS
NOVEMBER 20, 1860


## Burns, Robert

I cannot frame a toast to Burns. I can say nothing worthy of his generous heart and transcendent genius.

MEMORANDUM ON ROBERT BURNS
JANUARY 25, 1865


## Cabinet

The West is not only entitled to, but is in need of, one member of the cabinet.

LETTER TO WILLIAM SCHOULER
FEBRUARY 2, 1849

In the formation of my cabinet, I shall aim as nearly as possible at perfection. Any man whom I may appoint to such a position must be, as far as possible, like Caesar's wife, pure and above suspicion, of unblemished reputation and undoubted integrity.

REMARKS TO A PENNSYLVANIA DELEGATION
JANUARY 24, 1861

I must myself be the judge how long to retain in and when to remove any of you from his position. It would greatly pain me to discover any of you endeavoring to procure another's removal or in any way to prejudice him before the public. Such endeavor would be a wrong to me; and much worse, a wrong to the country. My wish is that on this subject no remark be made, nor question asked, by any of you, here or elsewhere, now or hereafter.

MEMORANDUM READ TO CABINET
JULY 1864 (?)

In cabinet, my view is that in questions affecting the whole country there should be full and frequent consultations and that nothing should be done particularly affecting any department without consultation with the head of that department.

MEMORANDUM ON INTERVIEW WITH
STEPHEN P. FESSENDEN
JULY 4, 1864

## Capitalism

That men who are industrious and sober and honest in the pursuit of their own interests should after a while accumulate capital, and after that should be allowed to enjoy it in peace, and also if they should choose when they have accumulated it to use it to save themselves from actual labor and hire other people to labor for them is right. In doing so they do not wrong the man they employ, for they find men who have not of their own land to work upon, or shops to work in, and who are bene-

fited by working for others, hired laborers, receiving their capital
for it. Thus a few men that own capital hire a few others, and
these establish the relation of capital and labor rightfully.

SPEECH AT CINCINNATI, OHIO
SEPTEMBER 17, 1859

I take it that it is best for all to leave each man free to acquire
property as fast as he can. Some will get wealthy. I don't believe
in a law to prevent a man from getting rich; it would do more
harm than good. . . . I want every man to have the chance—
and I believe a black man is entitled to it—in which he *can*
better his condition; when he may look forward and hope to be
a hired laborer this year and the next, work for himself after-
ward, and finally to hire men to work for him!

SPEECH AT NEW HAVEN, CONNECTICUT
MARCH 6, 1860

That some should be rich shows that others may become rich,
and hence is just encouragement to industry and enterprise. Let
not him who is houseless pull down the house of another; but let
him labor diligently and build one for himself, thus by example
assuring that his own shall be safe from violence when built.

REPLY TO NEW YORK WORKINGMEN'S DEMOCRATIC
REPUBLICAN ASSOCIATION
MARCH 21, 1864

## Carelessness

When I received the letter I put it in my old hat and, buying
a new one the next day, the old one was set aside; and so, the letter lost sight of for a time.

LETTER TO RICHARD S. THOMAS
JUNE 27, 1850

## Caution

These things *look* like the cautious *patting* and *petting* a spirited horse, preparatory to mounting him, and when it is dreaded that he may give the rider a fall.

"A HOUSE DIVIDED" SPEECH, SPRINGFIELD, ILLINOIS
JUNE 16, 1858

Make haste slowly.

LETTER TO FRANCIS H. PEIRPOINT
MARCH 20, 1862

## Censorship

The Secretary of War, you know, holds a pretty tight rein on the press so that they shall not tell more than they ought to, and I'm afraid that if I blab too much he might draw a tight rein on me.

REMARKS AT JERSEY CITY, NEW JERSEY
JUNE 24, 1862

## Change

He may yet be taught to sing a different song.

REPLY TO JAMES ADAMS
OCTOBER 18, 1837

A man may rightfully be *wiser today* than he was *yesterday*— . . . he may rightfully *change* when he finds himself wrong. But can we, for that reason, run ahead and *infer* that he *will* make any particular change of which he, himself, has given no intimation? Can we *safely* base *our* action upon any such vague inference?

"A HOUSE DIVIDED" SPEECH, SPRINGFIELD, ILLINOIS
JUNE 16, 1858

## Children

The little rare-ripe sort that are smarter at about five than ever after.

LETTER TO JOSHUA F. SPEED
OCTOBER 22, 1846

## Churches

It seems . . . that there is danger of the different religious denominations having some collision in their ministering among the colored people. . . . I should think each church should minister according to its own rules, without interference by others differing from them; and if there still be difficulties about *places* of worship, a real Christian charity and forbearance on the part of all might obviate it.

LETTER TO EDWIN M. STANTON
SEPTEMBER 29, 1862

The U. S. government must not . . . undertake to run the churches. When an individual, in a church or out of it, becomes dangerous to the public interest, he must be checked; but let the churches as such take care of themselves. It will not do for the U.S. to appoint trustees, supervisors, or other agents for the churches.

LETTER TO SAMUEL R. CURTIS
JANUARY 2, 1863

I have written before, and now repeat, the United States Government must not undertake to run the churches. When an individual in a church or out of it becomes dangerous to the public interest he must be checked, but the churches as such must take care of themselves. It will not do for the United States to appoint trustees, supervisors, or other agents for the churches. I add if the military have military need of the church building, let them keep it; otherwise let them get out of it and leave it and its owners alone except for causes that justify the arrest of anyone.

MEMORANDUM ON CHURCHES
MARCH 4, 1864

If the building is needed for military purposes, take it; if it is not so needed, let its church people have it, dealing with any disloyal people among them as you deal with other disloyal people.

ENDORSEMENT CONCERNING CHURCHES IN NEW ORLEANS
MARCH 15, 1864

Nobly sustained as the government has been by all the churches, I would utter nothing which might, in the least, appear invidious against any. Yet, without this, it may fairly be said that the Methodist Episcopal Church, not less devoted than the best, is, by its greater numbers, the most important of all. It is no fault in others that the Methodist Church sends more soldiers to the field, more nurses to the hospital, and more prayers to Heaven than any. God bless the Methodist Church—bless all the churches —and blessed be God, Who, in this our great trial, giveth us the churches.

RESPONSE TO METHODISTS
MAY 18, 1864

## Civil Disorder

So far as practicable you will, by means of your military force, expel guerrillas, marauders and murderers, and all who are known to harbor, aid or abet them. But, in like manner, you will repress assumptions of unauthorized individuals to perform the same service; because under pretense of doing this they become ma-

rauders and murderers themselves. To now restore peace, let the
military obey orders and those not of the military leave each other
alone.

LETTER TO JOHN M. SCHOFIELD
OCTOBER 1, 1863

Destruction of property and life [in Missouri] is rampant
everywhere. Is not the cure for this within easy reach of the people themselves? It cannot be that every man, not naturally a robber or cutthroat, would gladly put an end to this state of things.
. . . Each leaving all others alone solves the problem. And surely
each would do this but for his apprehension that others will not
leave him alone.

LETTER TO THOMAS C. FLETCHER
FEBRUARY 20, 1865

## Civil Rights

By the Constitution, each state . . . has a number of Representatives, in proportion to the number of its people. . . . But in
ascertaining the number of people for this purpose, five slaves
are counted as being equal to three whites. The slaves do not
vote; they are only counted and so used as to swell the influence
of the white people's votes.

SPEECH AT PEORIA, ILLINOIS
OCTOBER 16, 1854

Now my opinion is that the different states have the power to
make a Negro a citizen under the Constitution of the United
States if they choose. The Dred Scott decision decides that they
have not that power.

FOURTH DEBATE WITH STEPHEN A. DOUGLAS,
CHARLESTON, ILLINOIS
SEPTEMBER 18, 1858

I do not understand there is any place where an alteration of
the social and political relations of the Negro and white man can

be made except in the state legislature—not in the Congress of the United States.

FOURTH DEBATE WITH STEPHEN A. DOUGLAS,
CHARLESTON, ILLINOIS
SEPTEMBER 18, 1858

Understanding the spirit of our institutions to aim at the *elevation* of men, I am opposed to whatever tends to *degrade* them. I have some little notoriety for commiserating the oppressed condition of the Negro; and I should be strangely inconsistent if I could favor any project for curtailing the existing rights of *white men*, even though born in different lands and speaking different languages from myself.

LETTER TO THEODORE CANISIUS
MAY 17, 1859

Prior to my installation here it had been inculcated that any state had a lawful right to secede from the national Union; and that it would be expedient to exercise the right whenever the devotees of the doctrine should fail to elect a President to their own liking. I was elected contrary to their liking; and accordingly, so far as it was legally possible, they had taken seven states out of the Union. . . . The rebellion thus begun soon ran into the present civil war; and, in certain respects, it began on very unequal terms between the parties. The insurgents had been preparing for it more than thirty years, while the government had taken no steps to resist them. The former had carefully considered all the means which could be turned to their account. It undoubtedly was a well-pondered reliance with them that in their own unrestricted effort to destroy Union, Constitution and law, all together, the government would in great degree be restrained by the same Constitution and law from arresting their progress. Their sympathizers pervaded all departments of the government and nearly all communities of people. From this material, under cover of "Liberty of speech," "Liberty of the press" and "*Habeas corpus*," they hoped to keep on foot amongst us a most efficient corps of spies, informers, suppliers, and aiders and abettors of their cause. . . . They knew that in times such as they were inaugurating, by the Constitution itself, the *"Habeas corpus"* might be suspended; but they also knew they had friends who would make a question as to *who* was to suspend it; meanwhile their spies and others might remain at large to help on their cause. Or if, as has happened, the executive should suspend the writ without ruinous waste of time, instances of arresting innocent persons might occur, as are always likely to occur in such cases; and then a clamor could be raised in regard to this, which might be, at least, of some service to the insurgent cause. . . . Yet, thoroughly imbued with a reverence for the guaranteed rights of individuals, I was slow to adopt the strong measures which by degrees I have been forced to regard as being within the exceptions of the Constitution and as indispensable to the public safety. Nothing is better known to history than that courts of justice are utterly incompetent to such cases. Civil courts are organized chiefly for trials of individuals, or, at most, a few individuals acting in concert; and this in quiet times and on charges of crimes well defined in the law. Even in times of peace, bands of horse thieves and robbers frequently grow too numerous and powerful for the ordinary courts of justice. But what comparison, in numbers, have such bands ever borne to the insurgent sympathizers even in many of the loyal states? Again, a jury too frequently have at least one member more ready to hang the panel than to hang the traitor.

LETTER TO ERASTUS CORNING AND OTHERS
JUNE 12, 1863

## Civil War

If this fight should begin, is it likely to take a very peaceful, Union-saving turn? Will not the first drop of blood so shed be the real knell of the Union?

SPEECH AT PEORIA, ILLINOIS
OCTOBER 16, 1854

There is no peaceful extinction of slavery in prospect for us.

LETTER TO GEORGE ROBERTSON
AUGUST 15, 1855

It is a consoling circumstance that when we look out there is nothing that really hurts anybody. We entertain different views on political questions, but nobody is suffering anything. This is a most consoling circumstance, and from it we may conclude that all we want is time, patience and a reliance on that God Who has never forsaken this people.

SPEECH TO OHIO LEGISLATURE, COLUMBUS, OHIO
FEBRUARY 13, 1861

While I have been proud to see today the finest military array, I think, that I have ever seen, allow me to say in regard to those men that they give hope of what may be done when war is inevitable. But, at the same time, allow me to express the hope that in the shedding of blood their services may never be needed, especially in the shedding of fraternal blood. It shall be my endeavor to preserve the peace of this country so far as it can possibly be done consistently with the maintenance of the institutions of the country. With my consent, or without my great displeasure, this country shall never witness the shedding of one drop of blood in fraternal strife.

REPLY TO GOVERNOR ANDREW J. CURTIN,
HARRISBURG, PENNSYLVANIA
FEBRUARY 22, 1861

There needs to be no bloodshed or violence, and there shall be none unless it be forced upon the national authority. . . . There will be no invasion—no using of force against or among the people anywhere.

FIRST INAUGURAL ADDRESS
MARCH 4, 1861

Suppose you go to war, you cannot fight always; and when, after much loss on both sides and no gain on either, you cease fighting, the identical questions as to terms of intercourse are again upon you.

FIRST INAUGURAL ADDRESS
MARCH 4, 1861

In *your* hands, my dissatisfied fellow countrymen, and not in *mine*, is the momentous issue of civil war. The government will not assail *you*. You can have no conflict without being yourselves the aggressors. *You* have no oath registered in Heaven to destroy the government, while *I* shall have the most solemn one to "preserve, protect, and defend" it. . . . We must not be enemies. Though passion may have strained, it must not break our bonds of affection. The mystic chords of memory, stretching from every battlefield and patriot grave to every living heart and hearthstone all over this broad land, will yet swell the chorus of the Union when again touched, as surely they will be, by the better angels of our nature.

FIRST INAUGURAL ADDRESS
MARCH 4, 1861

I have desired as sincerely as any man—I sometimes think more than any other man—that our present difficulties might be settled without the shedding of blood. I will not say that all hope is gone. But if the alternative is presented, whether the Union is to be broken into fragments and the liberties of the people lost, or blood be shed, you will probably make the choice, with which I shall not be dissatisfied.

REPLY TO THE FRONTIER GUARD
APRIL 26, 1861

You have kindly adverted to the trial through which this Republic is now passing. It is one of deep import. It involves the question whether a representative republic, extended and aggrandized so much as to be safe against foreign enemies, can save itself from the dangers of domestic faction. I have faith in a good result.

COMMUNICATION TO THE REGENT CAPTAINS
OF THE REPUBLIC OF SAN MARINO
MAY 7, 1861

I recommend that you give the legal means for making this contest a short and a decisive one.

FRAGMENT OF DRAFT OF MESSAGE TO CONGRESS
JULY 4, 1861

It is my duty, as I conceive, to suppress an insurrection existing within the United States. I wish to do this with the least possible disturbance or annoyance to well-disposed people anywhere. So far I have not sent an armed force into Kentucky, nor have I any present purpose to do so. I sincerely desire that no necessity for it may be presented, but I mean to say nothing which shall hereafter embarrass me in the performance of what may seem to be my duty.

COMMUNICATION TO SIMON B. BUCKNER
JULY 10, 1861

A nation which endures factious domestic division is exposed to disrespect abroad; and one party, if not both, is sure, sooner or later, to invoke foreign intervention.

ANNUAL MESSAGE TO CONGRESS
DECEMBER 3, 1861

Have you noticed the facts that less than one half-day's cost of this war would pay for all the slaves in Delaware, at four hundred dollars per head?—that eighty-seven days' cost of this war would pay for all in Delaware, Maryland, District of Columbia, Kentucky and Missouri at the same price? Were those states to take the step, do you doubt that it would shorten the war more than eighty-seven days, and thus be an actual saving of expense.

LETTER TO HENRY J. RAYMOND
MARCH 9, 1862

An important crisis which involves, in my judgment, not only the civil and religious liberties of our own dear land, but in a large degree the civil and religious liberties of mankind in many countries and through many ages.

RESPONSE TO EVANGELICAL LUTHERANS
MAY 13, 1862

I expect to maintain this contest until successful, or till I die, or am conquered, or my term expires, or Congress or the country forsakes me.

LETTER TO WILLIAM H. SEWARD
JUNE 28, 1862

If we could somehow get a vote of the people of Tennessee and have it result properly it would be worth more to us than a battle gained.

LETTER TO GOVERNOR ANDREW JOHNSON OF TENNESSEE
JULY 3, 1862

The people of Louisiana—all intelligent people everywhere—know full well that I never had a wish to touch the foundations of their society or any right of theirs. With perfect knowledge of this, they forced a necessity upon me to send armies among them; and it is their own fault, not mine, that they are annoyed by the presence of General [John S.] Phelps. They also know the remedy—know how to be cured of General Phelps. Remove the necessity of his presence. And might it not be well for them to consider whether they have not already had *time* enough to do this? . . . If they will not do this, should they not receive harder blows rather than lighter ones? . . . I am a patient man—always willing to forgive on the Christian terms of repentance; and also to give ample *time* for repentance. Still I must save this government if possible. What I *cannot* do, of course, I *will* not do; but it may as well be understood, once for all, that I shall not surrender this game leaving any available card unplayed.

LETTER TO REVERDY JOHNSON
JULY 26, 1862

That the Secession Ordinance of Louisiana was adopted against the will of a majority of the people . . . is probably true; and in that fact may be found some instruction. . . . The paralysis—the dead palsy—of the government in this whole struggle is that this class of men will do nothing for the government, nothing for themselves, except demanding that the government shall not strike its open enemies, lest they be struck by accident! . . . They are to touch neither a sail nor a pump, but to be merely passengers—deadheads at that—to be carried snug and dry throughout the storm and safely landed right side up. Nay, more; even a mutineer is to go untouched lest these sacred passengers receive an accidental wound. . . . The people of Louisiana who

wish protection to person and property have but to reach forth
their hands and take it. . . . . If they will not do this, if they prefer to hazard all for the sake of destroying the government, it is
for them to consider whether it is probable I will surrender the
government to save them from losing all. . . . What would you
do in my position? Would you drop the war where it is? Or,
would you prosecute it in future with elder-stalk squirts charged
with rose water?

LETTER TO CUTHBERT BULLITT
JULY 28, 1863

If I had had my way, this war would never have been commenced; if I had been allowed my way this war would have been
ended before this.

REPLY TO ELIZA P. GURNEY
OCTOBER 26, 1862

Our national strife springs not from our permanent part, not
from the land we inhabit, not from our national homestead. . . .
Our strife pertains to ourselves—to the passing generations of
men; and it can, without convulsion, be hushed forever with the
passing of one generation.

ANNUAL MESSAGE TO CONGRESS
DECEMBER 1, 1862

The dogmas of the quiet past are inadequate to the stormy
present. The occasion is piled high with difficulty, and we must
rise with the occasion. As our case is new, so we must think anew
and act anew. We must disenthrall ourselves, and then we shall
save our country.

ANNUAL MESSAGE TO CONGRESS
DECEMBER 1, 1862

Insomuch as . . . nations like individuals are subjected to
punishments and chastisements in this world, may we not justly
fear that the awful calamity of civil war which now desolates the
land may be but a punishment inflicted upon us for our pre-

sumptuous sins, to the needful end of our national reformation as a whole people?

PROCLAMATION APPOINTING A NATIONAL FAST DAY
MARCH 30, 1863

From the beginning I saw that the issues of our great struggle depended on the Divine interposition and favor. If we had that, all would be well. The proportions of this rebellion were not for a long time understood. I saw that it involved the greatest difficulties, and would call forth all the powers of the whole country. The end is not yet.

REPLY TO MEMBERS OF THE PRESBYTERIAN
GENERAL ASSEMBLY
JUNE 2, 1863

This war is an appeal . . . from the ballot to the sword; and a great object with me has been to teach the futility of such appeal —to teach that there can be no successful appeal from a fair election, but to the next election.

FRAGMENT
AUGUST 1863 (?)

In the autumn of 1861, certain persons in armed rebellion against the United States . . . laid down their arms upon certain terms then proposed to them by Genl. [John A.] Dix. . . . It is now said that these persons, or some of them, are about to be forced into the military lines of the existing rebellion unless they will take an oath prescribed to them since, and not included in, Genl. Dix's proclamation. . . . Now, my judgment is that no one of these men should be forced from his home who has not broken faith with the government, according to the terms fixed by Gen. Dix and these men. It is bad faith in the government to force new terms upon such as have kept faith with it.

LETTER TO EDWIN M. STANTON
AUGUST 21, 1863

There are those who are dissatisfied with me. To such I would say: You desire peace; and you blame me that we do not have it. But how can we attain it? There are but three conceivable ways. First, to suppress the rebellion by force of arms. This, I am trying to do. Are you for it? If you are, so far we are agreed. If you are not for it, a second way is to give up the Union. I am against this. Are you for it? . . . If you are not for *force*, nor yet for *dissolution*, there only remains some imaginable *compromise*. I do not believe any compromise, embracing the maintenance of the Union, is now possible. . . . The strength of the rebellion is its military—its army. That army dominates all the country, and all the people, within its range. . . . No paper compromise to which the controllers of Lee's army are not agreed can at all affect that army. In an effort at such compromise we should waste time, which the enemy would improve to our disadvantage; and that would be all. A compromise, to be effective, must be made either with those who control the rebel army, or with the people first liberated from the domination of that army by the success of our own army.

LETTER TO JAMES C. CONKLING
AUGUST 26, 1863

It is easy to see that under the sharp discipline of civil war, the nation is beginning a new life.

ANNUAL MESSAGE TO CONGRESS
DECEMBER 8, 1863

By no people were the burdens incident to a great war ever more cheerfully borne.

ANNUAL MESSAGE TO CONGRESS
DECEMBER 8, 1863

War, at the best, is terrible; and this war of ours, in its magnitude and in its duration, is one of the most terrible.

SPEECH AT GREAT CENTRAL SANITARY FAIR,
PHILADELPHIA, PENNSYLVANIA
JUNE 16, 1864

When is the war to end? Surely I feel as deep an interest in this question is any other can, but I do not wish to name a day, or month, or a year when it is to end. I do not wish to run any risk of seeing the time come without our being ready for the end; and for fear of disappointment because the time had come and not the end. We accepted this war for an object, a worthy object, and the war will end when that object is attained. Under God, I hope it never will until that time. . . .

SPEECH AT GREAT CENTRAL SANITARY FAIR,
PHILADELPHIA, PENNSYLVANIA
JUNE 16, 1864

The preservation of our Union was *not* the sole avowed object for which the war was commenced. It was commenced for precisely the reverse object—*to destroy our Union.*

LETTER TO ISAAC M. SCHERMERHORN
SEPTEMBER 12, 1864

On the occasion corresponding to this four years ago, all thoughts were anxiously directed to an impending civil war. All dreaded it—all sought to avert it. While the inaugural address was being delivered from this place, devoted altogether to *saving* the Union without war, insurgent agents were in the city seeking to *destroy* it without war—seeking to dissolve the Union, and divide effects by negotiation. Both parties deprecated war; but one of them would *make* war rather than let the nation survive; and the other would *accept* war rather than let it perish. And the war came. . . . Neither party expected for the war the magnitude, or the duration, which it has already attained. Neither anticipated that the *cause* of the conflict might cease with, or even before, the conflict itself should cease. Each looked for an easier triumph and a result less fundamental and astounding. Both read the same Bible and pray to the same God; and each invokes His aid against the other. . . . The prayers of both could not be answered; that of neither has been answered fully. . . . Fondly do we hope— fervently do we pray—that this mighty scourge of war may speedily pass away. Yet, if God wills that it continue until all the wealth piled by the bondman's two hundred and fifty years of unrequited toil shall be sunk, and until every drop of blood drawn with the lash shall be paid by another drawn with the sword, as was said three thousand years ago, so still it must be said, "The judgments of the Lord are true and righteous altogether." With malice toward none, with charity for all, with firmness in the right as God gives us to see the right, let us strive on to finish the work we are in; to bind up the nation's wounds; to care for him who shall have borne the battle, and for his widow and his orphan—to do all which may achieve and cherish a just and a lasting peace, among ourselves and with all nations.

SECOND INAUGURAL ADDRESS
MARCH 4, 1865

## Civil War: Conduct

You would have me break my oath and surrender the Government without a blow. There is no Washington in that—no Jackson in that—no manhood or honor in that. I have no desire to invade the South, but I must have troops to defend this Capital. Geographically it lies surrounded by the soil of Maryland. . . . Our men are not moles, and can't dig under the earth; they are not birds, and can't fly through the air. There is no way but to march them across. . . . Keep your rowdies in Baltimore and there will be no bloodshed. Go home and tell your people that if they will not attack us, we will not attack them; but if they do attack us, we will return it, and that severely.

REPLY TO A BALTIMORE COMMITTEE
APRIL 22, 1861

You do not receive arms from us as fast as you need them, but it is because we have not near enough to meet all pressing demands; and we are obliged to share around what we have, sending the larger share to the points which appear to need them most. We have great hope that our own supply will be ample before long, so that you and all others can have as many as you need.

LETTER TO GOVERNOR OLIVER P. MORTON OF INDIANA
SEPTEMBER 29, 1861

I state my general idea of this war to be that we have the *greater* numbers and the enemy has the *greater* facility of concentrating forces upon points of collision; that we must fail unless we can find some way of making *our* advantage an overmatch for *his*; and that this can only be done by menacing him with superior forces at *different* points at the *same* time; so that we can safely attack one, or both, if he makes no change; and if he *weakens* one to *strengthen* the other, forbear to attack the strengthened one, but seize and hold the weakened one.

LETTER TO DON C. BUELL
JANUARY 13, 1862

You are probably engaged with the enemy. I suppose he made the attack. Stand well on your guard—hold all your ground, or yield any only inch by inch and in good order.

LETTER TO GEORGE B. MCCLELLAN
JUNE 1, 1862

I would come and see you, were it not that I fear my presence might divert you and the army from more important matters.

DISPATCH TO GEORGE B. MCCLELLAN
JUNE 15, 1862

I do not say you have not done all you could. I presume you met unexpected difficulties; and I beg you to believe that as surely as you have done your best, so have I.

DISPATCH TO JOHN C. FRÉMONT
JUNE 16, 1862

I would be very glad to talk with you, but you cannot leave your camp, and I cannot well leave here.

DISPATCH TO GEORGE B. MCCLELLAN
JUNE 21, 1862

Talking of where the responsibility will belong pains me very much. I give you all I can and act on the presumption that you will do the best you can with what you have while you continue, ungenerously I think, to assume that I could give you more if I would. I have omitted and shall omit no opportunity to send you reinforcements whenever I possibly can.

DISPATCH TO GEORGE B. MCCLELLAN
JUNE 26, 1862

I have not said you were ungenerous for saying you needed reinforcement. I thought you were ungenerous in assuming that I did not send them as fast as I could. I feel any misfortune to you and your army quite as keenly as you feel it yourself.

DISPATCH TO GEORGE B. MCCLELLAN
JUNE 28, 1862

If you are not strong enough to face the enemy you must find a place of security and wait, rest, and repair. Maintain your ground if you can, but save the army at all events. . . . We still have strength enough in the country and will bring it out.

LETTER TO GEORGE B. MCCLELLAN
JULY 1, 1862

I should not want the half of three hundred thousand new troops, if I could have them *now*. If I had fifty thousand additional troops here *now*, I believe I could substantially close the war in two weeks. But *time* is *everything;* and if I get fifty thousand new men in a month, I shall have lost twenty thousand old ones during the same month—having gained only thirty thousand—with the difference between old and new troops still against me. The quicker you send, the fewer you will have to send. *Time* is everything.

LETTER TO E. D. MORGAN, GOVERNOR OF NEW YORK,
AND ALL UNION GOVERNORS
JULY 3, 1862

If the military commanders in the field cannot be successful, not only the Secretary of War but myself, for the time being the master of both, cannot be but failures.

ADDRESS AT WASHINGTON
AUGUST 6, 1862

You remember my speaking to you of what I called your overcautiousness. Are you not overcautious when you assume that you cannot do what the enemy is constantly doing?

> LETTER TO GEORGE B. MCCLELLAN
> OCTOBER 13, 1862

I have just read your dispatch about sore-tongued and fatigued horses. Will you pardon me for asking what the horses of your army have done since the battle of Antietam that fatigue anything?

> DISPATCH TO GEORGE B. MCCLELLAN
> OCTOBER 25, 1862

This expanding and piling up of *impedimenta* has been, so far, almost our ruin; and will be our final ruin if it is not abandoned.

> LETTER TO NATHANIEL P. BANKS
> NOVEMBER 22, 1862

I fear we shall at last find out that the difficulty is in our case, rather than in particular generals.

> LETTER TO CARL SCHURZ
> NOVEMBER 24, 1862

And now, beware of rashness. Beware of rashness, but with energy and sleepless vigilance go forward and give us victories.

> LETTER TO JOSEPH HOOKER
> JANUARY 26, 1863

In no other way does the enemy give us so much trouble, at so little expense to himself, as by the *raids* of rapidly moving small bodies of troops (largely, if not wholly, mounted) harassing and discouraging loyal residents, supplying themselves with provisions, clothing, horses and the like, surprising and capturing small detachments of our forces, and breaking our communications. And this will increase just in proportion as his larger armies shall weaken, and wane. Nor can these raids be successfully met by even larger forces of our own, of the same kind, acting merely on the *defensive*. I think we should organize proper forces and make *counterraids*. We should not capture so much of supplies from them as they have done from us; but it would trouble them more to repair railroads and bridges than it does us.

LETTER TO WILLIAM S. ROSECRANS<br>FEBRUARY 17, 1863

We should continually harass and menace him [the enemy], so that he shall have no leisure, nor safety in sending away detachments. If he weakens himself, then pitch into him.

MEMORANDUM ON JOSEPH HOOKER'S PLAN OF<br>CAMPAIGN AGAINST RICHMOND<br>APRIL 1863 (?)

I have a single idea of my own about harbor defenses. It is a steam-ram built so as to sacrifice nearly all capacity for carrying to those of speed and strength, so as to be able to split any vessel having hollow enough in her to carry supplies for a voyage of any distance. . . . Her business would be to guard a particular harbor as a bulldog guards his master's door.

MEMORANDUM ON HARBOR DEFENSES<br>APRIL 4, 1863

Let your military measures be strong enough to repel the invader and keep the peace, and not so strong as to unnecessarily harass and persecute the people. It is a difficult *role*, and so much greater will be the honor if you perform it well. If both factions, or neither, shall abuse you, you will probably be about right. Beware of being assailed by one and praised by the other.

LETTER TO JOHN M. SCHOFIELD<br>MAY 27, 1863

In one word, I would not take any risk of being entangled upon the river, like an ox jumped half over a fence and liable to be torn by dogs front and rear, without a fair chance to gore one way or kick the other.

LETTER TO JOSEPH HOOKER
JUNE 5, 1863

I think *Lee's* army, and not *Richmond*, is your true objective point. If he comes towards the Upper Potomac, follow on his flank and on the inside track, shortening your lines whilst he lengthens his. Fight him when opportunity offers. If he stays where he is, fret him and fret him.

LETTER TO JOEPH HOOKER
JUNE 10, 1863

If the head of Lee's army is at Martinsburg and the tail of it on the Plank road between Fredericksburg and Chancellorsville, the animal must be very slim somewhere. Could you not break him?

LETTER TO JOSEPH HOOKER
JUNE 14, 1863

I do not believe you appreciate the magnitude of the misfortune involved in Lee's escape. He was within your easy grasp and to have closed upon him would, in connection with our other late successes, have ended the war. As it is, the war will be prolonged indefinitely. . . . Your golden opportunity is gone, and I am distressed immeasurably because of it.

LETTER TO GEORGE G. MEADE
JULY 14, 1863

I was deeply mortified by the escape of Lee across the Potomac, because the substantial destruction of his army would have ended the war, and because I believed such destruction was perfectly easy—believed that Gen. Meade and his noble army had expended all the skill, and toil, and blood, up to the ripe harvest, and then let the crop go to waste. Perhaps my mortification was heightened because I had always believed—making my belief a hobby possibly—that the main rebel army going north of the Potomac could never return if well attended to; and because I was so greatly flattered in this belief by the operations at Gettysburg. A few days having passed, I am now profoundly grateful for what was done, without criticism for what was not done.

LETTER TO OLIVER O. HOWARD
JULY 21, 1863

If our army cannot fall upon the enemy and hurt him where he is, it is plain to me it can gain nothing by attempting to follow him over a succession of entrenched lines into a fortified city.

LETTER TO HENRY W. HALLECK
SEPTEMBER 19, 1863

I think it very important for Gen. [William S.] Rosecrans to hold his position at or about Chattanooga, because . . . if he can only maintain this position without more, the rebellion can only eke out a short and feeble existence, as an animal sometimes may with a thorn in its vitals.

LETTER TO HENRY W. HALLECK
SEPTEMBER 21, 1863

If Gen. [George G.] Meade can now attack him [Lee] on a field no worse than equal to us and will do so with all the skill and courage which he, his officers and men possess, the honor will be his if he succeeds and the blame may be mine if he fails.

COMMUNICATION TO HENRY W. HALLECK
OCTOBER 16, 1863

## Clay, Henry

Henry Clay, my beau ideal of a statesman, the man for whom I fought all my humble life—Henry Clay once said of a class of men who would repress all tendencies to liberty and ultimate emancipation, that they must, if they would do this, go back to the era of our Independence and muzzle the cannon which thunders its annual joyous return; they must blow out the moral lights around us; they must penetrate the human soul and eradicate there the love of liberty; and then, and not till then, could they perpetuate slavery in this country!

FIRST DEBATE WITH STEPHEN A. DOUGLAS,
OTTAWA, ILLINOIS
AUGUST 21, 1858

Clay always opposed the rightfulness of slavery. . . . I can express all my views on the slavery question by quotations from Henry Clay.

SECOND DEBATE WITH STEPHEN A. DOUGLAS,
FREEPORT, ILLINOIS
AUGUST 27, 1858

## Clemency

I cannot listen to a man's own story, unsupported by any evidence, who has been convicted of violating the law; because that would put an end to all law.

MEMORANDUM ON FREDERICK MOELICH
SEPTEMBER 10, 1863

## Cliques

Of all things, avoid if possible a dividing into cliques among the friends of the common object. Be firm and resolute against such as you can perceive would make confusion and division.

LETTER TO FREDERICK STEELE
JANUARY 30, 1864

## Commitments

Remembering that Peter denied his Lord with an oath, after most solemnly protesting that he never would, I will not swear I will make no committals, but I do think I will not.

LETTER TO LYMAN TRUMBULL
JUNE 5, 1860

## Complacency

They smile as complacently . . . as the Christian does at Satan's rage.

LETTER TO MARY S. OWENS
DECEMBER 13, 1836

## Compromise

Discourage litigation. Persuade your neighbors to compromise whenever you can.

NOTES FOR A LAW LECTURE
JULY 1850 (?)

My name is new in the field, and I suppose I am not the *first* choice of a very great many. Our policy, then, is to give no offense to others—leave them in a mood to come to us if they shall be compelled to give up their first love. This, too, in dealing justly with all and leaving us in a mood to support heartily whoever shall be nominated.

LETTER TO SAMUEL GALLOWAY
MARCH 24, 1860

## Confidence

If I have . . . done anything, either by design or misadventure, which, if known, would subject me to a forfeiture of . . . confidence [of the people], he that knows of that thing and conceals it is a traitor to his country's interest.

LETTER TO ROBERT ALLEN
JUNE 21, 1836

## Confiscation

I think there is great danger that the . . . confiscation of property and the liberating [of] slaves of traitorous owners will alarm our Southern Union friends and turn them against us.

LETTER TO JOHN C. FRÉMONT
SEPTEMBER 2, 1861

## Confusion

In one faculty at least, there can be no dispute of the gentleman's [Usher F. Linder's] superiority over me and most other men, and that is the faculty of entangling a subject so that neither himself or any other man can find head or tail to it.

SPEECH IN ILLINOIS LEGISLATURE
JANUARY 11, 1837

## Congress

The Congress of the United States has no power under the Constitution to interfere with the institution of slavery in the different states.

PROTEST IN ILLINOIS LEGISLATURE
MARCH 3, 1837

Were I President, I should desire the legislation of the country to rest with Congress, uninfluenced by the executive in its origin or progress and undisturbed by the veto unless in very special and clear cases.

SUGGESTIONS ON WHAT ZACHARY TAYLOR SHOULD SAY IF
SELECTED AS WHIG CANDIDATE FOR PRESIDENT
MARCH 1848 (?)

Every fellow must say something and offer an amendment; and so time is wasted, it is shoved by and is a long while coming up again.

LETTER TO WALTER DAVIS
APRIL 14, 1848

A member will prefer voting for a bill which contains an appropriation for his district to voting for one which does not.

SPEECH ON INTERNAL IMPROVEMENTS
IN HOUSE OF REPRESENTATIVES
JUNE 20, 1848

Congress ought to prohibit slavery wherever it can be done without violation of the Constitution or of good faith.

FRAGMENT OF A SPEECH
MAY 1858

Congress cannot dictate a constitution to a new state. All it can do at that point is to secure the people a fair chance to form one for themselves and then to accept or reject it when they ask admission into the Union.

FRAGMENT OF A SPEECH
MAY 1858

I am impliedly, if not expressly, pledged to a belief in the *right* and *duty* of Congress to prohibit slavery in all the United States territories.

SECOND DEBATE WITH STEPHEN A. DOUGLAS,
FREEPORT, ILLINOIS
AUGUST 27, 1858

My political education strongly inclines me against a very free use of any . . . means by the Executive to control the legislation of the country. As a rule, I think it better that Congress should originate as well as perfect its measures without external bias.

SPEECH AT PITTSBURGH, PENNSYLVANIA
FEBRUARY 15, 1861

## Conscientious Objectors

On principle and faith opposed to both war and oppression, they can only practically oppose oppression by war. In this hard dilemma, some have chosen one horn and some the other. For those appealing to me on conscientious grounds, I have done, and shall do, the best I could and can in my own conscience under my oath to the law.

LETTER TO ELIZA P. GURNEY
SEPTEMBER 4, 1864

## Consistency

It is desired that I shall shift the ground upon which I have been elected. I can not do it. . . . It would make me appear as if I repented for the crime of having been elected and was anxious to apologize and beg forgiveness.

LETTER TO JOHN A. GILMER
DECEMBER 15, 1860

## Constitution

On the general proposition of amending the Constitution, as a general rule I think we would much better let it alone. No slight occasion should tempt us to touch it. Better not take the first step, which may lead to a habit of altering it. Better, rather, habituate ourselves to thinking of it as unalterable. It can scarcely be made better than it is. New provisions would introduce new difficulties and thus create and increase appetite for still further change.

SPEECH ON INTERNAL IMPROVEMENTS
IN HOUSE OF REPRESENTATIVES
JUNE 20, 1848

The Constitution . . . must be maintained, for it is the only safeguard of our liberties.

SPEECH AT KALAMAZOO, MICHIGAN
AUGUST 27, 1856

The institution of slavery is only mentioned in the Constitution of the United States two or three times, and in neither of these cases does the word "slavery" or "Negro race" occur: . . . in regard to the prohibition of the African slave trade [Art. I, Sec. 9], . . . on the subject of the basis of representation [Art. I, Sec. 3], and . . . in the provision for the reclamation of fugitive slaves [Art. IV, Sec. 3]. . . . In all three of these places, being the only allusions to slavery in the instrument, covert language is used. Language is used not suggesting that slavery existed or that the black race were among us. And I understand the contemporaneous history of those times to be that covert language was used with a purpose, and that purpose was that in our Constitution, which it was hoped and is still hoped will endure forever—when it should be read by intelligent and patriotic men, after the institution of slavery had passed from among us—there should be nothing on the face of the great charter of liberty suggesting that such a thing as Negro slavery had ever existed among us.

SEVENTH DEBATE WITH STEPHEN A. DOUGLAS,
ALTON, ILLINOIS
OCTOBER 15, 1858

The Constitution alludes to slavery three times without mentioning it once. . . . They speak of the "immigration of persons" and mean the importation of slaves, but do not say so. In establishing a basis of representation they say "all other persons" when they mean to say slaves—why did they not use the shortest phrase? In providing for the return of fugitives they say "persons held to service or labor." If they had said slaves it would have been plainer and less liable to misconstruction. Why didn't they do it? We cannot doubt that it was done on purpose. Only one reason is possible, and that is supplied us by one of the framers of the Constitution—and it is not possible for man to conceive of any other—they expected and desired that the system would come to an end and meant that, when it did, the Constitution should not show that there ever had been a slave in this good free country of ours!

SPEECH AT NEW HAVEN, CONNECTICUT
MARCH 6, 1860

I do not desire any amendment of the Constitution. Recognizing, however, that questions of such amendment rightfully belong to the American people, I should not feel justified nor inclined to withhold from them, if I could, a fair opportunity of expressing their will thereon.

LETTER TO DUFF GREEN
DECEMBER 28, 1860

It is said the devil takes care of his own. Much more should a good spirit—the spirit of the Constitution and the Union—take care of its own. I think it cannot do less and live.

OPINION ON ADMISSION OF WEST VIRGINIA
INTO THE UNION
DECEMBER 31, 1862

The Constitution is different *in its application* in cases of rebellion or invasion involving the public safety from what it is in times of profound peace and public security; and this opinion I adhere to, simply because by the Constitution itself things may be done in the one case which may not be done in the other.

LETTER TO MATTHEW BIRCHARD AND OTHERS
JUNE 29, 1863

The oath I took that I would, to the best of my ability, preserve, protect and defend the Constitution of the United States . . . imposed upon me the duty of preserving, by every indispensable means, that government—that nation—of which that Constitution was the organic law. Was it possible to lose the nation and yet preserve the Constitution? By general law, life *and* limb must be protected; yet often a limb must be amputated to save a life; but a life is never wisely given to save a limb. I felt that measures otherwise unconstitutional might become lawful by becoming indispensable to the preservation of the Constitution through the preservation of the nation. Right or wrong, I assumed this ground and now avow it. I could not feel that, to the best of my ability, I had even tried to preserve the Constitution if, to save slavery or any minor matter, I should permit the wreck of government, country and Constitution all together.

LETTER TO ALBERT G. HODGES
APRIL 4, 1864

## Correspondence

I have not sufficient composure to write a long letter.

LETTER TO JOHN T. STUART
JANUARY 20, 1841

Never let your correspondence fall behind.

NOTES FOR A LAW LECTURE
JULY 1850 (?)

You are in error if you suppose any important portion of my correspondence escapes my notice. Everything requiring my action or attention is brought to my notice.

LETTER TO WILLIAM H. FRY
JULY 19, 1862

I care little for the publication of any letter I have written.

LETTER TO JOHN M. SCHOFIELD
JULY 13, 1863

## Corruption

The great volcano at Washington, aroused and directed by the evil spirit that reigns there,* is belching forth the lava of political corruption in a current broad and deep, which is sweeping with frightful velocity over the whole length and breadth of the land, bidding fair to leave unscathed no green spot of living thing, while on its bosom are riding like demons on the waves of Hell the imps of that evil spirit and fiendishly taunting all those who dare resist its destroying course with the hopelessness of their effort.

SPEECH ON THE SUB-TREASURY
DECEMBER 26, 1839

## Cowardice

Singular indeed that the people should be writhing under oppression and injury, and yet not one among them to be found to raise the voice of complaint.

SPEECH IN ILLINOIS LEGISLATURE
JANUARY 11, 1837

A witty Irish soldier, who was always boasting of his bravery when no danger was near, but who invariably retreated without orders at the first charge of an engagement, being asked by his Captain why he did so, replied: "Captain, I have as brave a *heart* as Julius Caesar ever had; but somehow or other, whenever danger approaches, my *cowardly* legs will run away with it."

SPEECH ON THE SUB-TREASURY
DECEMBER 26, 1839

* A reference to President Martin Van Buren.

## Crime Prevention

How effectual have penitentiaries . . . been in preventing the crimes they were established to suppress?

SPEECH ON THE SUB-TREASURY
DECEMBER 26, 1839

The gallows has long been the penalty of murder, and yet we scarcely open a newspaper that does not relate a new case of that crime.

SPEECH ON THE SUB-TREASURY
DECEMBER 26, 1839

Will the punishment of the thief bring back the stolen money? No more so than the hanging of a murderer restores his victim to life.

SPEECH ON THE SUB-TREASURY
DECEMBER 26, 1839

## Criticism

It is so easy and so common to ascribe motives to men . . . other than those they profess to act upon.

SPEECH TO WASHINGTON TEMPERANCE SOCIETY,
SPRINGFIELD, ILLINOIS
FEBRUARY 22, 1842

Senators and Representatives speak of me in their places as they please, without question; . . . officers of the army must cease addressing insulting letters to them for taking no greater liberty with them.

LETTER TO GEORGE B. MCCLELLAN
MAY 9, 1862

I am constantly pressed by those who *scold* before they *think*.

LETTER TO JOHN A. MCCLERNAND
AUGUST 12, 1863

## Currency

Fluctuations in the value of currency are always injurious, and to reduce these fluctuations to the lowest possible point will always be a leading purpose in wise legislation.

ANNUAL MESSAGE TO CONGRESS
DECEMBER 1, 1862

## Davis, Jefferson

If Mr. Davis is still so hostile to the Government and so determined to aid its enemies in destroying it, he makes his own choice.

NOTE TO JOHN W. DAVIS
SEPTEMBER 1861

If Jefferson Davis wishes, for himself or for the benefit of his friends at the North, to know what I would do if he were to offer peace and reunion, saying nothing about slavery, let him try me.

LETTER TO CHARLES D. ROBINSON
AUGUST 17, 1864

## Death

Death, abstractly considered, is the same with the high as with the low; but, practically, we are not so much aroused as to the contemplation of our own mortal natures by the fall of *many* undistinguished as that of *one* great and well-known name.

EULOGY ON ZACHARY TAYLOR
JULY 25, 1850

If it be his lot to go now, he will soon have a joyous meeting with many loved ones gone before, and where the rest of us, through the help of God, hope ere long to join them.

LETTER TO JOHN D. JOHNSTON
JANUARY 12, 1851

## Deception

Reports are often false, and always false when made by a knave to cloak his knavery.

SPEECH ON THE SUB-TREASURY
DECEMBER 26, 1839

Long experience has shown that nothing short of an actual demand of the money will expose an adroit peculator. Ask him for reports and he will give them to your heart's content; send agents to examine and count the money in his hands and he will borrow of a friend, merely to be counted and then returned, a sufficient sum to make the sum square. Try what you will, it will all fail till you demand the money—then, and not till then, the truth will come.

SPEECH ON THE SUB-TREASURY
DECEMBER 26, 1839

It would be amusing, if it were not disgusting, to see how quick these compromise-breakers administer on the political effects of their dead adversaries, trumping up claims never before heard of, and dividing the assets among themselves. If I should be found dead tomorrow morning, nothing but my insignificance could prevent a speech being made on my authority before the end of next week.

SPEECH AT SPRINGFIELD, ILLINOIS
JULY 17, 1858

This may be reality and yet may only be contrivance for deception; and to determine which is perplexing.

DISPATCH TO GEORGE B. MCCLELLAN
JUNE 20, 1862

## Declaration of Independence

Our Declaration of Independence was [once] held sacred by all and thought to include all; but now, to aid in making the bondage of the Negro universal and eternal, it is assailed and sneered at and construed and hawked at and torn till, if its framers could rise from their graves, they could not at all recognize it.

SPEECH AT SPRINGFIELD, ILLINOIS
JUNE 26, 1857

I think the authors of that notable instrument intended to include *all* men, but they did not intend to declare all men equal *in all respects*. They did not mean to say all were equal in color, size, intellect, moral developments or social capacity. They defined with tolerable distinction in what respects they did consider all men created equal—equal in "certain inalienable rights, among which are life, liberty, and the pursuit of happiness." This they said, and this meant. They did not mean to assert the obvious untruth that all were then actually enjoying that equality, nor yet that they were about to confer it immediately upon them. In fact they had no power to confer such a boon. They meant simply to declare the *right*, so that the *enforcement* of it might follow as fast as circumstances should permit. They meant to set up a standard maxim for free society, which should be familiar to all and revered by all; constantly looked to, constantly labored for, and even though never perfectly attained, constantly approximated, and thereby constantly spreading and deepening its influence and augmenting the happiness and value of life to all people of all colors everywhere. The assertion that "all men are created equal" was of no practical use in effecting our separation from Great Britain; and it was placed in the Declaration not for that, but for future use. Its authors meant it to be, thank God it is now proving itself, a stumbling block to those who in after times might seek to turn a free people back into the hateful paths of despotism. They knew the proneness of prosperity to breed tyrants, and they meant when such should reappear in this fair land and commence their vocation they should find left for them at least one hard nut to crack.

SPEECH AT SPRINGFIELD, ILLINOIS
JUNE 26, 1857

We have besides these men—descended by blood from our ancestors—among us perhaps half our people who are not descendants at all of these men; they are men who have come from Europe—German, Irish, French and Scandinavian—men that have come from Europe themselves, or whose ancestors have come hither and settled here, finding themselves our equals in all things. If they look back through this history to trace their connection with those days by blood, they find they have none, they cannot carry themselves back into that glorious epoch and make themselves feel that they are part of us, but when they look through that old Declaration of Independence they find that those old men say that "We hold these truths to be self-evident, that all men are created equal," and then they feel that that moral sentiment taught in that day evidences their relation to those men, that it is the father of all moral principle in them, and that they have a right to claim it as though they were blood of the blood and flesh of the flesh of the men who wrote that Declaration, and so they are. That is the electric cord in that Declaration that links the hearts of patriotic and liberty-loving men together, that will link those patriotic hearts as long as the love of freedom exists in the minds of men throughout the world.

SPEECH AT CHICAGO, ILLINOIS
JULY 10, 1858

I have often inquired of myself what great principle or idea it was that kept this Confederacy so long together. It was not the mere matter of the separation of the colonies from the mother land, but something in that Declaration giving liberty, not alone to the people of this country, but hope to the world for all future time. It was that which gave promise that in due time the weights should be lifted from the shoulders of all men and that *all* should have an equal chance.

SPEECH AT PHILADELPHIA, PENNSYLVANIA
FEBRUARY 22, 1861

I adhere to the Declaration of Independence. If Judge [Stephen A.] Douglas and his friends are not willing to stand by it, let them come up and amend it. Let them make it read that all men are created equal except Negroes. Let us have it decided whether the Declaration of Independence, in this blessed year of 1858, shall be thus amended. In his construction of the Declaration last year, he said it only meant that Americans in America were equal to Englishmen in England. Then, when I pointed out to him that by the rule he excludes the Germans, the Irish, the Portuguese and all the other people who have come amongst us since the Revolution, he reconstructs his construction. In his last speech he tells us it meant Europeans. I press him a little further, and ask if it meant to include the Russians in Asia? Or does he mean to exclude that vast population from the principles of our Declaration of Independence? I expect ere long he will introduce another amendment to his definition. He is not at all particular. He is satisfied with anything which does not endanger the nationalizing of Negro slavery. It may draw white men down, but it must not lift Negroes up. Who shall say, "I am the superior and you are the inferior"?

SPEECH AT SPRINGFIELD, ILLINOIS
JULY 17, 1858

If you have been taught doctrines conflicting with the great landmarks of the Declaration of Independence; if you have listened to suggestions which would take away from its grandeur and mutilate the fair symmetry of its proportions; if you have been inclined to believe that all men are *not* created equal in those inalienable rights enumerated by our chart of liberty, let me entreat you to come back. Return to the fountain whose waters spring close by the blood of the Revolution. Think nothing of me —take no thought for the political fate of any man whomsoever—

but come back to the truths that are in the Declaration of Independence. You may do anything with me you choose, if you will but heed these sacred principles. You may not only defeat me for the Senate, but you may take me and put me to death. While pretending no indifference to earthly honors, I *do claim* to be actuated in this contest by something higher than an anxiety for office. I charge you to drop every paltry and insignificant thought for any man's success. It is nothing; I am nothing; Judge Douglas is nothing. *But do not destroy that immortal emblem of Humanity—the Declaration of American Independence.*

SPEECH AT LEWISTOWN, ILLINOIS
AUGUST 17, 1858

## Defiance

If ever I feel the soul within me elevate and expand to those dimensions not wholly unworthy of its Almighty Architect, it is when I contemplate the cause of my country, deserted by all the world beside, and I standing up boldly and alone and hurling defiance at her victorious oppressors.

SPEECH ON THE SUB-TREASURY
DECEMBER 26, 1839

## Deliberation

Nothing valuable can be lost by taking time.

FIRST INAUGURAL ADDRESS
MARCH 4, 1861

## Democracy

I go for all sharing the privileges of the government who assist in bearing its burdens.

LETTER TO THE *Sangamo* (ILLINOIS) *Journal*
JUNE 13, 1836

The people know their rights, and they are never slow to assert and maintain them when they are invaded.

SPEECH IN ILLINOIS LEGISLATURE
JANUARY 11, 1837

The experiment is successful; and thousands have won their deathless names in making it so.

SPEECH TO YOUNG MEN'S LYCEUM,
SPRINGFIELD, ILLINOIS
JANUARY 27, 1838

The primary, the cardinal, the one great living principle of all democratic representative government [is] the principle that the representative is bound to carry out the known will of his people.

SPEECH IN HOUSE OF REPRESENTATIVES
JULY 27, 1848

In leaving the people's business in their hands, we cannot be wrong.

SPEECH IN HOUSE OF REPRESENTATIVES
JULY 27, 1848

We made the experiment, and the fruit is before us.

FRAGMENT
JULY 1854 (?)

As I would not be a *slave*, so I would not be a *master*. This expresses my idea of democracy. Whatever differs from this, to the extent of the difference, is no democracy.

FRAGMENT
AUGUST 1858 (?)

By the frame of the government under which we live, this same people have wisely given their public servants but little power for mischief; and have, with equal wisdom, provided for the return of that little to their own hands at very short intervals.

FIRST INAUGURAL ADDRESS
MARCH 4, 1861

The distinct issue, "Immediate dissolution or blood" . . . embraces more than the fate of these United States. It presents to the whole family of man the question whether a constitutional republic or democracy—a government of the people, by the same people—can or cannot maintain its territorial integrity against its own domestic foes. It presents the question whether discontented individuals—too few in numbers to control administration, according to organic law, in any case—can always, upon the pretenses made in this case or on any other pretenses, or arbitrarily without any pretense, break up their government and thus practically put an end to free government upon the earth. It forces us to ask: "Is there, in all republics, this inherent and fatal weakness? Must a government, of necessity, be too *strong* for the liberties of its own people, or too *weak* to maintain its own existence?"

MESSAGE TO CONGRESS IN SPECIAL SESSION
JULY 4, 1861

This country, Sir, maintains, and means to maintain, the rights of human nature and the capacity of man for self-government.

REPLY TO EDWARD COUNT PIPER, MINISTER RESIDENT
FROM SWEDEN AND NORWAY
NOVEMBER 8, 1861

## Demonstrations

Too much reliance is placed in noisy demonstrations— . . . They excite prejudice and close the avenues to sober reason.

LETTER TO ANDREW MCCALLEN
JUNE 19, 1858

## Deserters

Long experience has shown that armies can not be maintained unless desertion shall be punished by the severe penalty of death. The case requires, and the law and the Constitution sanction this punishment. Must I shoot a simple-minded soldier boy who deserts, while I must not touch a hair of a wily agitator who induces him to desert? This is none the less injurious when effected by getting a father or brother or friend into a public meeting, and there working upon his feelings till he is persuaded to write the soldier boy that he is fighting in a bad cause, for a wicked administration of a contemptible government too weak to arrest and punish him if he shall desert. I think that in such a case, to silence the agitator and save the boy is not only constitutional but, withal, a great mercy.

LETTER TO ERASTUS CORNING AND OTHERS
JUNE 12, 1863

Let him fight instead of being shot.

LETTER TO JOSEPH HOLT
JULY 18, 1863

I am unwilling for any boy under eighteen to be shot.

LETTER TO GEORGE G. MEADE
OCTOBER 8, 1863

## Despondency

Should excessive pleasure . . . be accompanied with a painful counterpart at times, still let me urge you . . . to remember, in the depth and even the agony of despondency, that very shortly you are to feel well again.

LETTER TO JOSHUA F. SPEED
FEBRUARY 13, 1842

## Despotism

When the white man governs himself, that is self-government; but when he governs himself and also governs *another* man, that is *more* than self-government—that is despotism.

SPEECH IN PEORIA, ILLINOIS
OCTOBER 16, 1854

## Destruction

If destruction be our lot, we must ourselves be its author and finisher.

SPEECH TO YOUNG MEN'S LYCEUM,
SPRINGFIELD, ILLINOIS
JANUARY 27, 1838

## Detectives

I do not perceive anything necessarily inconsistent with the practice of detectives and others engaged in the business of "rascal-catching."

LETTER TO SALMON P. CHASE
FEBRUARY 20, 1864

## Determination

Let none falter who thinks he is right.

SPEECH ON THE SUB-TREASURY
DECEMBER 26, 1839

Before I resolve to do one thing or the other, I must regain my confidence in my own ability to keep my resolves when they are made.

LETTER TO JOSHUA F. SPEED
JULY 4, 1842

Determine that the thing can and shall be done, and then we shall find the way.

SPEECH ON INTERNAL IMPROVEMENTS
IN HOUSE OF REPRESENTATIVES
JUNE 20, 1884

I hope those with whom I am surrounded have principle enough to nerve themselves for the task and leave nothing undone that can be fairly done to bring about the right result.

SPEECH AT SPRINGFIELD, ILLINOIS
JULY 17, 1858

By all means don't say, "If I can"; say, "*I will.*"

LETTER TO JOHN C. BAGBY
SEPTEMBER 6, 1858

The cause of civil liberty must not be surrendered at the end of *one* or even one *hundred* defeats.

LETTER TO HENRY ASBURY
NOVEMBER 19, 1858

Neither let us be slandered from our duty by false accusations against us, nor frightened from it by menaces of destruction to the Government nor of dungeons to ourselves. LET US HAVE FAITH THAT RIGHT MAKES MIGHT; AND IN THAT FAITH LET US, TO THE END, DARE TO DO OUR DUTY AS WE UNDERSTAND IT.

ADDRESS AT NEW YORK CITY
FEBRUARY 27, 1860

This puts the case in the hardest shape for us. But fight we must; and conquer we shall in the end.

LETTER TO CYRUS M. ALLEN
MAY 1, 1860

I am not wanting in the purpose, though I may fail in the strength, to maintain my freedom from bad influences. . . . May the Almighty grant that the cause of truth, justice and humanity shall in no wise suffer at my hands.

LETTER TO JOSHUA R. GIDDINGS
MAY 21, 1860

The thing starts well everywhere—too well, I almost fear, to last. But we are in, and stick or go through must be the word.

LETTER TO CALEB B. SMITH
MAY 26, 1860

I appreciate the danger against which you would guard me; nor am I wanting in the *purpose* to avoid it.

LETTER TO WILLIAM C. BRYANT
JUNE 28, 1860

Having made the attempt, you *must* succeed in it. *"Must"* is the word. I know not how to aid you save in the assurance of one of mature age, and much severe experience, that you *can* not fail if you resolutely determine that you *will* not.

LETTER TO GEORGE C. LATHAM
JULY 22, 1860

Hold firm as with a chain of steel.

LETTER TO ELIHU B. WASHBURNE
DECEMBER 13, 1860

I shall not surrender this game leaving any available card unplayed.

LETTER TO REVERDY JOHNSON
JULY 26, 1862

## Dictatorship

I have heard, in such a way as to believe it, of your recently saying that both the Army and the Government needed a dictator. Of course it was not *for* this, but in spite of it, that I have given you the command. Only those generals who gain successes can set up dictators. What I now ask of you is military success and I will risk the dictatorship.

LETTER TO JOSEPH HOOKER
JANUARY 26, 1863

## Dignity

It is difficult to make a man miserable while he feels he is worthy of himself and claims a kindred to the great God who made him.

SPEECH ON COLONIZATION TO A
DEPUTATION OF NEGROES
AUGUST 14, 1862

## Disappointment

I have been too familiar with disappointments.

COMMUNICATION TO THE PEOPLE OF
SANGAMON COUNTY, ILLINOIS
MARCH 9, 1832

## Discouragement

Let nothing discourage or baffle you.

LETTER TO ELIHU B. WASHBURNE
APRIL 30, 1848

## Distance

Great distance, in either time or space, has wonderful power to lull and render quiescent the human mind.

SPEECH TO WASHINGTON TEMPERANCE SOCIETY,
SPRINGFIELD, ILLINOIS
FEBRUARY 22, 1842

## District of Columbia

The Congress of the United States has the power under the Constitution to abolish slavery in the District of Columbia, but that . . . power ought not to be exercised unless at the request of the people of said District.

PROTEST IN ILLINOIS LEGISLATURE
MARCH 3, 1837

No person not now within the District of Columbia, nor now owned by any person or persons now resident within it, nor hereafter born within it, shall ever be held in slavery within said District. . . . No person now within said District, or now owned by any person or persons now resident within the same, or hereafter born within it, shall ever be held in slavery without the limits of said District: *Provided*, that officers of the government of the United States being citizens of the slave-holding states, coming into said District on public business and remaining only so long as may be reasonably necessary for that object, may be attended into and out of said District and, while there, by the necessary servants of themselves and their families, without their right to hold such servants in service being thereby impaired. . . . All children born of slave mothers within said District on, or after the first day of January in the year of our Lord one thousand, eight hundred and fifty shall be free; but shall be reasonably supported and educated by the respective owners of their mothers or by their heirs or representatives, and

shall owe reasonable service, as apprentices, to such owners, heirs
and representatives until they respectively arrive at the age of
—— years* when they shall be entirely free. . . . All persons
now within said District lawfully held as slaves, or now owned
by any person or persons now resident within said District, shall
remain such at the will of their respective owners, their heirs
and legal representatives: *Provided,* that any such owner or his
legal representative may at any time receive from the Treasury
of the United States the full value of his or her slave of the
class in this section mentioned, upon which such slave shall be
forthwith and forever free; and *provided further,* that the President of the United States, the Secretary of State, and the Secretary of the Treasury shall be a board for determining the value
of such slaves as their owners may desire to emancipate under
this section.

DRAFT OF RESOLUTION, NEVER INTRODUCED
IN HOUSE OF REPRESENTATIVES
JANUARY 10, 1849

I do not stand today pledged to the abolition of slavery in
the District of Columbia. . . . I have my mind very distinctly
made up. I should be exceedingly glad to see slavery abolished
in the District of Columbia. I believe that Congress possesses
the constitutional power to abolish it. Yet as a member of Congress I should not, with my present views, be in favor of *endeavoring* to abolish slavery in the District of Columbia unless
it would be upon these conditions: *First,* that the abolition should
be gradual; *second,* that it should be on a vote of the majority
of qualified voters in the District; and *third,* that compensation
should be made to unwilling owners. With these three conditions,
I confess I would be exceedingly glad to see Congress abolish
slavery in the District of Columbia, and, in the language of Henry
Clay, "sweep from our Capital that foul blot upon our nation."

SECOND DEBATE WITH STEPHEN A. DOUGLAS,
FREEPORT, ILLINOIS
AUGUST 27, 1858

* Age was never filled in as the matter was dropped by Lincoln, who
felt he had too little influence to introduce and pass a Slavery bill at that
time.

I have never doubted the constitutional authority of Congress to abolish slavery in this District; and I have ever desired to see the national capital freed from the institution in some satisfactory way.

MESSAGE TO CONGRESS
APRIL 16, 1862

## *"Dixie"*

I have always thought "Dixie" one of the best tunes I have ever heard. Our adversaries over the way attempted to appropriate it, but I insisted yesterday that we fairly captured it. I presented the question to the Attorney General, and he gave it as his legal opinion that it is our lawful prize.

RESPONSE TO A SERENADE
APRIL 10, 1865

## *Douglas, Stephen A.*

When the builders of the tower of Babel got into difficulty about language, if they had just called on Judge Douglas, he would at once have construed away the difficulty and enabled them to finish the structure upon the truly democratic platform on which they were building.

SPEECH TO THE SCOTT CLUB, SPRINGFIELD, ILLINOIS
AUGUST 14, 1852

With *me*, the race of ambition has been a failure—a flat failure; with *him* it has been one of splendid success. His name fills the nation, and is not unknown even in foreign lands. I affect no contempt for the high eminence he has reached. So reached, that the oppressed of my species might have shared with me in the elevation, I would rather stand on that eminence than wear the richest crown that ever pressed a monarch's brow.

FRAGMENT ON DOUGLAS
DECEMBER 1856

A *living* dog is better than a *dead* lion. Judge Douglas, if not a *dead* lion *for this work*, is at least a *caged* and *toothless* one. How can he oppose the advances of slavery: he don't *care* anything about it. His avowed *mission is impressing* the "public heart" to *care* nothing about it.

"A HOUSE DIVIDED" SPEECH, SPRINGFIELD, ILLINOIS
JUNE 16, 1858

I suppose that Judge Douglas will claim in a little while that he is the inventor of the idea that the people should govern themselves, that nobody ever thought of such a thing until he brought it forward.

SPEECH AT CHICAGO
JULY 10, 1858

He says that I am in favor of making war by the North upon the South for the extinction of slavery, that I am also in favor of inviting (as he expresses it) the South to a war upon the North for the purpose of nationalizing slavery.

SPEECH AT CHICAGO
JULY 10, 1858

His tactics just now, in part, is to make it appear that he is having a triumphal entry into, and march through, the country; but it is all as bombastic and hollow as Napoleon's bulletins sent back from his campaign in Russia.

LETTER TO GUSTAVE P. KOERNER
JULY 15, 1858

There is no solid shot in these bombastic parades of his.

LETTER TO GUSTAVE P. KOERNER
JULY 15, 1858

"Popular Sovereignty" . . . is to be labeled upon the cars in which he travels; put upon the hacks he rides in; to be flaunted upon the arches he passes under and the banners which wave over him. It is to be dished up in as many varieties as a French cook can produce soups from potatoes. Now, as this is so great a staple of the plan of the campaign it is worthwhile to examine it carefully; and if we examine a very little and do not allow ourselves to be misled, we shall be able to see that the whole thing is the most arrant quixotism that was ever enacted before a community.

SPEECH AT SPRINGFIELD, ILLINOIS<br>JULY 17, 1858

Does Judge Douglas, when he says that several of the past years of his life have been devoted to the question of "popular sovereignty" and that all the remainder of his life shall be devoted to it, does he mean to say that he has been devoting his life to securing to the people of the territories the right to exclude slavery from the territories? If he means so to say, he means to deceive; because he and everyone knows that the decision of the Supreme Court [the Dred Scott decision], which he approves and makes especial ground of attack upon me for disapproving, forbids the people of a territory to exclude slavery. This covers the whole ground, from the settlement of a territory till it reaches the degree of maturity entitling it to form a state constitution. So far as all that ground is concerned, the Judge is not sustaining popular sovereignty, but absolutely opposing it. He sustains the decision which declares that the popular will of the territories has no constitutional power to exclude slavery during their territorial existence. This being so, the period of time from the first settlement of a territory till it reaches the point of forming a state constitution, is not the thing that the Judge has fought for or is fighting for; but on the contrary, he has fought for, and is fighting for, the thing that annihilates and crushes out that same popular sovereignty.

SPEECH AT SPRINGFIELD, ILLINOIS<br>JULY 17, 1858

What is Judge Douglas going to spend his life for? Is he going to spend his life in maintaining a principle that nobody on earth opposes? Does he expect to stand up in majestic dignity and go through his *apotheosis* and become a god in the maintaining of a principle which neither a man nor a mouse in all God's creation is opposing?

SPEECH AT SPRINGFIELD, ILLINOIS
JULY 17, 1858

He says I have a proneness for quoting Scripture. If I should do so now, it occurs that perhaps he places himself somewhat upon the ground of the parable of the lost sheep which went astray upon the mountains, and when the owner of the hundred sheep found the one that was lost, and threw it upon his shoulders, and came home rejoicing, it was said that there was more rejoicing over the one sheep that was lost and had been found, than over the ninety and nine in the fold. The application is made by the Saviour in this parable thus, "Verily, I say unto you, there is more rejoicing in heaven over one sinner that repenteth, than over ninety and nine just persons that need no repentance." And now, if the Judge claims the benefit of this parable, *let him repent*. Let him come up here and say: I am the only just person; and you are the ninety-nine sinners! *Repentance* before *forgiveness* is a provision of the Christian system, and on that condition alone will the Republicans grant his forgiveness.

SPEECH AT SPRINGFIELD, ILLINOIS
JULY 17, 1858

I will not say that he willfully misquotes, but he does fail to quote accurately.

SPEECH AT SPRINGFIELD, ILLINOIS
JULY 17, 1858

Cannot the Judge perceive the distinction between a *purpose* and an *expectation?* I have often expressed an expectation to die, but I have never expressed a *wish* to die.

SPEECH AT SPRINGFIELD, ILLINOIS
JULY 17, 1858

The Judge's inference [is] that because I wish to see slavery placed in the course of ultimate extinction—placed where our fathers originally placed it—I wish to annihilate the state legislatures—to force cotton to grow upon the tops of the Green Mountains—to free ice in Florida—to cut lumber on the broad Illinois prairies—that I am in favor of all these ridiculous and impossible things.

SPEECH AT SPRINGFIELD, ILLINOIS
JULY 17, 1858

I wish to stand erect before the country, as well as Judge Douglas, on [the] question of judicial authority; and therefore I add something to the authority in favor of my own position. I wish to show that I am sustained by authority in addition to that heretofore presented. I do not expect to convince the Judge. It is part of the plan of his campaign, and he will cling to it with a desperate grip. Even, turn it upon him—turn the sharp point against him and gaff him through—he will still cling to it till he can invent some new dodge to take the place of it.

SPEECH AT SPRINGFIELD, ILLINOIS
JULY 17, 1858

I wish to know what the Judge can charge upon me with respect to decisions of the Supreme Court which does not lie in all its length, breadth and proportions at his own door. The plain truth is simply this: Judge Douglas is *for* Supreme Court decisions when he likes them and against them when he does not like them.

SPEECH AT SPRINGFIELD, ILLINOIS
JULY 17, 1858

I never stood opposed to a decision of the Supreme Court till this [Dred Scott decision]. On the contrary, I have no recollection that he was ever particularly in favor of one till this. He never was in favor of any nor opposed to any till the present one, which helps to nationalize slavery.

SPEECH AT SPRINGFIELD, ILLINOIS
JULY 17, 1858

One more point on this Springfield speech which Judge Douglas says he has read so carefully. I expressed my belief in the existence of a conspiracy to perpetuate and nationalize slavery. I did not profess to know it, nor do I now. I showed the part Judge Douglas had played in the string of facts constituting, to my mind, the proof of that conspiracy. I showed the parts played by others. I charged that the people had been deceived into carrying the last Presidential election by the impression that the people of the territories might exclude slavery if they chose, when it was known in advance by the conspirators that the court was to decide that neither Congress nor the people could so exclude slavery. These charges are more distinctly made than anything else in the speech. Judge Douglas has carefully read and reread that speech. He has not, so far as I know, contradicted those charges. In the two speeches which I heard, he certainly did not. On his own tacit admission I renew that charge. I charge him with having been a party to that conspiracy and to that deception for the sole purpose of nationalizing slavery.

SPEECH AT SPRINGFIELD, ILLINOIS
JULY 17, 1858

Will it be agreeable to you to make an arrangement for you and myself to divide time and address the same audiences during the present canvass?

LETTER TO STEPHEN A. DOUGLAS
JULY 24, 1858

I do not wish Douglas to put words into my mouth. I do not wish him to construe my words as he pleases and then represent me as meaning what he wishes me to mean, but I do wish the people to read and judge for themselves.

SPEECH AT CLINTON, ILLINOIS
JULY 27, 1858

Although, by the terms, as you propose, you take *four* openings and closes to my *three*, I accede and thus close the arrangement [for debates].

LETTER TO STEPHEN A. DOUGLAS
JULY 31, 1858

He cares nothing for the South—he knows he is already dead there.

LETTER TO HENRY ASBURY
JULY 31, 1858

He will instantly take ground that slavery cannot actually exist in the territories unless the people desire it and so give it protective territorial legislation. If this offends the South, he will let it offend them.

LETTER TO HENRY ASBURY
JULY 31, 1858

Friends write me from all the places where Douglas is speaking, and they all say he gains nothing. This shows at least that he does not scare and cow our friends where he goes.

LETTER TO JOSEPH O. GLOVER
AUGUST 9, 1858

Judge Douglas helped to *vote down* a clause giving the people of the territories the right to *exclude* slavery if they chose.

SPEECH AT BEARDSTOWN, ILLINOIS
AUGUST 12, 1858

I am informed that my distinguished friend yesterday became a little excited, nervous perhaps, and he said something about *fighting*, as though referring to a pugilistic encounter between him and myself.

SPEECH AT HAVANA, ILLINOIS
AUGUST 14, 1858

He and I are about the best friends in the world, and when we get together he would no more think of fighting me than of fighting his wife. Therefore, ladies and gentlemen, when the Judge talked about fighting, he was not giving vent to any ill-feeling of his own but merely trying to excite—well, *enthusiasm* against me on the part of his audience. And as I find he was tolerably successful, we will call it quits.

SPEECH AT HAVANA, ILLINOIS
AUGUST 14, 1858

All others, North and South, have at some time or another declared themselves in favor of it [slavery] or against it. All others have either said that it is right and just and should therefore be perpetuated, or that it is wrong and wicked and should be immediately swept from civilized society, or that it is an evil to be tolerated because it cannot be removed. But to Judge Douglas belongs the *distinction* of having never said that he regarded it either as an evil or a good, morally right or morally wrong. His speech at Bloomington would leave us to infer that he was opposed to the introduction of slavery into Illinois; but his effort in Lewistown, I am told, favors the idea that if you can make more money by flogging niggers than by flogging oxen, there is no moral consideration which should interfere to prevent your doing so.

SPEECH AT LEWISTOWN, ILLINOIS
AUGUST 17, 1858

I remind him of another piece of history on the question of respect for judicial decisions, and it is a piece of Illinois history belonging to a time when the large party to which Judge Douglas belonged were displeased with a decision of the Supreme Court of Illinois because they had decided that a Governor could not remove a Secretary of State. You will find the whole story in Ford's History of Illinois, and I know that Judge Douglas will not deny that he was then in favor of overslaughing that decision by the mode of adding five new Judges so as to vote down the four old ones. Not only so, but it ended in *the Judge's sitting down on that very bench as one of the five new Judges to break down the four old ones.* It was in this way precisely that he got his title of Judge. Now, when the Judge tells me that men appointed conditionally to sit as members of a court will have to be catechised beforehand upon some subject, I say, "You know, Judge; you have tried it." When he says a court of this kind will lose the confidence of all men, will be prostituted and disgraced by such a proceeding, I say, "You know best, Judge; you have been through the mill."

FIRST DEBATE WITH STEPHEN A. DOUGLAS,
OTTAWA, ILLINOIS
AUGUST 21, 1858

I say that "a house divided against itself cannot stand." Does the Judge say it *can* stand? . . . If he does, then there is a question of veracity, not between him and me, but between the Judge and an authority of a somewhat higher character.

FIRST DEBATE WITH STEPHEN A. DOUGLAS,
OTTAWA, ILLINOIS
AUGUST 21, 1858

Douglas and I, for the first time this canvass, crossed swords here yesterday; the fire flew some, and I am glad to know I am yet alive.

LETTER TO JOSEPH O. CUNNINGHAM
AUGUST 22, 1858

Senator Douglas regularly argues against the doctrine of the equality of men, and while he does not draw the conclusion that the superiors ought to enslave the inferiors, he evidently wishes his hearers to draw that conclusion. He shirks the responsibility of pulling the house down, but he digs under it that it may fall of its own weight.

NOTES FOR SPEECHES
OCTOBER 1858 (?)

I see it rapidly approaching. Whatever may be the result of this ephemeral contest between Judge Douglas and myself, I see the day rapidly approaching when his pill of sectionalism, which he has been thrusting down the throats of Republicans for years past, will be crowded down his own throat.

FIFTH DEBATE WITH STEPHEN A. DOUGLAS,
GALESBURG, ILLINOIS
OCTOBER 7, 1858

Judge Douglas has intimated . . . that all this difficulty in regard to the institution of slavery is the mere agitation of office seekers and ambitious Northern politicians. He thinks we want to get "his place," I suppose. I agree that there are office seekers amongst us. The Bible says somewhere that we are desperately selfish. I think we would have discovered that fact without the Bible. I do not claim that I am any less so than the average of men, but I do claim that I am not more selfish than Judge Douglas.

SEVENTH DEBATE WITH STEPHEN A. DOUGLAS,
ALTON, ILLINOIS
OCTOBER 15, 1858

Douglas had the ingenuity to be supported in the late contest both as the best means to *break down* and to *uphold* the slave interest. No ingenuity can keep those antagonistic elements in harmony long.

LETTER TO HENRY ASBURY
NOVEMBER 19, 1858

Douglas managed to be supported both as the best instrument to *put down* and to *uphold* the slave power; but no ingenuity can long keep these antagonisms in harmony.

LETTER TO CHARLES H. RAY
NOVEMBER 20, 1858

## Draft

I am unwilling to give up a drafted man *now*, even for the *certainty*, much less for the mere *chance*, of getting a volunteer *hereafter*.

LETTER TO HORATIO SEYMOUR
AUGUST 16, 1863

At the beginning of the war, and ever since, a variety of motives pressing, some in one direction and some in the other, would be presented to the mind of each man physically fit for a soldier, upon the combined effect of which motives he would, or would not, voluntarily enter the service. Among these motives would be patriotism, political bias, ambition, personal courage, love of adventure, want of employment, and convenience, or the opposites of some of these. We already have . . . substantially all that can be obtained upon this voluntary weighing of motives. And yet we must somehow obtain more. . . . To meet this necessity, the law for the draft has been enacted. . . . They tell us the law is unconstitutional. It is the first instance, I believe, in which the power of Congress to do a thing has ever been questioned in a case when the power is given by the Constitution in express terms. Whether a power can be implied when it is not expressed, has often been the subject of controversy; but this is the first case in which the degree of effrontery has been ventured upon of denying a power which is plainly and distinctly written down in the Constitution. . . . The power is given fully, completely, unconditionally. It is not a power to raise armies *if* state authorities consent, nor *if* the men to compose the armies are entirely willing, but it is a power to raise and support armies given to Congress by the Constitution without an if. . . . The republican institutions and territorial integrity of our country cannot be maintained without the further raising and supporting of armies. There can be no army without men. Men can be had only voluntarily or involuntarily. We have ceased to obtain them voluntarily; and to obtain them involuntarily is the draft—the conscription. If you dispute the fact and declare that men can still be had voluntarily in sufficient numbers, prove the assertion by yourselves volunteering in such numbers, and I shall gladly give up the draft. . . . I do not say that all who would avoid serving in the war are unpatriotic; but I do think every patriot should willingly take his chance under a law made with great care in order to secure entire fairness. . . . The principle of the draft, which simply is involuntary or enforced service, is not new. It has been practiced in all ages of the world. It was well known to the framers of our Constitution. . . . It has been used, just before, in establishing our independence; and it was also used under the Constitution in 1812. Wherein is the peculiar hardship now? Shall we shrink from the necessary means to maintain our free government, which our grandfathers employed to establish it and our own fathers have already employed once to maintain it? Are we degenerate? Has the manhood of our race run out?

OPINION ON THE DRAFT
AUGUST or SEPTEMBER 1863 (?)

A man who offers to volunteer and is rejected should not afterwards be drafted and forced to serve.

LETTER TO EDWIN M. STANTON
DECEMBER 14, 1864

## Dred Scott Decision

The Dred Scott decision . . . may be reduced to three points. The first is that a Negro cannot be a citizen. That point is made in order to deprive the Negro, in every possible event, of the benefit of that provision of the United States Constitution which declares that "the citizens of each state shall be entitled to all privileges and immunities of citizens in the several states." The second point is that the United States Constitution protects slavery, as property, in all the United States territories and that neither Congress, nor the people of the territories, nor any other power, can prohibit it at any time prior to the formation of state constitutions. This point is made in order that the territories may safely be filled up with slaves before the formation of state constitutions, thereby to embarrass the free-state sentiment and enhance the chances of slave constitutions being adopted. The third point decided is that the voluntary bringing of Dred Scott into Illinois by his master and holding him here a long time as a slave did not operate his emancipation—did not make him free. This point is made, not to be pressed immediately; but if acquiesced in for a while, then to sustain the logical conclusion that what Dred Scott's master might lawfully do with any other one or one hundred slaves in Illinois or in any other free state.

FRAGMENT OF A SPEECH
MAY 1858

Somebody has to reverse that decision, since it is made; and we mean to reverse it, and we mean to do it peaceably.

SPEECH AT CHICAGO, ILLINOIS
JULY 10, 1858

Decisions apparently contrary to that decision, or that good lawyers thought were contrary to that decision, have been made by that very court [the Supreme Court] before. It is the first of its kind; it is an astonisher in legal history. It is a new wonder of the world. It is based upon falsehood in the main as to the facts—allegations of facts upon which it stands are not facts at all in many instances; and no decision made on any question—the first instance of a decision made under so many unfavorable circumstances—thus placed has ever been held by the profession as law, and it has always needed confirmation before the lawyers regarded it as settled law.

SPEECH AT CHICAGO, ILLINOIS
JULY 10, 1858

I never stood opposed to a decision of the Supreme Court till this.

SPEECH AT SPRINGFIELD, ILLINOIS
JULY 17, 1858

## Duty

Who that knows anything of human nature doubts that, in many instances, interest will prevail over duty.

SPEECH ON THE SUB-TREASURY
DECEMBER 26, 1839

It is *much* for the young to know that treading the hard path of duty . . . *will* be noticed and *will* lead to high places.

EULOGY ON ZACHARY TAYLOR
JULY 25, 1850

LET US HAVE FAITH THAT RIGHT MAKES MIGHT;
AND IN THAT FAITH LET US, TO THE END, DARE
TO DO OUR DUTY AS WE UNDERSTAND IT.

ADDRESS AT NEW YORK CITY
FEBRUARY 27, 1860

I shall not do *more* than I can, and I shall do *all* I can to save
the Government, which is my sworn duty as well as my personal
inclination.

LETTER TO CUTHBERT BULLITT
JULY 28, 1862

## Economics

It seems to be an opinion very generally entertained, that the
condition of a nation is *best* whenever it can *buy cheapest;* but
this is not necessarily true, because if, at the same time and by
the same cause, it is compelled to *sell* correspondingly cheap,
nothing is gained.

NOTES FOR A TARIFF DISCUSSION
DECEMBER 1847

## Education

That every man may receive at least a moderate education and
thereby be enabled to read the histories of his own and other
countries, by which he may duly appreciate the value of our free
institutions, appears to be an object of vital importance.

COMMUNICATION TO THE PEOPLE OF
SANGAMON COUNTY, ILLINOIS
MARCH 9, 1832

I desire to see the time when education—and by its means,
morality, sobriety, enterprise and industry—shall become much
more general than at present, and should be gratified to have it

in my power to contribute something to the advancement of any measure which might have a tendency to accelerate the happy period.

COMMUNICATION TO THE PEOPLE OF
SANGAMON COUNTY, ILLINOIS
MARCH 9, 1832

The old general rule was that *educated* people did not perform manual labor. They managed to eat their bread, leaving the toil of producing it to the uneducated. This was not an insupportable evil to the working bees, so long as the class of drones remained very small. But *now*, especially in these free states, nearly all are educated—quite too nearly all to leave the labor of the uneducated in any wise adequate to the support of the whole. It follows from this that henceforth educated people must labor. Otherwise education itself would become a positive and intolerable evil.

SPEECH AT MILWAUKEE, WISCONSIN
SEPTEMBER 30, 1859

## Elections

Trust the people to decide.

LETTER TO JOHN J. HARDIN
FEBRUARY 7, 1846

We . . . are in favor of making Presidential elections and the legislation of the country distinct matters, so that the people can elect whom they please, and afterwards legislate just as they please without any hindrance, save only so much as may guard against infractions of the Constitution, undue haste, and want of consideration.

SPEECH IN HOUSE OF REPRESENTATIVES
JULY 27, 1848

Every right-thinking man shall go to the polls and, without fear of prejudice, *vote* as he *thinks.*

FRAGMENT OF A SPEECH
MAY 1858

I do not deny the possibility that the people may err in an election; but if they do, the true remedy is in the next election.

FRAGMENT OF SPEECH INTENDED FOR KENTUCKIANS
FEBRUARY 1861

If defeated at one election, I believe in taking the chances next time.

REMARKS AT POUGHKEEPSIE, NEW YORK
FEBRUARY 19, 1861

It is not the qualified voters, but the qualified voters *who choose to vote,* that constitute the political power of the state.

OPINION ON ADMISSION OF WEST VIRGINIA INTO THE UNION
DECEMBER 31, 1862

There can be no successful appeal from a fair election, but to the next election.

FRAGMENT
AUGUST 1863 (?)

The present presidential contest will almost certainly be no other than a contest between a Union and a Disunion candidate, disunion certainly following the success of the latter. The issue is a mighty one for all people and all time.

LETTER TO ABRAM WAKEMAN
JULY 25, 1864

It has long been a grave question whether any government, not *too* strong for the liberties of its people, can be strong *enough* to maintain its own existence in great emergencies. On this point the present rebellion brought our republic to a severe test; and a presidential election occurring in regular course during the rebellion added not a little to the strain. If the loyal people, *united*, were put to the utmost of their strength by the rebellion, must they not fail when *divided* and partially paralyzed by a political war among themselves? But the election was a necessity. We cannot have free government without elections; and if the rebellion could force us to forego or postpone a national election, it might fairly claim to have already conquered and ruined us. . . . But the election . . . has demonstrated that a people's government can sustain a national election in the midst of a great civil war. Until now it has not been known to the world that this was a possibility. It shows also how *sound* and how *strong* we still are. It shows that, even among candidates of the same party, he who is most devoted to the Union, and most opposed to treason, can receive most of the people's votes.

RESPONSE TO A SERENADE
NOVEMBER 10, 1864

I can scarcely believe that Gen. John B. Houston has been arrested "for no other offense than opposition to my re-election," for if that had been deemed sufficient cause of arrest, I should have heard of more than one arrest in Kentucky on election day.

LETTER TO THOMAS E. BRAMLETTE
NOVEMBER 10, 1864

## Electoral College

I was once of your opinion . . . that presidential electors should be dispensed with; but a more thorough knowledge of the causes that first introduced them has made me doubt. Those causes were briefly these. The convention that framed the Constitution had this difficulty: the small states wished to so frame the new government as that they might be equal to the large ones regardless of the inequality of population. They compromised it, by basing the House of Representatives on *population*, and the Senate on *states* regardless of population; and the Executive on both principles, by electors in each state, equal in numbers to her senators *and* representatives. Now, throw away the machinery of electors and the compromise is broken up and the whole yielded to the principle of the large states. There is one thing more. In the slave states you have representatives and consequently, electors, partly upon the basis of your black population, which would be swept away by the change you seem to think desirable.

LETTER TO JOSEPHUS HEWETT
FEBRUARY 13, 1848

## Eloquence

Many eloquent men fail utterly; . . . they are not, as a class, generally successful.

EULOGY ON HENRY CLAY
JULY 6, 1852

## Emancipation

It is nothing but a miserable perversion of what I *have* said to assume that I have declared Missouri, or any other slave state, shall emancipate her slaves. I have proposed no such thing.

SEVENTH DEBATE WITH STEPHEN A. DOUGLAS,
ALTON, ILLINOIS
OCTOBER 15, 1858

If the General [Frémont] needs them [slaves], he can seize them and use them; but when the need is past, it is not for him to fix their permanent future condition. That must be settled according to laws made by lawmakers and not by military proclamations. . . . I do not say that Congress might not with propriety pass a law on the point . . . I do not say I might not, as a member of Congress, vote for it. What I object to is that I, as President, shall expressly or impliedly seize and exercise the permanent legislative functions of the government.

LETTER TO ORVILLE H. BROWNING
SEPTEMBER 22, 1861

The leaders of the existing insurrection entertain the hope that this government will ultimately be forced to acknowledge the independence of some part of the disaffected region. . . . To deprive them of this hope substantially ends the rebellion; and the initiation of emancipation completely deprives them of it, as to all states initiating it. . . . I say "initiation" because in my judgment gradual, and not sudden, emancipation is better for all.

MESSAGE TO CONGRESS
MARCH 6, 1862

If I were to suggest anything it would be that as the North are already for the measure, we should urge it *persuasively*, and not *menacingly*, upon the South. . . . I would like the bill to have the three main features: gradual; compensation; and vote of the people.

LETTER TO HORACE GREELEY
MARCH 24, 1862

To the people of those states [Georgia, Florida, South Carolina], I now earnestly appeal. I do not argue. I beseech you to make the arguments for yourselves. You cannot, if you would, be blind to the signs of the times. I beg of you a calm and enlarged consideration of them, ranging, if it may be, far above personal and partisan politics. This proposal makes common cause for a common object, casting no reproaches upon any. It acts not the pharisee. The change it contemplates would come gently as the dews of heaven, not rending or wrecking anything. Will you not embrace it? So much good has not been done by one effort in all past time, as, in the providence of God, it is now your high privilege to do. May the vast future not have to lament that you have neglected it.

PROCLAMATION REVOKING GENERAL HUNTER'S ORDER
OF MILITARY EMANCIPATION OF MAY 9, 1862
MAY 19, 1862

Let the states which are in rebellion see, definitely and certainly, that in no event will the states you represent ever join their proposed Confederacy, and they cannot much longer maintain the contest. But you cannot divest them of their hope to ultimately have you with them so long as you show a determination to perpetuate the institution within your own states. Beat them at elections, as you have overwhelmingly done, and, nothing daunted, they still claim you as their own. You and I know what the lever of their power is. Break that lever before their faces, and they can shake you no more forever.

APPEAL TO BORDER STATE REPRESENTATIVES TO
FAVOR COMPENSATED EMANCIPATION
JULY 12, 1862

You prefer that the constitutional relation of the states to the nation shall be practically restored, without disturbance of the institution; and if this were done, my whole duty in this respect, under the Constitution and my oath of office, would be performed. But it is not done, and we are trying to accomplish it by war. The incidents of the war cannot be avoided. If the war continue long, as it must if the object not be sooner attained, the institution in your states will be extinguished by mere friction and abrasion—by the mere incidents of war. It will be gone, and you will have nothing valuable in lieu of it. Much of its value is gone already. . . . How much better to thus save the money which else we sink forever in the war. . . . How much better for you as seller, and the nation as buyer, to sell out, and buy out, that without which the war could never have been, than to sink both the thing to be sold and the price of it in cutting one another's throats.

APPEAL TO BORDER STATE REPRESENTATIVES TO
FAVOR COMPENSATED EMANCIPATION
JULY 12, 1862

It is startling to say that Congress can free a slave within a state; and yet if it were said the ownership of the slave had first been transferred to the nation and that Congress had then liberated him, the difficulty would at once vanish. And this is the real case. The traitor against the general government forfeits his slave, at least as justly as he does any other property; and he forfeits both to the govern ent against which he offends. The government, so far as there can be ownership, thus owns the forfeited slaves; and the question for Congress in regard to them is, "Shall they be made free, or be sold to new masters?" I perceive no objection to Congress deciding in advance that they shall be free.

MESSAGE TO CONGRESS
JULY 17, 1862

I would save the Union, I would save it the shortest way under the Constitution. . . . If there be those who would not save the Union, unless they could at the same time *save* slavery, I do not agree with them. If there be those who would not save the Union unless they could at the same time *destroy* slavery, I do not agree with them. My paramount object in this struggle *is* to save the Union and is *not* either to save or to destroy slavery. If I could save the Union without freeing *any* slave I would do it, and if I could save it by freeing *all* the slaves I would do it; and if I could save it by freeing some and leaving others alone I would also do that. What I do about slavery and the colored race, I do because I believe it helps to save the Union; and what I forbear, I forbear because I do *not* believe it would help to save the Union.

LETTER TO HORACE GREELEY
AUGUST 22, 1862

I am approached with the most opposite opinions and advice, and that by religious men who are equally certain that they represent the Divine Will. I am sure that either the one or the other class is mistaken in that belief, and perhaps in some respects both. I hope it will not be irreverent for me to say that if it is probable that God would reveal his will to others on a point so connected with my duty, it might be supposed he would reveal it directly to me; for, unless I am more deceived in myself than I often am, it is my earnest desire to know the will of Providence in this matter. *And if I can learn what it is I will do it!* These are not, however, the days of miracles, and I suppose it will be granted that I am not to expect a direct revelation. I must study the plain physical facts of the case, ascertain what is possible and learn what appears to be wise and right. . . . What good would a proclamation of emancipation from me do, especially as we are now situated? I do not want to issue a document that the whole world will see must necessarily be inoperative, like the Pope's Bull against the comet.* Would *my word* free the slaves, when I cannot even enforce the Constitution in the rebel states? . . . And what reason is there to think it would have any greater effect upon the slaves than the late law of Congress, which I approved and which offers protection and freedom to the slaves of rebel masters who come within our lines? Yet I cannot learn that that law has caused a single slave to come over to us. And suppose they could be induced by a proclamation of freedom from me to throw themselves upon us, *what should we do with them?*

REPLY TO EMANCIPATION MEMORIAL PRESENTED BY
CHICAGO CHRISTIANS OF ALL DENOMINATIONS
SEPTEMBER 13, 1862

I admit that slavery is the root of the rebellion, or at least its *sine qua non.* . . . I will also concede that emancipation would help us in Europe and convince them that we are incited by something more than ambition. I grant further that it would help us *somewhat* in the North. . . . And then unquestionably it would weaken the rebels by drawing off their laborers, which is of great importance. But I am not sure we could do much with the blacks. If we were to arm them, I fear that in a few weeks the arms would be in the hands of the rebels. . . . I will mention another thing . . . : There are fifty thousand bayonets in the Union armies from the border slave states. It would be a serious

* Reference to a legend that a bull issued June 29, 1456, by Callistus III excommunicated Halley's Comet.

matter if, in consequence of a proclamation [of emancipation] . . . , they should go over to the rebels. . . . Let me say one thing more: I think you should admit that we already have an important principle to rally and unite the people in the fact that constitutional government is at stake. This is a fundamental idea, going down about as deep as any thing.

REPLY TO EMANCIPATION MEMORIAL PRESENTED BY
CHICAGO CHRISTIANS OF ALL DENOMINATIONS
SEPTEMBER 13, 1862

I have not decided against a proclamation of liberty to the slaves, but hold the matter under advisement. And I can assure you that the subject is on my mind, by day and night, more than any other. Whatever shall appear to be God's Will I will do.

REPLY TO EMANCIPATION MEMORIAL PRESENTED BY
CHICAGO CHRISTIANS OF ALL DENOMINATIONS
SEPTEMBER 13, 1862

On the first day of January, in the year of our Lord one thousand eight hundred and sixty-three, all persons held as slaves within any state or designated part of a state, the people whereof shall then be in rebellion against the United States, shall be then, thenceforward and forever free.

PRELIMINARY EMANCIPATION PROCLAMATION
SEPTEMBER 22, 1862

What I did, I did after very full deliberation and under a very heavy and solemn sense of responsibility. I can only trust in God I have made no mistake. . . . It is now for the country and the world to pass judgment on it.

REPLY TO A SERENADE IN HONOR OF
EMANCIPATION PROCLAMATION
SEPTEMBER 24, 1862

While I hope something from the Proclamation, my expectations are not as sanguine as are those of some friends. The time

for its effect southward has not come; but northward the effect
should be instantaneous. It is six days old, and while commenda-
tion in newspapers and by distinguished individuals is all that a
vain man could wish, the stocks have declined and troops come
forward more slowly than ever. . . . The North responds to the
Proclamation sufficiently in breath; but breath alone kills no
rebels.

LETTER TO HANNIBAL HAMLIN
SEPTEMBER 28, 1862

Emancipation, even without deportation, would probably enhance the wages of white labor and very surely would not reduce
them. Thus, the customary amount of labor would still have to
be performed; the freed people would surely not do more than
their old proportion of it and very probably for a time would do
less, leaving an increased part to white laborers, bringing their
labor into greater demand and, consequently, enhancing the
wages of it.

ANNUAL MESSAGE TO CONGRESS
DECEMBER 1, 1862

It is dreaded that the freed people will swarm forth and cover
the whole land? Are they not already in the land? Will liberation
make them any more numerous? Equally distributed among the
whites of the whole country, . . . there would be but one colored to seven whites. Could the one, in any way, greatly disturb
the seven? There are many communities now having more than
one free colored person to seven whites; and this, without any
apparent consciousness of evil from it. . . . But why should
Emancipation South send the free people North? People of any
color seldom run unless there be something to run from. *Heretofore* colored people, to some extent, have fled North from bondage; and *now*, perhaps, from both bondage and destitution. But
if gradual emancipation and deportation be adopted, they will
have neither to flee from. Their old masters will give them wages
at least until new laborers can be procured; and the freed men,
in turn, will gladly give their labor for the wages till new homes

can be found for them in congenial climes and with people of their own blood and race. . . . And, in any event, cannot the North decide for itself whether to receive them? . . .

ANNUAL MESSAGE TO CONGRESS<br>DECEMBER 1, 1862

In *giving* freedom to the *slave* we *assure* freedom to the *free*—honorable alike in what we give and what we preserve. We shall nobly save or meanly lose the last, best hope of earth. Other means may succeed; this could not fail. The way is plain, peaceful, generous, just—a way which, if followed, the world will forever applaud and God must forever bless.

ANNUAL MESSAGE TO CONGRESS<br>DECEMBER 1, 1862

I hereby enjoin upon the people so declared to be free to abstain from all violence, unless in necessary self-defense.

EMANCIPATION PROCLAMATION<br>JANUARY 1, 1863

Upon this act, sincerely believed to be an act of justice, warranted by the Constitution, upon military necessity, I invoke the considerable judgment of mankind, and the gracious favor of Almighty God.

EMANCIPATION PROCLAMATION<br>JANUARY 1, 1863

To use a coarse, but an expressive figure, broken eggs cannot be mended. I have issued the Emancipation Proclamation, and I cannot retract it. After the commencement of hostilities, I struggled nearly a year and a half to get along without touching the "institution"; and when finally I conditionally determined to touch it, I gave a hundred days' fair notice of my purpose to all the states and people within which time they could have turned it wholly aside by simply again becoming citizens of the United States. They chose to disregard it, and I made the peremptory proclamation on what appeared to me to be a military necessity. And being made, it must stand.

LETTER TO JOHN A. MCCLERNAND
JANUARY 8, 1863

The proclamation has been issued. We were not succeeding—at best, were progressing too slowly—without it. Now that we have it and bear all the disadvantages of it (as we do bear in certain quarters), we must also take some benefit from it if practicable.

LETTER TO JOHN A. DIX
JANUARY 14, 1863

Your dispatch, asking in substance whether, in case Missouri shall adopt gradual emancipation, the general government will protect slave owners in that species of property during the short time it shall be permitted by the state to exist within it, has been received. Desirous as I am that emancipation shall be adopted by Missouri and believing as I do that *gradual* can be made better than *immediate* for both black and white, except when military necessity changes the case, my impulse is to say that such protection would be given. I cannot know exactly what shape an act of emancipation may take. If the period from the initiation to the final end should be comparatively short, and the act should prevent persons being sold during that period into more lasting slavery, the whole would be easier. I do not wish to pledge the general government to the affirmative support of even temporary slavery beyond what can be fairly claimed under the Constitution. I suppose, however, this is not desired; but that it is desired for the military force of the United States, while in Missouri, to not be used in subverting the temporarily reserved legal rights in slaves during the progress of emancipation. This I would desire also. I have very earnestly urged the slave states to adopt emancipation; and it ought to be and is an object with me not to overthrow or thwart what any of them may in good faith do to that end.

LETTER TO JOHN M. SCHOFIELD
JUNE 22, 1863

The Emancipation Proclamation . . . is valid in law, and will be so held by the courts. I think I shall not retract or repudiate it. Those who shall have tasted actual freedom, I believe, can never be slaves or quasi-slaves again. For the rest, I believe some plan—substantially being gradual emancipation—would be better for both white and black. The Missouri plan, recently adopted, I do not object to on account of the time for *ending* the institution; but I am sorry the *beginning* should have been postponed for seven years, leaving all that time to agitate for the repeal of the whole thing. It should begin at once, giving at least the newborn a vested interest in freedom which could not be taken away.

LETTER TO STEPHEN A. HURLBUT
JULY 31, 1863

During my continuance here, the government will return no person to slavery who is free according to the proclamation or to any of the acts of Congress, unless such return shall be held to be a legal duty by the proper court of final resort, in which case I will promptly act as may then appear to be my personal duty.

FRAGMENT
AUGUST 1863 (?)

I would be glad for her [Louisiana] to make a new constitution recognizing the Emancipation Proclamation in those parts of the state to which the Proclamation does not apply. And while she is at it, I think it would not be objectionable for her to adopt some practical system by which the two races could gradually live themselves out of their old relations to each other and both come out better prepared for the new. Education for young blacks should be included in the plan.

LETTER TO NATHANIEL P. BANKS
AUGUST 5, 1863

The proclamation, as law, either is valid or is not valid. If it is not valid, it needs no retraction. If it is valid, it can not be retracted any more than the dead can be brought back to life. Some . . . profess to think its retraction would operate favorably for the Union. Why better *after* the retraction than *before* the issue? There was more than a year and a half of trial to suppress the rebellion before the proclamation issued, the last one hundred days of which passed under an explicit notice that it was coming, unless averted by those in revolt returning to their allegiance. The war has certainly progressed as favorably for us since the issue of the proclamation as before.

LETTER TO JAMES C. CONKLING
AUGUST 26, 1863

The original proclamation has no constitutional or legal justification except as a military measure. The exemptions were made because the military necessity did not apply to the exempted localities. Nor does that necessity apply to them now any more than it did then. If I take the step, must I not do so without the argument of military necessity and so without any argument except the one that I think the measure politically expedient and morally right? Would I not thus give up all footing upon Constitution or law? Would I not thus be in the boundless field of absolutism? Could this pass unnoticed or unresisted? . . . Would not many of our own friends shrink away appalled? Would it not lose us the elections and with them the very cause we seek to advance?

LETTER TO SALMON P. CHASE
SEPTEMBER 2, 1863

I see you have declared in favor of emancipation in Tennessee, for which may God bless you. Get emancipation into your new state government—constitution—and there will be no such word as fail for your case.

LETTER TO ANDREW JOHNSON
SEPTEMBER 11, 1863

My wishes are in a general way expressed as well as I can express them in the proclamation issued on the 8th of the present month. . . . It there appears that I deem the sustaining of the Emancipation Proclamation, where it applies, as indispensable. . . . I have not put forth the plan in that proclamation as a Pro-

crustean bed, to which exact conformity is to be indispensable.
. . . I wish that labor already done, which varies from that plan
in no important particular, may not be thrown away. . . . As to
the particulars of what I may think best to be done in any state,
I have publicly stated certain points which I have thought indispensable to the re-establishment and maintenance of the national
authority; and I go no further than this because I wish to avoid
both the substance and the appearance of dictation.

LETTER TO THOMAS COTTMAN
DECEMBER 15, 1863

You have inquired how the government would regard and
treat cases wherein the owners of plantations, in Arkansas for
instance, might fully recognize the freedom of those formerly
slaves and, by fair contracts of hire with them, recommence the
cultivation of their plantations. I answer I should regard such
cases with great favor and should, as the principle, treat them
precisely as I would treat the same number of free white people
in the same relation and condition. Whether white or black, reasonable effort should be made to give government protection. In
neither case should the giving of aid and comfort to the rebellion,
or other practices injurious to the government, be allowed on
such plantations; and in either, the government would claim the
right to take if necessary those of proper ages and conditions
into the military service. Such plan must not be used to break
up existing leases or arrangements of abandoned plantations
which the government may have made to give employment and
sustenance to the idle and destitute people. With the foregoing
qualifications and explanations, and in view of its tendency to advance freedom and restore peace and prosperity, such hiring and
employment of the freed people would be regarded by me with
rather especial favor.

LETTER TO ALPHEUS LEWIS
JANUARY 23, 1864

I think it probable that my expressions of a preference for
*gradual* over *immediate* emancipation are misunderstood. I had
thought the *gradual* would produce less confusion and destitu-

tion and therefore would be more satisfactory; but if those who are better acquainted with the subject and are more deeply interested in it prefer the *immediate*, most certainly I have no objection to their judgment prevailing. My wish is that all who are for emancipation *in any form* shall co-operate, all treating all respectfully, and all adopting and acting upon the major opinion when fairly ascertained. What I have dreaded is the danger that by jealousies, rivalries and consequent ill-blood—driving one another out of meetings and conventions, perchance from the polls —the friends of emancipation themselves may divide and lose the measure altogether.

LETTER TO JOHN A. J. CRESWELL
MARCH 7, 1864

Emancipation in Maryland . . . would aid much to end the rebellion.

LETTER TO JOHN A. J. CRESWELL
MARCH 17, 1864

When, early in the war, Gen. [John C.] Frémont attempted military emancipation, I forbade it because I did not then think it an indispensable necessity. When, a little later, Gen. [Simon] Cameron, then Secretary of War, suggested arming of the blacks, I objected because I did not yet think it an indispensable necessity. When, still later, Gen. [David] Hunter attempted military emancipation, I again forbade it because I did not yet think the indispensable necessity had come. When, in March and May and July 1862, I made earnest and successive appeals to the border states to favor compensated emancipation, I believed the indispensable necessity for military emancipation and arming the blacks would come unless averted by that measure. They declined the proposition; and I was, in my best judgment, driven to the alternative of either surrendering the Union, and with it the Constitution, or of laying strong hand upon the colored element. I chose the latter.

LETTER TO ALBERT G. HODGES
APRIL 4, 1864

More than a year of trial now shows no loss by it in our foreign relations, none in our home popular sentiment, none in our white military force—no loss by it anyhow or anywhere.

LETTER TO ALBERT G. HODGES
APRIL 4, 1864

## Embarrassment

I have found that when one is embarrassed usually the shortest way to get through with it is to quit talking or thinking about it and go at something else.

SPEECH AT CINCINNATI, OHIO
SEPTEMBER 17, 1859

## Employment

We must look not merely to *buying* cheap, nor yet to buying cheap *and* selling dear, but also to have constant employment so that we may have the largest possible of something to sell.

NOTES FOR TARIFF DISCUSSION
DECEMBER 1847

## Enemies

I have *bad* men also to deal with, both North and South—men who are eager for something new upon which to base misrepresentations—men who would like to frighten me or, at least, to fix upon me the character of timidity and cowardice. . . . I intend keeping my eye upon these gentlemen and to not unnecessarily put any weapons in their hands.

LETTER TO GEORGE D. PRENTICE
OCTOBER 29, 1860

## Equality

A few but an increasing number of men, . . . for the sake of perpetuating slavery, are beginning to assail and to ridicule the white man's charter of freedom—the declaration that "all men are created free and equal."

EULOGY ON HENRY CLAY
JULY 6, 1852

Most *governments* have been based, practically, on the denial of equal rights of men; . . . *ours* began by *affirming* those rights. *They* said some men are too *ignorant* and *vicious* to share in government. Possibly so, said we; and, by your system, you would always keep them ignorant and vicious. We proposed to give *all* a chance, and we expected the weak to grow stronger, the ignorant wiser, and all better and happier together.

FRAGMENT
JULY 1854 (?)

Let it not be said I am contending for the establishment of political and social equality between the whites and blacks. I have already said the contrary.

SPEECH AT PEORIA, ILLINOIS
OCTOBER 16, 1854

Near eighty years ago we began by declaring that all men are created equal; but now from that beginning we have run down to the other declaration that for SOME *men* to enslave OTHERS is a "sacred right of self-government." These principles cannot stand together. They are as opposite as God and mammon, and whoever holds to the one must despise the other.

SPEECH AT PEORIA, ILLINOIS
OCTOBER 16, 1854

When we were the political slaves of King George and wanted to be free, we called the maxim that "all men are created equal" a self-evident truth; but now when we have grown fat and have lost all dread of being slaves ourselves, we have become so greedy to be *masters* that we call the same maxim "a self-evident lie."

LETTER TO GEORGE ROBERTSON
AUGUST 15, 1855

Our progress in degeneracy appears to me to be pretty rapid. As a nation, we began by declaring *"all men are created equal."* We now practically read it "all men are created equal, *except Negroes.*" When the Know-Nothings get control, it will read "all men are created equal, except Negroes, *and foreigners, and Catholics.*" When it comes to this I should prefer emigrating to some country where they make no pretense of loving liberty—to Russia, for instance, where despotism can be taken pure and without the base alloy of hypocrisy.

LETTER TO JOSHUA F. SPEED
AUGUST 24, 1855

It is a truth that cannot be denied, that in all the free states no white man is the equal of the white man of the slave states.

SPEECH AT KALAMAZOO, MICHIGAN
AUGUST 27, 1856

Public opinion . . . always has a *"central idea"* from which all its minor thoughts radiate. That "central idea" in our political public opinion at the beginning was, and until recently has continued to be, "the equality of men." And although it has always submitted patiently to whatever of inequality there seemed to be as matter of actual necessity, its constant working has been a steady progress toward the practical equality of all men.

SPEECH AT CHICAGO, ILLINOIS
DECEMBER 10, 1856

I protest against that counterfeit logic which concludes that, because I do not want a black woman for a *slave*, I must necessarily want her for a *wife.* I need not have her for either; I can just leave her alone. In some respects she is certainly not my equal; but in her natural right to eat the bread she earns with her own hands without asking leave of any one else, she is my equal and the equal of all others.

SPEECH AT SPRINGFIELD, ILLINOIS
JUNE 26, 1857

Arguments . . . are made that the inferior race are to be treated with as much allowance as they are capable of enjoying; that as much is to be done for them as their condition will allow. What are these arguments? They are the arguments that kings have made for enslaving the people in all ages of the world. You will find that all the arguments in favor of king-craft were of this class; they always bestrode the necks of the people, not that they wanted to do it, but because the people were better off for being ridden. That is their argument, and this argument of the Judge [Stephen A. Douglas] is the same old serpent that says you work and I eat, you toil and I will enjoy the fruits of it. Turn in whatever way you will—whether it come from the mouth of a king, an excuse for enslaving the people of his country; or from the mouth of men of one race as a reason for enslaving the men of another race—it is all the same old serpent, and I hold if that course of argumentation that is made for the purpose of convincing the public mind that we should not care about this should be granted, it does not stop with the Negro. I should like to know if taking this old Declaration of Independence, which declares that all men are equal upon principle, and making exceptions to it— where will it stop? If one man says it does not mean a Negro, why not another say it does not mean some other man? If that Declaration is not the truth, let us get the statute book in which we find it and tear it out! Who is so bold as to do it! If it is not true, let us tear it out!

SPEECH AT CHICAGO, ILLINOIS
JULY 10, 1858

The Saviour, I suppose, did not expect that any human creature could be perfect as the Father in Heaven; but He said, "As your Father in Heaven is perfect, be ye also perfect." He set that up as a standard, and he who did most towards reaching that standard attained to the highest degree of moral perfection. So I say in relation to the principle that all men are created equal, let it be as nearly reached as we can. If we cannot give freedom to every creature, let us do nothing that will impose slavery upon any other creature. Let us then turn this government back into the channel in which the framers of the Constitution originally placed it. Let us stand firmly by each other. If we do not do so we are turning in the contrary direction that our friend Judge Douglas proposes—not intentionally—as working in the traces that tend to make this one universal slave nation. He is one that runs in that direction, and as such I resist him.

SPEECH AT CHICAGO, ILLINOIS<br>JULY 10, 1858

Let us discard all this quibbling about this man and the other man, this race and that race and the other race being inferior, and therefore they must be placed in an inferior position—discarding our standard that we have left us. Let us discard all these things and unite as one people throughout this land, until we shall once more stand up declaring that all men are created equal.

SPEECH AT CHICAGO, ILLINOIS<br>JULY 10, 1858

I leave you, hoping that the lamp of liberty will burn in your bosoms until there shall no longer be a doubt that all men are created free and equal.

SPEECH AT CHICAGO, ILLINOIS<br>JULY 10, 1858

Last night Judge [Stephen A.] Douglas tormented himself with horrors about my disposition to make Negroes perfectly equal with white men in social and political relations. He did not stop to show that I have said any such thing or that it legitimately follows from anything I have said, but he rushes on with his assertions.

SPEECH AT SPRINGFIELD, ILLINOIS<br>JULY 17, 1858

Who shall say, "I am the superior and you are the inferior"?

SPEECH AT SPRINGFIELD, ILLINOIS
JULY 17, 1858

I do not understand the Declaration [of Independence] to mean that all men were created equal in all respects. They [Negroes] are not our equal in color; but I suppose that it does mean to declare that all men are equal in some respects; they are equal in their right to "life, liberty, and the pursuit of happiness." Certainly the Negro is not our equal in color—perhaps not in many other respects; still, in the right to put into his mouth the bread that his own hands have earned, he is the equal of every other man, white or black. In pointing out that more has been given you, you cannot be justified in taking away the little which has been given him. All I ask for the Negro is that if you do not like him, let him alone. If God gave him but little, that little let him enjoy.

SPEECH AT SPRINGFIELD, ILLINOIS
JULY 17, 1858

I hold that . . . there is no reason in the world why the Negro is not entitled to all the natural rights enumerated in the Declaration of Independence: the right to life, liberty and the pursuit of happiness. I hold that he is as much entitled to these as the white man. I agree with Judge Douglas he is not my equal in many respects—certainly not in color, perhaps not in moral or intellectual endowment. But in the right to eat the bread, without leave of anybody else, which his own hand earns, *he is my equal and the equal of Judge Douglas, and the equal of every living man.*

FIRST DEBATE WITH STEPHEN A. DOUGLAS,
OTTAWA, ILLINOIS
AUGUST 21, 1858

I have no purpose to introduce political and social equality between the white and the black races. There is a physical difference between the two which, in my judgment, will probably forever forbid their living together upon the footing of perfect equality, and inasmuch as it becomes a necessity that there must be a difference, I . . . am in favor of the race to which I belong having the superior position.

FIRST DEBATE WITH STEPHEN A. DOUGLAS,
OTTAWA, ILLINOIS
AUGUST 21, 1858

I am not, nor ever have been, in favor of bringing about in any way the social and political equality of the white and black races. . . . I am not, nor ever have been, in favor of making voters or jurors of Negroes, nor of qualifying them to hold office, nor to intermarry with white people.

FOURTH DEBATE WITH STEPHEN A. DOUGLAS,
CHARLESTON, ILLINOIS
SEPTEMBER 18, 1858

Advancement—improvement in condition—is the order of things in a society of equals.

FRAGMENT ON FREE LABOR
SEPTEMBER 1859 (?)

The restoration of the rebel states to the Union must rest upon the principle of civil and political equality of both races.

LETTER TO JAMES S. WADSWORTH
JANUARY 1864 (?)

## Equanimity

Do nothing further about it. Although it wrongs me, and annoys me some, I prefer letting it run its course.

LETTER TO GEORGE G. FOGG
AUGUST 29, 1860

## Error

Holding it a sound maxim that it is better to be only sometimes right than at all times wrong, so soon as I discover my opinions to be erroneous I shall be ready to renounce them.

COMMUNICATION TO THE PEOPLE OF
SANGAMON COUNTY, ILLINOIS
MARCH 9, 1832

## Ethics

A public expose, . . . though it might confound the guilty, I fear might also injure some who are innocent.

LETTER TO JOHN ADDISON
AUGUST 9, 1850

I don't want to be unjustly accused of dealing illiberally or unfairly with an adversary, either in court or in a political canvass or anywhere else. I would despise myself if I supposed myself ready to deal less liberally with an adversary than I was willing to be treated myself.

FOURTH DEBATE WITH STEPHEN A. DOUGLAS,
CHARLESTON, ILLINOIS
SEPTEMBER 18, 1858

I confess, when I propose a certain measure of policy, it is not enough for me that I do not intend anything evil in the result, but it is incumbent on me to show that it has not a *tendency* to that result.

SEVENTH DEBATE WITH STEPHEN A. DOUGLAS,
ALTON, ILLINOIS
OCTOBER 15, 1858

## Evidence

We better know there is fire whence we see much smoke rising than [we] could know it by one or two witnesses swearing to it. The witnesses may commit perjury, but the smoke cannot.

LETTER TO JOHN R. UNDERWOOD AND HENRY GRIDER
OCTOBER 26, 1864

## Evil

An *evil* tree cannot bring forth *good* fruit.

LETTER TO WILLIAMSON DURLEY
OCTOBER 3, 1845

The true rule in determining to embrace or reject anything is not whether it have *any* evil in it, but whether it have more of evil than of good.

SPEECH ON INTERNAL IMPROVEMENTS
IN HOUSE OF REPRESENTATIVES
JUNE 20, 1848

There are few things *wholly* evil or *wholly* good.

SPEECH ON INTERNAL IMPROVEMENTS
IN HOUSE OF REPRESENTATIVES
JUNE 20, 1848

## Executions

I am trying to evade the butchering business lately.

ENDORSEMENT CONCERNING HENRY ANDREWS
JANUARY 7, 1864

## Expansion

When that flag was originally raised here it had but thirteen stars. I wish to call your attention to the fact that, under the blessing of God, each additional star added to that flag has given additional prosperity and happiness to this country. . . . Cultivating the spirit that animated our fathers, . . . cherishing that fraternal feeling which has so long characterized us as a nation, excluding passion, ill-temper and precipitate action on all occasions, I think we may promise ourselves that not only the new star placed upon that flag shall be permitted to remain there to our permanent prosperity for years to come; but additional ones shall from time to time be placed there, until we shall number as was anticipated by the great historian, five hundred millions of happy and prosperous people.

SPEECH AT THE FLAG-RAISING BEFORE INDEPENDENCE HALL,
PHILADELPHIA, PENNSYLVANIA
FEBRUARY 22, 1861

## Expediency

If I cannot rightfully murder a man, I may tie him to the tail of a kicking horse and let him kick the man to death.

SPEECH AT BLOOMINGTON, ILLINOIS
APRIL 10, 1860

Do we gain anything by opening one leak to stop another? Do we gain anything by quieting one clamor merely to open another and, probably, a larger one?

LETTER TO ALEXANDER K. MCCLURE
JUNE 30, 1863

## Experience

We all feel that we know that a blast of wind would extinguish the flame of the candle. . . . How do we know it? . . . We know it because we have seen through all our lives that a blast of wind extinguishes the flame of a candle whenever it is thrown fully upon it.

SPEECH ON THE SUB-TREASURY
DECEMBER 26, 1839

We all feel to *know* that we have to die. How? We have never died yet. We know it because we know, or at least we think we know, that of all the beings just like ourselves who have been coming into the world for six thousand years, not one is now living who was here two hundred years ago.

SPEECH ON THE SUB-TREASURY
DECEMBER 26, 1839

## Extremism

Often a limb must be amputated to save a life; but a life is never wisely given to save a limb.

LETTER TO ALBERT G. HODGES
APRIL 4, 1864

## Failure

If after all we shall fail, be it so.

SPEECH ON THE SUB-TREASURY
DECEMBER 26, 1839

I find quite as much material for a lecture in those points wherein I have failed as in those wherein I have been moderately successful.

NOTES FOR A LAW LECTURE
JULY 1850 (?)

## Fair Play

Fair play is a jewel.

LETTER TO SIMON CAMERON
AUGUST 10, 1861

## Faith

I never despair of sustaining myself before the people upon any measure that will stand a full investigation.

LETTER TO WILLIAM S. WAIT
MARCH 2, 1839

We shall not fail—if we stand firm, we shall not fail.

"A HOUSE DIVIDED" SPEECH, SPRINGFIELD, ILLINOIS
JUNE 16, 1858

The political horizon looks dark and lowering; but the people, under Providence, will set all right.

LETTER TO PETER H. SILVESTER
DECEMBER 22, 1860

## Falsehood

You were not very prudent, John, in stating a falsehood in this instance: but you were as prudent as possible, under the circumstances, to quote no authority by which to prove it.

LETTER TO JOHN HILL
SEPTEMBER 1860

## Falsification

I ought to know that the man who makes a charge without knowing it to be true falsifies as much as he who knowingly tells a falsehood.

FIRST DEBATE WITH STEPHEN A. DOUGLAS,
OTTAWA, ILLINOIS
AUGUST 21, 1858

## Farmers

My opinion of them [farmers] is that, in proportions to numbers, they are neither better nor worse than other people. In the nature of things they are more numerous than any other class; and I believe there really are more attempts at flattering them than any other, the reason of which I cannot perceive unless it be that they can cast more votes than any other.

SPEECH AT MILWAUKEE, WISCONSIN
SEPTEMBER 30, 1859

Farmers being the most numerous class, it follows that their interest is the largest interest. It also follows that that interest is most worthy of all to be cherished and cultivated—that if there be inevitable conflict between that interest and any other, that other should yield.

SPEECH AT MILWAUKEE, WISCONSIN
SEPTEMBER 30, 1859

## Farming

No other human occupation opens so wide a field for the profitable and agreeable combination of labor with cultivated thought as agriculture.

SPEECH AT MILWAUKEE, WISCONSIN
SEPTEMBER 30, 1859

## Favors

No one has needed favors more than I, and generally few have been less unwilling to accept them.

LETTER TO ROBERT ALLEN
JUNE 21, 1836

## Fiction

I am not much of a reader of this sort of literature.

LETTER TO JOHN MARSHALL
FEBRUARY 8, 1854

## Filing

When you can't find *it* any where else look into this.

SLIP WRITTEN ON FILE OF MISCELLANEOUS PAPERS
NO DATE

## Fishing

As the United States have, in common with Great Britain and France, a deep interest in the preservation and development of the fisheries adjacent to the northeastern coast and islands of this continent, it seems proper that we should concert with the governments of those countries such measures as may be conducive to those important objects.

MESSAGE TO CONGRESS
JULY 19, 1861

## Flattery

When my friend, Judge Douglas, came to Chicago on the 9th of July . . . he made an harangue there in which he . . . complimented me as being a "kind, amiable, and intelligent gentleman." . . . With these pleasant titles (I must confess to my weakness) I was a little "taken," for it came from a great man. I was not very much accustomed to flattery, and it came the sweeter to me. I was rather like the Hoosier with the gingerbread when he said he reckoned he loved it better than any other man and got less of it. . . .

FIRST DEBATE WITH STEPHEN A. DOUGLAS,
OTTAWA, ILLINOIS
AUGUST 21, 1858

## Forefathers

We find ourselves under the government of a system of political institutions conducing more essentially to the ends of civil and religious liberty than any of which the history of former times tells us. We, when mounting the stage of existence, found ourselves the legal inheritors of these fundamental blessings. We toiled not in the acquirement or establishment of them—they are a legacy bequeathed us by a *once* hardy, brave, and patriotic, but *now* lamented and departed race of ancestors.

SPEECH TO YOUNG MEN'S LYCEUM,
SPRINGFIELD, ILLINOIS
JANUARY 27, 1838

Theirs was the task (and nobly they performed it) to possess themselves, and through themselves, us, of this goodly land; and to uprear upon its hills and its valleys a political edifice of liberty and equal rights; 'tis ours only to transmit these—the former, unprofaned by the foot of an invader; the latter, undecayed by the lapse of time and untorn by usurpation—to the latest generation that fate shall permit the world to know. This task of gratitude to our fathers, justice to ourselves, duty to posterity, and love for our species in general, all imperatively require us faithfully to perform.

SPEECH TO YOUNG MEN'S LYCEUM,
SPRINGFIELD, ILLINOIS
JANUARY 27, 1838

I love the sentiments of those old-time men and shall be most happy to abide by their opinions.

SPEECH AT PEORIA, ILLINOIS
OCTOBER 16, 1854

Our fathers and grandfathers . . . were iron men; they fought for the principle that they were contending for; and we understood that by what they then did, it has followed that the degree of prosperity that we now enjoy has come to us.

SPEECH AT CHICAGO, ILLINOIS
JULY 10, 1858

The work of the Plymouth emigrants was the glory of their age. While we reverence their memory, let us not forget how vastly greater is our opportunity.

LETTER TO JOSEPH H. CHOATE
DECEMBER 19, 1864

## Foreign Relations

The United States have no enmities, animosities or rivalries, and no interests which conflict with the welfare, safety and rights or interests of any other nation. Their own prosperity, happiness and aggrandizement are sought most safely and advantageously through the preservation not only of peace on their own part, but peace among all other nations.

REPLY TO FEDERICO BARREDA,
MINISTER FROM PERU
MARCH 4, 1862

Republicanism is demonstrating its adaptation to the highest interests of society—the preservation of the state itself against the violence of faction. Elsewhere on the American continent it is struggling against the inroads of anarchy, which invites foreign intervention. Let the American States, therefore, draw closer together and animate and reassure each other and thus prove to the world that, although we have inherited some of the errors of ancient systems, we are nevertheless capable of completing and establishing the new one which we have chosen. On the result largely depends the progress, civilization and happiness of mankind.

REPLY TO LORENZO˙MONTUFAR,
MINISTER FROM SAN SALVADOR
APRIL 24, 1862

Several of the republics of this hemisphere . . . are alarmed at a supposed sentiment tending to reactionary movements against republican institutions on this continent. It seems therefore to be proper that we should show to any of them who may apply for that purpose that, compatibly with our cardinal policy and with an enlightened view of our own interests, we are willing to encourage them by strengthening our ties of good will and good neighborhood with them.

MESSAGE TO THE SENATE
MAY 30, 1862

We remain in peace and friendship with foreign powers. The efforts of disloyal citizens of the United States to involve us in foreign wars, to aid an inexcusable insurrection, have been unavailing. Her Britannic Majesty's government, as was justly expected, have exercised their authority to prevent the departure of new hostile expeditions from British ports. The Emperor of France has, by a like proceeding, promptly vindicated the neutrality which he proclaimed at the beginning of the contest. Questions of great intricacy and importance have arisen out of the blockade and other belligerent operations between the government and several of the maritime powers, but they have been discussed and, as far as was possible, accommodated in a spirit

of frankness, justice and mutual good will. It is especially gratifying that our prize courts, by the impartiality of their adjudica-
tions, have commanded the respect and confidence of maritime
powers.

ANNUAL MESSAGE TO CONGRESS
DECEMBER 8, 1863

When Congress assembled a year ago, the war had already
lasted nearly twenty months, and there had been many conflicts
on both land and sea with varying results. The rebellion had
been pressed back into reduced limits; yet the tone of public
feeling and opinion, at home and abroad, was not satisfactory.
With other signs, the popular elections, then just past, indicated
uneasiness among ourselves; while amid much that was cold and
menacing the kindest words coming from Europe were uttered
in accents of pity, that we were too blind to surrender a hopeless cause. Our commerce was suffering greatly by a few armed
vessels built upon and furnished from foreign shores, and we
were threatened with such additions from the same quarter
as would sweep our trade from the sea and raise our blockade.
We had failed to elicit from European governments anything
hopeful upon this subject. The . . . Emancipation Proclamation
came, including the announcement that colored men of suitable
condition would be received into the war service. The policy of
emancipation, and of employing black soldiers, gave to the future
a new aspect about which hope and fear and doubt contended
in uncertain conflict. . . . Eleven months having now passed, we
are permitted to take another review. . . . No servile insurrection, or tendency to violence or cruelty, has marked the measures
of emancipation and arming the blacks. These measures have
been much discussed in foreign countries, and contemporary
with such discussion the tone of public sentiment there is much
improved. . . . The crisis which threatened to divide the friends
of the Union is past.

ANNUAL MESSAGE TO CONGRESS
DECEMBER 8, 1863

## Foreign Trade

The United States, I think, ought not to be exceptionally illiberal to international trade and commerce.

ANNUAL MESSAGE TO CONGRESS
DECEMBER 8, 1863

## Freedom

As a nation of freemen, we must live through all time, or die by suicide.

SPEECH TO YOUNG MEN'S LYCEUM,
SPRINGFIELD, ILLINOIS
JANUARY 27, 1838

In our greedy chase to make profit of the Negro, let us beware lest we "cancel and tear to pieces" even the white man's charter of freedom.

SPEECH AT PEORIA, ILLINOIS
OCTOBER 16, 1854

This is a world of compensations; and he who would *be* no slave must consent to *have* no slave. Those who deny freedom to others deserve it not themselves; and, under a just God, cannot long retain it.

LETTER TO HENRY L. PIERCE AND OTHERS
APRIL 6, 1859

No oppressed people will *fight* and *endure* as our fathers did without the promise of something better than a mere change of masters.

FRAGMENT ON THE CONSTITUTION AND THE UNION
JANUARY 1861

The resources, advantages and powers of the American people are very great, and they have, consequently, succeeded to equally great responsibilities. It seems to have devolved upon them to test whether a government established on the principles of human freedom can be maintained against an effort to build one upon the exclusive foundation of human bondage.

LETTER TO THE WORKINGMEN OF LONDON, ENGLAND
FEBRUARY 2, 1863

## Free Enterprise

There is not, of necessity, any such thing as the free hired laborer being fixed to that condition for life. Many independent men everywhere in these states, a few years back in their lives, were hired laborers. The prudent, penniless beginner in the world labors for wages a while, saves a surplus with which to buy tools or land for himself; then labors on his own account for another while, and at length hires another new beginner to help him. This is the just, and generous, and prosperous system which opens the way to all—gives hope to all—and consequent energy, and progress, and improvement of condition to all. No men living are more worthy to be trusted than those who toil up from poverty—none less inclined to take, or touch, aught which they have not honestly earned. Let us beware of surrendering a political power which they already possess and which, if surrendered, will surely be used to close the door of advancement against such as they and to fix new disabilities and burdens upon them till all of liberty shall be lost.

ANNUAL MESSAGE TO CONGRESS
DECEMBER 3, 1861

## Frémont, John C.

He is losing the confidence of men near him whose support any man in his position must have to be successful. His cardinal mistake is that he isolates himself and allows nobody to see him, and by which he does not know what is going on in the very matter he is dealing with.

LETTER TO DAVID HUNTER
SEPTEMBER 9, 1861

No impression has been made on my mind against the honor or integrity of Gen. Frémont, and I now enter my protest against being understood as acting in any hostility towards him.

LETTER TO MRS. FRÉMONT
SEPTEMBER 12, 1861

## Friends

All our friends—They are too numerous to be now named individually, while there is no one of them who is not too dear to be forgotten or neglected.

TOAST AT A DINNER, SPRINGFIELD, ILLINOIS
JULY 25, 1837

How miserably things seem to be arranged in this world. If we have no friends, we have no pleasure; and if we have them, we are sure to lose them and be doubly pained by the loss.

LETTER TO JOSHUA F. SPEED
FEBRUARY 25, 1842

It is a delicate matter to oppose the wishes of a friend.

LETTER TO WILLIAM B. PRESTON
MAY 16, 1849

The better part of one's life consists of his friendships.

LETTER TO JOSEPH GILLESPIE
JULY 13, 1849

You distinguish between yourself and my *original* friends—
a distinction which, by your leave, I propose to forget.

LETTER TO SCHUYLER COLFAX
MAY 26, 1860

When I have friends who disagree with each other, I am very
slow to take sides in their quarrel.

LETTER TO ANDREW G. CURTIN
FEBRUARY 4, 1861

I think . . . all our friends should have absolute freedom of
choice among our friends.

MEMORANDUM ON INTERVIEW WITH CORNELIUS A. WALBORN
JUNE 20, 1864

## Fugitive Slave Law

I do not now, nor ever did, stand in favor of the unconditional
repeal of the fugitive slave law. . . . I have never hesitated to
say . . . that I think, under the Constitution of the United States,
the people of the Southern states are entitled to a congressional
fugitive slave law. . . . The existing fugitive slave law . . . I
think . . . should have been framed so as to be free from some
of the objections that pertain to it, without lessening its ef-
ficiency.

SECOND DEBATE WITH STEPHEN A. DOUGLAS,
FREEPORT, ILLINOIS
AUGUST 27, 1858

A member of Congress swears to support the Constitution of
the United States; and if he sees a right established by that
Constitution which needs specific legislative protection can he
clear his oath without giving that protection? Let me ask you
why many of us who are opposed to slavery upon principle
give our acquiescence to a fugitive slave law? Why do we hold
ourselves under obligations to pass such a law, and abide by

it when it is passed? Because the Constitution makes provision that the owners of slaves shall have the right to reclaim them. It gives the right to reclaim slaves, and that right is . . . a barren right unless there is legislation that will enforce it.

THIRD DEBATE WITH STEPHEN A. DOUGLAS,
JONESBORO, ILLINOIS
SEPTEMBER 15, 1858

I am for honest enforcement of the Constitution—fugitive slave clause included.

LETTER TO LYMAN TRUMBULL
DECEMBER 17, 1860

I may as well surrender this contest directly as to make any order the obvious purpose of which would be to return fugitive slaves.

LETTER TO GEORGE ROBERTSON
NOVEMBER 20, 1862

## Gamblers

If they were annually swept from the stage of existence by the plague or smallpox, honest men would, perhaps, be much profited.

SPEECH TO YOUNG MEN'S LYCEUM,
SPRINGFIELD, ILLINOIS
JANUARY 27, 1838

## Genius

Towering genius disdains a beaten path.

SPEECH TO YOUNG MEN'S LYCEUM,
SPRINGFIELD, ILLINOIS
JANUARY 27, 1838

## German-Americans

Ever true to *Liberty*, the *Union* and the Constitution—true to Liberty, not *selfishly*, but upon *principle*—not for special *classes* of men, but for *all* men; true to the Union and Constitution as the best means to advance that liberty.

LETTER TO ANTON C. HESING, HENRY WENDT AND
ALEXANDER FISHER
JUNE 30, 1858

The Germans are true and patriotic.

LETTER TO HENRY W. HALLECK
JANUARY 15, 1862

## Gettysburg

On this last Fourth of July just passed, when we have a gigantic rebellion, at the bottom of which is an effort to overthrow the principle that all men were created equal, we have the surrender of a most powerful position and army on that very day, and not only so, but in a succession of battles in Pennsylvania—near to us—through three days, so rapidly fought that they might be called one great battle on the 1st, 2d and 3d of the month of July; and on the 4th the cohorts of those who opposed the declaration that all men are created equal "turned tail" and run.

RESPONSE TO A SERENADE
JULY 7, 1863

## Gettysburg Address

I expected to see you here at Cabinet meeting and to say something about going to Gettysburg. There will be a train to take and return us. The time for starting is not yet fixed; but when it shall be, I will notify you.

LETTER TO SALMON P. CHASE
NOVEMBER 17, 1863

FIRST DRAFT

Fourscore and seven years ago our fathers brought forth, upon this continent, a new nation, conceived in liberty, and dedicated to the proposition that "all men are created equal." Now we are engaged in a great civil war, testing whether that nation, or any nation so conceived, and so dedicated, can long endure. We are met on a great battle field of that war. We have come to dedicate a portion of it, as a final resting place for those who died here, that the nation might live. This we may, in all propriety do. But, in a larger sense, we can not dedicate—we can not consecrate—we can not hallow, this ground. The brave men, living and dead, who struggled here, have hallowed it, far above our poor power to add or detract. The world will little note, nor long remember what we say here; while it can never forget what they did here.

It is rather for us, the living, to stand here, we here be dedicated to the great task remaining before us—that, from these honored dead we take increased devotion to that cause for which they here, gave the last full measure of devotion—that we here highly resolve these dead shall not have died in vain; that the nation, shall have a new birth of freedom, and that government of the people by the people for the people, shall not perish from the earth.

DRAFT OF SPEECH TO BE DELIVERED AT DEDICATION
OF CEMETERY AT GETTYSBURG, PENNSYLVANIA
NOVEMBER 19, 1863

FINAL TEXT

Fourscore and seven years ago our fathers brought forth on this continent, a new nation, conceived in Liberty, and dedicated to the proposition that all men are created equal.

Now we are engaged in a great civil war, testing whether that nation, or any nation so conceived and so dedicated, can long endure. We are met on a great battle-field of that war. We have come to dedicate a portion of that field, as a final resting place for those who here gave their lives that that nation might live. It is altogether fitting and proper that we should do this.

But, in a larger sense, we cannot dedicate—we cannot consecrate—we cannot hallow—this ground. The brave men, living and dead, who struggled here, have consecrated it, far above our poor power to add or detract. The world will little note, nor long remember what we say here, but it can never forget what they did here. It is for us the living, rather, to be dedicated here to the unfinished work which they who fought here have thus far so nobly advanced. It is rather for us to be here dedicated to the great task remaining before us—that from these honored dead we take increased devotion to that cause for which they gave the last full measure of devotion—that we here highly resolve that these dead shall not have died in vain—that this nation, under God, shall have a new birth of freedom—and that government of the people, by the people, for the people, shall not perish from the earth.

SPEECH DELIVERED AT DEDICATION
OF CEMETERY AT GETTYSBURG, PENNSYLVANIA
NOVEMBER 19, 1863

In our respective parts yesterday, you could not have been excused to make a short address, nor I a long one. I am pleased to know that, in your judgment, the little I did say was not entirely a failure.

LETTER TO EDWARD EVERETT
NOVEMBER 20, 1863

## God

He renders the worst of human conditions tolerable, while He permits the best to be nothing better than tolerable.

LETTER TO MARY SPEED
SEPTEMBER 27, 1841

He notes the fall of a sparrow and numbers the hair of our heads; and He will not forget the dying man who puts his trust in Him.

LETTER TO JOHN D. JOHNSTON

JANUARY 12, 1851

Call upon and confide in our great and good and merciful Maker, who will not turn away . . . in any extremity.

LETTER TO JOHN D. JOHNSTON

JANUARY 12, 1851

The will of God prevails. In great contests each party claims to act in accordance with the will of God. Both *may* be, and one *must* be wrong. God cannot be *for* and *against* the same thing at the same time. In the present civil war it is quite possible that God's purpose is something quite different from the purpose of either party—and yet the human instrumentalities, working just as they do, are of the best adaptation to effect His purpose. I am almost ready to say this is probably true—that God wills this contest and wills that it shall not yet end. By His mere quiet power on the minds of the now contestants, He could either have *saved* or *destroyed* the Union without a human contest. Yet the contest began. And having begun, He could give the final victory to either side any day. Yet the contest proceeds.

MEDITATION ON THE DIVINE WILL

SEPTEMBER 1862

Whatever shall be sincerely, and in God's name, devised for the good of the soldier and seaman in their hard spheres of duty can scarcely fail to be blest. And whatever shall tend to turn our thoughts from the unreasoning and uncharitable passions, prejudices and jealousies incident to a great national trouble, such as ours, and to fix them upon the vast and long-enduring consequences, for weal or for woe, which are to result from the struggle; and especially to strengthen our reliance on the Supreme Being for the final triumph of the right, can not but be well for us all.

LETTER TO ALEXANDER REED

FEBRUARY 22, 1863

We have been the recipients of the choicest bounties of Heaven. We have been preserved these many years in peace and prosperity. We have grown in numbers, wealth and power as no other nation has ever grown. But we have forgotten God. . . . We have vainly imagined, in the deceitfulness of our hearts, that all these blessings were produced by some superior wisdom and virtue of our own. Intoxicated with unbroken success, we have become too self-sufficient to feel the necessity of redeeming and preserving grace, too proud to pray to the God that made us!

PROCLAMATION APPOINTING A NATIONAL FAST DAY
MARCH 30, 1863

Amid the greatest difficulties of my administration, when I could not see any other resort, I would place my whole reliance in God, knowing that all would go well and that He would decide for the right.

REMARKS TO BALTIMORE PRESBYTERIAN SYNOD
OCTOBER 24, 1863

Another year of health and of sufficiently abundant harvests has passed. For these, and especially for the improved condition of our national affairs, our renewed and profoundest gratitude to God is due.

ANNUAL MESSAGE TO CONGRESS
DECEMBER 8, 1863

If God now wills the removal of a great wrong, and wills also that we of the North as well as you of the South shall pay fairly for our complicity in that wrong, impartial history will find therein new cause to attest and revere the justice and goodness of God.

LETTER TO ALBERT G. HODGES
APRIL 4, 1864

The Almighty has His own purposes. "Woe unto the world because of offenses! for it must needs be that offenses come; but woe to that man by whom the offense cometh!" If we shall suppose that American slavery is one of those offenses which, in the providence of God, must needs come, but which, having continued through His appointed time, He now wills to remove, and that He gives to both North and South this terrible war, as the woe due to those by whom the offense came, shall we discern therein any departure from those attributes which the believers in a Living God always ascribe to Him?

SECOND INAUGURAL ADDRESS

MARCH 4, 1865

Men are not flattered by being shown that there has been a difference of purpose between the Almighty and them. To deny it, however, . . . is to deny that there is a God governing the world.

LETTER TO THURLOW WEED

MARCH 15, 1865

## Government

That our government should have been maintained in its original form from its establishment until now is not much to be wondered at.

SPEECH TO YOUNG MEN'S LYCEUM, SPRINGFIELD, ILLINOIS

JANUARY 27, 1838

In all that the people can individually do as well for themselves, government ought not to interfere.

FRAGMENT

JULY 1854 (?)

The legitimate object of government is to do for a community of people whatever they need to have done but cannot do *at all*, or cannot *so well do*, for themselves in their separate and individual capacities.

FRAGMENT

JULY 1854 (?)

The desirable things which the individuals of a people cannot do or cannot well do for themselves fall into two classes: those which have relations to *wrongs*, and those which have not.

FRAGMENT
JULY 1854 (?)

The best-framed and best-administered governments are necessarily expensive.

FRAGMENT
JULY 1854 (?)

Government is a combination of the people of a country to effect certain objects by joint effort.

FRAGMENT
JULY 1854 (?)

If all men were just, there would still be *some*, though not so *much*, need of government.

FRAGMENT
JULY 1854 (?)

According to our ancient faith, the just powers of government are derived from the consent of the governed.

SPEECH AT PEORIA, ILLINOIS
OCTOBER 16, 1854

No man is good enough to govern another man *without that other's consent*. I say this is the leading principle, the sheet anchor, or American republicanism.

SPEECH AT PEORIA, ILLINOIS
OCTOBER 16, 1854

What use for the general government when there is nothing left for it [to] govern?

SPEECH AT PEORIA, ILLINOIS
OCTOBER 16, 1854

I believe each individual is naturally entitled to do as he pleases with himself and the fruit of his labor so far as it in no wise interferes with any other man's rights—that each community, as a state, has a right to do exactly as it pleases with all the concerns within that state that interfere with the rights of no other state, and that the general government, upon principle, has no right to interfere with anything other than that general class of things that does concern the whole.

SPEECH AT CHICAGO, ILLINOIS
JULY 10, 1858

It is no just function of government to prohibit what is *not wrong*.

NOTES FOR SPEECHES AT COLUMBUS AND CINCINNATI, OHIO
SEPTEMBER 16, 17, 1859

We admit that the U. S. general government is not charged with the duty of redressing or preventing all the wrongs in the world. But that government rightfully may and, subject to the Constitution, ought to redress and prevent all wrongs which are wrongs to the nation itself.

NOTES FOR SPEECHES AT COLUMBUS AND CINCINNATI, OHIO
SEPTEMBER 16, 17, 1859

The republican system of government, which has been adopted so generally on this continent, has proved its adaptation to what is the first purpose of government everywhere—the maintenance of national independence. It is my confident hope and belief that this system will be found, after sufficient trials, to be better adapted everywhere than any other to other great interests of human society—namely, the preservation of peace, order and national prosperity.

REPLY TO DON MARCELINO HURTADO, ENVOY OF GRENADA
JUNE 4, 1861

It is not always in the power of governments to enlarge or restrict the scope of moral results which follow the policies that they may deem it necessary for the public safety, from time to time, to adopt.

LETTER TO THE WORKINGMEN OF MANCHESTER, ENGLAND
JANUARY 19, 1863

Let the friends of the government first save the government, and then administer it to their own liking.

LETTER TO HENRY W. DAVIS
MARCH 18, 1863

While we must, by all available means, prevent the overthrow of the government, we should avoid planting and cultivating too many thorns in the bosom of society.

LETTER TO EDWIN M. STANTON
MARCH 18, 1864

Government should not act for revenge.

LETTER TO EDWIN M. STANTON
MAY 17, 1864

## Grant, Ulysses S.

Grant is a copious worker and fighter, but a very meager writer or telegrapher.

LETTER TO AMBROSE E. BURNSIDE
JULY 27, 1863

The nation's appreciation of what you have done and its reliance upon you for what remains to do in the existing great struggle are now presented with this commission, constituting you Lieutenant General in the Army of the United States. With this high honor devolves upon you also a corresponding responsibility. As the country herein trusts you, so, under God, it will sustain you. I scarcely need to add that with what I here speak for the nation goes my own hearty personal concurrence.

SPEECH TO ULYSSES S. GRANT
MARCH 9, 1864

I have seen your dispatch expressing your unwillingness to break your hold where you are. . . . Hold on with a bulldog grip, and chew and choke as much as possible.

TELEGRAM TO ULYSSES S. GRANT
AUGUST 17, 1864

## Greed

After an angry and dangerous controversy, the parties made friends by dividing the bone of contention. The one party first appropriates her own share, beyond all power to be disturbed in the possession of it, and then seizes the share of the other party. It is as if two starving men had divided their only loaf, the one had hastily swallowed his half and then grabbed the other half just as he was putting it in his mouth!

SPEECH AT PEORIA, ILLINOIS
OCTOBER 16, 1854

## Greeley, Horace

*I* consider him incapable of corruption or falsehood.

LETTER TO CHARLES L. WILSON
JUNE 1, 1858

## Habeas Corpus

It was decided that we have a case of rebellion, and the public safety does require the qualified suspension of the writ which was authorized to be made. Now it is insisted that Congress, and not the Executive, is vested with this power. But the Constitution itself is silent as to which, or who, is to exercise the power; and as the provision was plainly made for a dangerous emergency it cannot be believed the framers of the instrument contended that in every case the danger should run its course until Congress could be called together, the very assembling of which might be prevented, as was intended in this case, by the rebellion.

MESSAGE TO CONGRESS IN SPECIAL SESSION

JULY 4, 1861

Suspension [of Habeas Corpus] is allowed by the Constitution on purpose that men may be arrested and held who cannot be proved to be guilty of defined crime, "when, in cases of rebellion or invasion the public safety may require it." This is precisely our present case—a case of rebellion wherein the public safety does require the suspension. Indeed, arrests by process of courts and arrests in cases of rebellion do not proceed altogether upon the same basis. The former is directed at the small percentage of ordinary and continuous perpetration of crime; while the latter is directed at sudden and extensive uprisings against the government which, at most, will succeed or fail in no great length of time. In the latter case arrests are made not so much for what has been done as for what probably would be done. The latter is more for the preventive and less for the vindictive than the former. . . . I concede that the class of arrests complained of can be constitutional only when, in cases of rebellion or invasion, the public safety may require them; and I insist that in such cases they are constitutional *wherever* the public safety does require them—as well in places to which they may prevent the rebellion extending as in those where it may be already prevailing —as well where they may restrain mischievous interference with the raising and supplying of armies to suppress the rebellion as where the rebellion may actually be—as well where they may restrain the enticing men out of the army as where they would prevent mutiny in the army—equally constitutional at all places where they will conduce to the public safety as against the dangers of rebellion or invasion.

LETTER TO ERASTUS CORNING AND OTHERS

JUNE 12, 1863

The benefit of the writ of Habeas Corpus is the great means through which the guarantees of personal liberty are conserved.

LETTER TO MATTHEW BIRCHARD AND OTHERS
JUNE 29, 1863

## Happiness

Nothing would make me more miserable than to believe you miserable—nothing more happy than to know you were so.

LETTER TO MARY S. OWENS
AUGUST 16, 1837

## Haste

There is not a moment of time to be lost.

LETTER TO JOSIAH B. HERRICK
JUNE 3, 1849

## Hawaii

In every light in which the state of the Hawaiian Islands can be contemplated, it is an object of profound interest to the United States. Virtually it was once a colony. It is now a near and intimate neighbor. It is a haven of shelter and refreshment for our merchant fishermen, seamen and other citizens, when on their lawful occasions they are navigating the eastern seas and oceans. Its people are free, and its laws, language and religion are largely the fruits of our own teaching and example.

REPLY TO A SPEECH BY ELISHA H. ALLEN,
ENVOY AND MINISTER FROM HAWAII
JUNE 9, 1864

## Heckling

I am quite willing to answer any gentleman in the crowd who asks an *intelligent* question.

SPEECH AT CHICAGO, ILLINOIS
JULY 10, 1858

## History

What invading foemen could *never do,* the silent artillery of time *has done.*

SPEECH TO YOUNG MEN'S LYCEUM,
SPRINGFIELD, ILLINOIS
JANUARY 27, 1838

What has once happened will invariably happen again when the same circumstances which combined to produce it shall again combine in the same way.

SPEECH ON THE SUB-TREASURY
DECEMBER 26, 1839

·We know nothing of what will happen in future but by the analogy of experience.

SPEECH ON THE SUB-TREASURY
DECEMBER 26, 1839

Fellow citizens, *we* cannot escape history. We of this Congress and this administration will be remembered in spite of ourselves. No personal significance, or insignificance, can spare one or another of us. The fiery trial through which we pass will light us down, in honor or dishonor, to the latest generation. We *say* we are for the Union. The world will not forget that we say this. We know how to save the Union. The world knows we do know how to save it. We—even *we here*—hold the power, and bear the responsibility.

ANNUAL MESSAGE TO CONGRESS
DECEMBER 1, 1862

A fair examination of history has seemed to authorize a belief that the past action and influence of the United States were generally regarded as having been beneficent towards mankind.

LETTER TO THE WORKINGMEN OF MANCHESTER, ENGLAND
JANUARY 19, 1863

## Honesty

Upon the subjects of which I have treated, I have spoken as I thought.

COMMUNICATION TO THE PEOPLE OF
SANGAMON COUNTY, ILLINOIS
MARCH 9, 1832

The noblest work of God—an honest man.

EULOGY ON BENJAMIN FERGUSON
TO THE WASHINGTON TEMPERANCE SOCIETY,
SPRINGFIELD, ILLINOIS
FEBRUARY 8, 1842

## Human Nature

I believe it is universally understood and acknowledged that all men will ever act correctly, unless they have a motive to do otherwise.

SPEECH IN ILLINOIS LEGISLATURE
JANUARY 11, 1837

Pleasures to be enjoyed or pains to be endured *after* we shall be dead and gone are but little regarded even in our *own* cases, and much less in the cases of others.

ADDRESS TO WASHINGTON TEMPERANCE SOCIETY,
SPRINGFIELD, ILLINOIS
FEBRUARY 22, 1842

Slavery is founded in the selfishness of man's nature—opposition to it is [in] his love of justice. These principles are an eternal antagonism; and when brought into collision so fiercely, as slavery extension brings them, shocks and throes and convulsions must ceaselessly follow. . . . Repeal all compromises—repeal the Declaration of Independence—repeal all past history; you still cannot repeal human nature.

SPEECH AT PEORIA, ILLINOIS
OCTOBER 16, 1854

When a not very great man begins to be mentioned for a very great position, his head is very likely to be a little turned.

LETTER TO RICHARD M. CORWINE
APRIL 6, 1860

Human nature will not change. In any future great national trial, compared with the men of this, we shall have as weak and as strong; as silly and as wise; as bad and good. Let us, therefore, study the incidents of this as philosophy to learn wisdom from.

RESPONSE TO A SERENADE
NOVEMBER 10, 1864

## Humor

The fisherman's wife, whose drowned husband was brought home with his body full of eels, said when she was asked what was to be done with him—*"Take the eels out and set him again."*

FIFTH DEBATE WITH STEPHEN A. DOUGLAS,
GALESBURG, ILLINOIS
OCTOBER 7, 1858

He said he was riding *bass-ackwards* on a *jass-ack*, through a *patton-cotch*, on a pair of *baddle-sags*, stuffed full of *binger-gred*, when the animal *steered* at a *scump*, and the *lirrup-steather* broke, and throwed him in the *forner* of the *kence* and broke his *pishing-fole*. He said he would not have minded it much, but he fell right in a great *tow-curd*; in fact, he said it give him a right smart *sick* of *fitness*—he had the *molera-corbus* pretty bad. He said, about *bray dake* he come to himself, ran home, seized up a *stick* of *wood* and split the *axe* to make a light, rushed into the house, and found the *door* sick abed, and his *wife* standing open. But thank goodness she is getting right *hat* and *farty* again.

IDENTIFIED AS A "PIECE" WHICH LINCOLN WROTE<br>
AND GAVE THE BAILIFF OF<br>
THE COURT IN SPRINGFIELD, ILLINOIS<br>
NO DATE

Some specimens of your soap have been used at our house and Mrs. L. declares it is a superb article. She at the same time protests that *I* have never given sufficient attention to the "soap question" to be a competent judge.

LETTER TO DANIEL P. GARDNER<br>
SEPTEMBER 28, 1860

## Immigration

In regard to Germans and foreigners, I esteem foreigners no better than other people, nor any worse. They are all of the great family of men, and if there is one shackle upon any of them it would be far better to lift the load from them than to pile additional loads upon them. And inasmuch as the continent of America is a comparatively new country and the other countries of the world are old countries, there is more room here, comparatively speaking, than there is there; and if they can better their condition by leaving their old homes, there is nothing in my heart to forbid them coming; and I bid them all Godspeed.

SPEECH AT CINCINNATI, OHIO<br>
FEBRUARY 12, 1861

I again submit to your consideration the expediency of establishing a system for the encouragement of immigration. Although this source of national wealth and strength is again flowing with greater freedom than for several years before the insurrection occurred, there is still a great deficiency of laborers in every field of industry, especially in agriculture and in our mines, as well of iron and coal as of the precious metals. While the demand for labor is thus increased here, tens of thousands of persons, destitute of remunerative occupation, are thronging our foreign consulates and offering to emigrate to the United States if essential, but very cheap, assistance can be afforded them. It is easy to see that, under the sharp discipline of civil war, the nation is beginning a new life. This noble effort demands the aid and ought to receive the attention of the government.

ANNUAL MESSAGE TO CONGRESS
DECEMBER 8, 1863

## Impartiality

I think very much of the people as an old friend said he thought of woman. He said when he lost his first wife, who had been a great help to him in his business, he thought he was ruined—that he could never find another to fill her place. At length, however, he married another who he found did quite as well as the first, and that his opinion now was that any woman would do well who was well done by. So I think of the whole people of this nation—they will ever do well if well done by. We will try to do well by them in all parts of the country, North and South, with entire confidence that all will be well with all of us.

REMARKS AT BLOOMINGTON, ILLINOIS
NOVEMBER 21, 1860

I intend . . . to accommodate the people in the several localities if they themselves will allow me to accommodate them. In one word, I never have been, am not now and probably never shall be in a mood of harassing the people, North or South.

LETTER TO JOHN A. GILMER
DECEMBER 15, 1860

It is proper that I should avail myself of all the information and all the time at my command in order that when the time arrives in which I must speak officially I shall be able to take the ground which I deem the best and safest and from which I may have no occasion to swerve. I shall endeavor to take the ground I deem most just to the North, the East, the West, the South and the whole country. I take it, I hope, in good temper—certainly no malice toward any section.

ADDRESS AT TRENTON, NEW JERSEY
FEBRUARY 21, 1861

As President, in the administration of the government, I hope to be man enough not to know one citizen of the United States from another, nor one section from another.

REPLY TO A MASSACHUSETTS DELEGATION
MARCH 5, 1861

## Impatience

While I am anxious, please do not suppose I am impatient.

LETTER TO JOSEPH HOOKER
APRIL 28, 1863

## Inconsistency

No party can command respect which sustains this year what it opposed last.

LETTER TO SAMUEL GALLOWAY
JULY 28, 1859

## Independence Day

The Fourth of July has not quite dwindled away; it is still a great day—*for burning firecrackers!!!*

LETTER TO GEORGE ROBERTSON
AUGUST 15, 1855

We hold this annual celebration to remind ourselves of all the good done in this process of time, of how it was done and who did it, and how we are historically connected with it.

SPEECH AT CHICAGO, ILLINOIS
JULY 10, 1858

## Indians

The pale-faced people are numerous and prosperous because they cultivate the earth, produce bread and depend upon the products of the earth rather than wild game for a subsistence. . . . We are not, as a race, so much disposed to fight and kill one another as our red brethren.

SPEECH TO INDIANS
MARCH 27, 1863

Sound policy and our imperative duty to these wards of the government demand our anxious and constant attention to their material well-being, to their progress in the arts of civilization, and, above all, to that moral training which, under the blessing of Divine Providence, will confer upon them the elevated and sanctifying influences, the hopes and consolation of the Christian faith.

ANNUAL MESSAGE TO CONGRESS
DECEMBER 8, 1863

## Industrial Arts

Citizens of the United States may justly pride themselves upon their proficiency in industrial arts.

MESSAGE TO CONGRESS
JULY 16, 1861

## Inequality

Inequality is certainly never to be embraced for its own sake; but is every good thing to be discarded which may be inseparably connected with some degree of it? If so, we must discard all government.

SPEECH ON INTERNAL IMPROVEMENTS
IN HOUSE OF REPRESENTATIVES
JUNE 20, 1848

## Injustice

There is no keeping men silent when they feel they are wronged by their friends.

LETTER TO WILLIAM B. PRESTON
APRIL 20, 1849

I intend no injustice to any; and if I have done any, I deeply regret it.

LETTER TO GEORGE B. MCCLELLAN
OCTOBER 27, 1862

## Insanity

> And here's an object more of dread
> Than ought the grave contains—
> A human-form, with reason fled,
> While wretched life remains.

STANZA FROM "MY CHILDHOOD HOME I SEE AGAIN"
FEBRUARY 1846 (?)

## Interference

The interference of outsiders generally does more harm than good. It breeds confusion and, with it, delays and neglect.

LETTER TO WILLIAM M. COOPER
JULY 23, 1863

## Internal Improvements

Time and experience have verified to a demonstration the public utility of internal improvements.

COMMUNICATION TO THE PEOPLE OF
SANGAMON COUNTY, ILLINOIS
MARCH 9, 1832

## Jackson, Andrew

Like a horde of hungry ticks you have stuck to the tail of the Hermitage lion to the end of his life; and you are sticking to it, and drawing a loathsome sustenance from it, after he is dead. A fellow once advertised that he had made a discovery by which he could make a new man out of an old one, and have enough of the stuff left to make a little yellow dog. Just such a discovery has Gen. Jackson's popularity been to you. You have not only twice made President of him out of it, but you have had enough of the stuff left to make Presidents of several comparatively small men since; and it is your chief reliance now to make still another.

SPEECH IN HOUSE OF REPRESENTATIVES
JULY 27, 1848

*Jefferson, Thomas*

Mr. Jefferson . . . was, is, and perhaps will continue to be, the most distinguished politician of our history.

SPEECH AT PEORIA, ILLINOIS
OCTOBER 16, 1854

The liberty of making slaves of other people—Jefferson never thought of.

SPEECH AT PEORIA, ILLINOIS
OCTOBER 16, 1854

Bearing in mind that about seventy years ago two great political parties were first formed in this country, that Thomas Jefferson was the head of one of them and Boston the headquarters of the other, it is both curious and interesting that those supposed to descend politically from the party opposed to Jefferson should now be celebrating his birthday in their own original seat of empire, while those claiming political descent from him have nearly ceased to breathe his name everywhere. . . . All honor to Jefferson—to the man who, in the concrete pressure of a struggle for national independence by a single people, had the coolness, forecast and capacity to introduce into a merely revolutionary document an abstract truth applicable to all men and all times, and so to embalm it there that today, and in all coming days, it shall be a rebuke and a stumbling block to the very harbingers of reappearing tyranny and oppression.

LETTER TO HENRY L. PIERCE AND OTHERS
APRIL 6, 1859

## Jury

A jury too frequently have at least one member more ready
to hang the panel than to hang the traitor.

LETTER TO ERASTUS CORNING AND OTHERS
JUNE 12, 1863 (?)

## Justice

If some men will kill, or beat, or constrain others, or despoil
them of property by force, fraud or noncompliance with contracts, it is a common object with peaceful and just men to
prevent it.

FRAGMENT
JULY 1854 (?)

## Labor

All *carrying*, and incidents of carrying, of articles from the
place of their production to a *distant* place for consumption,
which articles could be produced of as good quality, in sufficient
quantity, and with as little labor at the place of consumption as
at the place carried from, is useless labor.

NOTES FOR A TARIFF DISCUSSION
DECEMBER 1847

In the early days of the world, the Almighty said to the first
of our race, "In the sweat of thy face shalt thou eat bread";
and since then, if we except the *light* and the *air* of heaven, no
good thing has been or can be enjoyed by us without having
fir t cost labor.

NOTES FOR A TARIFF DISCUSSION
DECEMBER 1847

To each laborer the whole product of his labor, or as nearly as possible, is a most worthy object of any good government.

NOTES FOR A TARIFF DISCUSSION
DECEMBER 1847

The habits of our whole species fall into three great classes—*useful* labor, *useless* labor and *idleness*. Of these the first only is meritorious, and to it all the products of labor rightfully belong; but the two latter, while they exist, are heavy pensioners upon the first, robbing it of a large portion of its just rights.

NOTES FOR A TARIFF DISCUSSION
DECEMBER 1847

Inasmuch as most good things are produced by labor, it follows that all such things of right belong to those whose labor has produced them. But it has so happened in all ages of the world that *some* have labored and others *have*, without labor, enjoyed a large proportion of the fruits. This is wrong and should not continue.

NOTES FOR A TARIFF DISCUSSION
DECEMBER 1847

If at any time all *labor* should cease, and all existing provisions be equally divided among the people, at the end of a single year there could scarcely be one human being left alive—all would have perished by want of subsistence.

NOTES FOR A TARIFF DISCUSSION
DECEMBER 1847

Labor is the great source from which nearly all, if not all, human comforts and necessities are drawn. There is a difference in opinion about the elements of labor in society. Some men assume that there is a necessary connection between capital and labor and that connection draws within it the whole of the labor of the community. They assume that nobody works unless capital excites them to work. They begin next to consider what is the best way. They say that there are but two ways: one is to hire men and to allure them to labor by their consent; the other is to buy the men and drive them to it, and that is slavery. Having assumed that, they proceed to discuss the question of whether the laborers themselves are better off in the condition of slaves or of hired laborers, and they usually decide that they are better off in the condition of slaves.

SPEECH AT CINCINNATI, OHIO
SEPTEMBER 17, 1859

It is assumed that labor and education are incompatible and any practical combination of them impossible. According to that theory, a blind horse upon a treadmill is a perfect illustration of what a laborer should be—all the better for being blind that he could not tread out of place or kick understandingly. According to that theory, the education of laborers is not only useless, but pernicious and dangerous. In fact, it is in some sort deemed a misfortune that laborers should have heads at all. Those same heads are regarded as explosive materials only to be safely kept in damp places, as far as possible from that peculiar sort of fire which ignites them.

SPEECH AT MILWAUKEE, WISCONSIN
SEPTEMBER 30, 1859

The workingmen are the basis of all governments, for the plain reason that they are the most numerous.

SPEECH AT CINCINNATI, OHIO
FEBRUARY 12, 1861

Labor is the true standard of value.

SPEECH AT PITTSBURGH, PENNSYLVANIA
FEBRUARY 15, 1861

Labor is prior to, and independent of, capital. Capital is only the fruit of labor and could never have existed if labor had not first existed. Labor is the superior of capital and deserves much the higher consideration. Capital has its rights, which are as worthy of protection as any other rights. Nor is it denied that there is, and probably always will be, a relation between labor and capital, producing mutual benefits.

ANNUAL MESSAGE TO CONGRESS
DECEMBER 3, 1861

None are so deeply interested to resist the present rebellion as the working people.

REPLY TO NEW YORK WORKINGMEN'S DEMOCRATIC
REPUBLICAN ASSOCIATION
MARCH 21, 1864

The strongest bond of human sympathy, outside of the family relation, should be one uniting all working people, of all nations and tongues and kindreds.

REPLY TO NEW YORK WORKINGMEN'S DEMOCRATIC
REPUBLICAN ASSOCIATION
MARCH 21, 1864

Let not him who is houseless pull down the house of another; but let him labor diligently and build one for himself, thus by example assuring that his own shall be safe from violence when built.

REPLY TO NEW YORK WORKINGMEN'S DEMOCRATIC
REPUBLICAN ASSOCIATION
MARCH 21, 1864

## Lawlessness

I am opposed to encouraging that lawless and mobocratic spirit . . . which is already abroad in the land and is spreading with rapid and fearful impetuosity to the ultimate overthrow of every institution, or even moral principle, in which persons and property have hitherto found security.

SPEECH IN ILLINOIS LEGISLATURE
JANUARY 11, 1837

There is, even now, something of an ill omen amongst us. I mean the increasing disregard for law which pervades the country; the growing disposition to substitute the wild and furious passions, in lieu of the sober judgment of courts; and the worse than savage mobs, for the executive ministers of justice.

SPEECH TO YOUNG MEN'S LYCEUM,
SPRINGFIELD, ILLINOIS
JANUARY 27, 1838

## Laws

Bad laws, if they exist, should be repealed as soon as possible; still, while they continue in force, . . . they should be religiously observed.

SPEECH TO YOUNG MEN'S LYCEUM,
SPRINGFIELD, ILLINOIS
JANUARY 27, 1838

Let me not be understood as saying there are no bad laws, nor that grievances may not arise for the redress of which no legal provisions have been made.

SPEECH TO YOUNG MEN'S LYCEUM,
SPRINGFIELD, ILLINOIS
JANUARY 27, 1838

Let reverence for the laws be breathed by every American mother to the lisping babe that prattles on her lap—let it be taught in schools, in seminaries, and in colleges. . . . In short, let it become the *political religion* of the nation; and let the old and the young, the rich and the poor, the grave and the gay, of all sexes and tongues, and colors and conditions, sacrifice unceasingly upon its altars.

SPEECH TO YOUNG MEN'S LYCEUM,
SPRINGFIELD, ILLINOIS
JANUARY 27, 1838

Let every man remember that to violate the law is to trample on the blood of his father and to tear the charter of his own and his children's liberty.

SPEECH TO YOUNG MEN'S LYCEUM,
SPRINGFIELD, ILLINOIS
JANUARY 27, 1838

Let every American, every lover of liberty, every well-wisher to his posterity, swear by the blood of the Revolution never to violate in the least particular the laws of the country and never to tolerate their violation by others.

SPEECH TO YOUNG MEN'S LYCEUM,
SPRINGFIELD, ILLINOIS
JANUARY 27, 1838

An unconstitutional act is not a law.

SPEECH AT GALENA, ILLINOIS
JULY 23, 1856

Judicial decisions are of greater or less authority as precedents, according to circumstances.

SPEECH AT SPRINGFIELD, ILLINOIS
JUNE 26, 1857

*Legislation* and *adjudication* must follow, and conform to, the progress of society.

NOTES OF ARGUMENT IN LAW CASE
JUNE 1858

It seems to me very important that the statute laws should be made as plain and intelligible as possible and be reduced to as small a compass as may consist with the fullness and precision of the will of the legislature and the perspicuity of its language. This, well done, would, I think, greatly facilitate the labors of those whose duty it is to assist in the administration of the laws and would be a lasting benefit to the people by placing before them, in a more accessible and intelligible form, the laws which so deeply concern their interests and their duties.

ANNUAL MESSAGE TO CONGRESS
DECEMBER 3, 1861

## Lawyers

In law it is good policy never to *plead* what you *need* not, lest you oblige yourself to *prove* what you *can* not.

LETTER TO USHER F. LINDER
FEBRUARY 20, 1848

Never stir up litigation. A worse man can scarcely be found than one who does this.

NOTES FOR A LAW LECTURE
JULY 1850 (?)

The leading rule for a lawyer, as for the man of every other calling, is diligence.

NOTES FOR A LAW LECTURE
JULY 1850 (?)

However able and faithful he may be in other respects, people are slow to bring him business if he cannot make a speech. And yet there is not a more fatal error to young lawyers than relying too much on speech making. If anyone, upon his rare powers of speaking, shall claim an exemption from the drudgery of law, his case is a failure in advance.

NOTES FOR A LAW LECTURE
JULY 1850 (?)

As a peacemaker the lawyer has a superior opportunity of being a good man.

NOTES FOR A LAW LECTURE
JULY 1850 (?)

There is a vague popular belief that lawyers are necessarily dishonest. . . . Let no young man choosing the law for a calling for a moment yield to the popular belief. Resolve to be honest at all events; and if in your own judgment you cannot be an honest lawyer, resolve to be honest without being a lawyer. Choose some other occupation rather than one in the choosing of which you do, in advance, consent to be a knave.

NOTES FOR A LAW LECTURE
JULY 1850 (?)

If you are resolutely determined to make a lawyer of yourself, the thing is more than half done already. It is but a small matter whether you read *with* anybody or not. I did not read with anyone. Get the books and read and study them till you understand them in their principal features, and that is the main thing. It is of no consequence to be in a large town while you are reading. I read at New Salem, which never had three hundred people living in it. The *books*, and your *capacity* for understanding them, are just the same in all places.

LETTER TO ISHAM REAVIS
NOVEMBER 5, 1855

If you wish to be a lawyer, attach no consequence to the *place* you are in or the *person* you are with; but get books, sit down anywhere and go to reading for yourself. That will make a lawyer of you quicker than any other way.

LETTER TO WILLIAM H. GRIGSBY
AUGUST 3, 1858

I am absent altogether too much to be a suitable instructor for a law student. When a man has reached the age that Mr. [John H.] Widmer has and has already been doing for himself, my judgment is that he reads the books for himself without an instructor. That is precisely the way I came to the law. . . . That is my judgment of the cheapest, quickest and best way.

LETTER TO JAMES T. THORNTON
DECEMBER 2, 1858

The mode is very simple, though laborious and tedious. It is only to get the books and read and study them carefully. . . . Work, work, work is the main thing.

LETTER TO JOHN M. BROCKMAN
SEPTEMBER 25, 1860

## Leadership

Some single mind must be master, else there will be no agreement in anything.

LETTER TO WILLIAM M. FISHBACK
FEBRUARY 17, 1864

## Liberty

I submit that the proposition that the thing which determines whether a man is free or slave is rather *concrete* than *abstract*. I think you would conclude that it was if your liberty depended upon it, and so would Judge Douglas if his liberty depended upon it.

SPEECH AT SPRINGFIELD, ILLINOIS
JULY 17, 1858

What constitutes the bulwark of our own liberty and independence? It is not our frowning battlements, our bristling seacoasts, the guns of our war steamers, or the strength of our gallant and disciplined army. These are not our reliance against a resumption of tyranny in our fair land. All of them may be turned against our liberties, without making us stronger or weaker for the struggle. Our reliance is in the *love of liberty* which God has planted in our bosoms. Our defense is in the preservation of the spirit which prizes liberty as the heritage of all men, in all lands, everywhere. Destroy this spirit, and you have planted the seeds of despotism around your doors. Familiarize yourselves with the chains of bondage, and you are preparing your own limbs to wear them. Accustomed to trample on the rights of those around you, you have lost the genius of your own independence, and become the fit subjects of the first cunning tyrant who rises. And let me tell you, all these things are prepared for you with the logic of history, if the elections shall promise that the next Dred Scott decision and all future decisions will be quietly acquiesced in by the people.

SPEECH AT EDWARDSVILLE, ILLINOIS
SEPTEMBER 11, 1858

Without the *Constitution* and the *Union*, we could not have attained the result; but even these are not the primary cause of our great prosperity. There is something back of these, entwining itself more closely about the human heart. That something is the principle of "liberty to all"—the principle that clears the *path* for all—gives *hope* to all—and, by consequence, *enterprise* and *industry* to all.

FRAGMENT ON THE CONSTITUTION AND THE UNION
JANUARY 1861

"Liberty to all" . . . the assertion of that *principle* . . . has proved an "apple of gold" to us. The *Union* and the *Constitution* are the *picture* of *silver* subsequently framed around it. The picture was made not to *conceal* or *destroy* the apple, but to *adorn* and *preserve* it. The *picture* was made *for* the apple—*not* the apple for the picture.

FRAGMENT ON THE CONSTITUTION AND THE UNION
JANUARY 1861 (?)

The world has never had a good definition of the word liberty, and the American people, just now, are much in want of one. We all declare for liberty; but in using the same *word* we do not all mean the same *thing*. With some the word liberty may mean for each man to do as he pleases with himself and the product of his labor; while with others the same word may mean for some men to do as they please with other men and the product of other men's labor. Here are two not only different but incompatible things called by the same name—liberty. And it follows that each of the things is, by the respective parties, called by two different and incompatible names—liberty and tyranny. The shepherd drives the wolf from the sheep's throat, for which the sheep thanks the shepherd as a *liberator*, while the wolf denounces him for the same act as the destroyer of liberty, especially as the sheep was a black one. Plainly the sheep and the wolf are not agreed upon a definition of the word liberty; and precisely the same difference prevails today among us human creatures, even in the North, and all professing to love liberty.

SPEECH AT SANITARY FAIR,
BALTIMORE, MARYLAND
APRIL 18, 1864

## Lincoln, Abraham

Abraham Lincoln
his hand and pen
he will be good but
god knows When*

FROM LINCOLN'S SELF-MADE ARITHMETIC BOOK
NO DATE

Abraham Lincoln is my name
And with my pen I wrote the same
I wrote in both hast and speed
and left it here for fools to read

FROM LINCOLN'S SELF-MADE ARITHMETIC BOOK
NO DATE

Abraham Lincoln his hand and pen he will be good
but god knows When   Time What an emty vaper
tis and days how swift they are   swift as an indian arrow

* It has been suggested that this was a traditional verse in the Lincoln family.

fly on like a shooting star  the presant moment Just is here
then slides away in haste that we can never say they're ours but
only say they're past

LATER ENTRY FROM LINCOLN'S SELF-MADE ARITHMETIC BOOK
NO DATE

I was born and have ever remained in the most humble walks
of life. I have no wealthy or popular relations to recommend
me. My case is thrown exclusively upon the independent voters
of this county, and if elected they will have conferred a favor
upon me for which I shall be unremitting in my labors to com-
pensate. But if the good people in their wisdom shall see fit to
keep me in the background, I have been too familiar with disappointments to be very much chagrined.

COMMUNICATION TO THE PEOPLE OF
SANGAMON COUNTY, ILLINOIS
MARCH 9, 1832

I am never sanguine.

LETTER TO JOHN T. STUART
JANUARY 20, 1840

My old, withered, dry eyes are full of tears yet.

LETTER TO WILLIAM H. HERNDON
FEBRUARY 2, 1848

I am not a very sentimental man.

LETTER TO C. U. SCHLATER
JANUARY 5, 1849

I do not . . . question the patriotism or . . . assail the motives
of any man or class of men.

SPEECH AT PEORIA, ILLINOIS
OCTOBER 16, 1854

It pains me a little that you have deemed it necessary to point out to me how I may be compensated for throwing myself in the breach now. This assumes that I am merely calculating the chances of personal advancement. Let me assure you that I decline to be a candidate for Congress on my clear conviction that my running would *hurt* and not *help* the cause. I am willing to make any personal sacrifice, but I am not willing to do what, in my own judgment, is a sacrifice of the cause itself.

LETTER TO JULIAN M. STURTEVANT
SEPTEMBER 27, 1856

I have never professed an indifference to the honors of official station; and were I to do so now, I should make myself ridiculous. Yet I have never failed—do not now fail—to remember that in the republican cause there is a higher aim than that of mere office.

FRAGMENT ON THE STRUGGLE AGAINST SLAVERY
JULY 1858 (?)

I am not master of language; I have not a fine education; I am not capable of entering into a disquisition upon dialectics.

SPEECH AT CHICAGO, ILLINOIS
JULY 10, 1858

Nobody has ever expected me to be President.

SPEECH AT SPRINGFIELD, ILLINOIS
JULY 17, 1858

I set out in this campaign with the intention of conducting it strictly as a gentleman, in substance at least if not in the outside polish. The latter I shall never be, but that which constitutes the inside of a gentleman I hope I understand and am not less inclined to practice than others. It was my purpose and expectations that this canvass would be conducted upon principle and with fairness on both sides; and it shall not be my fault if this purpose and expectation shall be given up.

SPEECH AT SPRINGFIELD, ILLINOIS
JULY 17, 1858

The Judge is woefully at fault about his early friend Lincoln being a "grocery keeper." I don't know as it would be a great sin if I had been, but he is mistaken. Lincoln never kept a grocery anywhere in the world. It is true that Lincoln did work the latter part of one winter in a small still house up at the head of a hollow.

> FIRST DEBATE WITH STEPHEN A. DOUGLAS,
> OTTAWA, ILLINOIS
> AUGUST 21, 1858

I must, in candor, say I do not think myself fit for the Presidency.

> LETTER TO THOMAS J. PICKETT
> APRIL 16, 1859

You suggest that a visit to the place of my nativity might be pleasant to me. Indeed it would. But would it be safe? Would not the people lynch me?

> LETTER TO SAMUEL HAYCRAFT
> JUNE 4, 1860

I am rather inclined to silence, . . . and whether that be wise or not, it is at least more unusual nowadays to find a man who can hold his tongue than to find one who cannot.

> REMARKS AT PITTSBURGH, PENNSYLVANIA
> FEBRUARY 14, 1861

I trust that in the course I shall pursue I shall be sustained, not only by the party that elected me but by the patriotic people of the whole country.

> REMARKS AT PEEKSKILL, NEW YORK
> FEBRUARY 19, 1861

I am exceedingly anxious that this Union, the Constitution, and the liberties of the people shall be perpetuated in accordance with the original idea for which that struggle was made, and I shall be most happy indeed if I shall be an humble instrument in the hands of the Almighty and of this, his chosen people, for perpetuating the object of that great struggle.

SPEECH AT TRENTON, NEW JERSEY
FEBRUARY 21, 1861

Whoever in later times shall see this and look at the date will readily excuse the writer for not having indulged in sentiment or poetry.

INSCRIPTION IN ALBUM OF MARY REBECCA DARBY SMITH
APRIL 19, 1861

I shall do nothing in malice. What I deal with is too vast for malicious dealing.

LETTER TO CUTHBERT BULLITT
JULY 28, 1862

I can only say that I have acted upon my best convictions without selfishness or malice and that, by the help of God, I shall continue to do so.

LETTER TO AGÉNOR-ETIENNE DE GASPARIN
AUGUST 4, 1862

I am very little inclined on any occasion to say anything unless I hope to produce some good by it.

SPEECH AT WASHINGTON, D.C.
AUGUST 6, 1862

I . . . wish to make the personal acknowledgment that you were right and I was wrong.

LETTER TO ULYSSES S. GRANT
JULY 13, 1863

Do not lean a hair's breadth against your own feelings, or your judgment of the public service, on the idea of gratifying me.

LETTER TO GEORGE G. MEADE
JULY 27, 1863

I appear before you, fellow citizens, merely to thank you for this compliment. The inference is a very fair one that you would hear me for a little while at least, were I to commence to make a speech. I do not appear before you for the purpose of doing so, and for several substantial reasons. The most substantial of these is that I have no speech to make. In my position, it is somewhat important that I should not say any foolish things. It very often happens that the only way to help it is to say nothing at all.

REMARKS TO CITIZENS OF GETTYSBURG, PENNSYLVANIA
NOVEMBER 18, 1863

I am very glad the elections this autumn have gone favorably and that I have not, by native depravity or under evil influences, done anything bad enough to prevent the good result.

LETTER TO ZACHARIAH CHANDLER
NOVEMBER 20, 1863

I claim not to have controlled events, but confess plainly that events have controlled me.

LETTER TO ALBERT G. HODGES
APRIL 4, 1864

So far as able, within my sphere, I have always acted as I believed to be right and just; and I have done all I could for the good of mankind generally.

REPLY TO LOYAL NEGROES OF BALTIMORE
UPON PRESENTATION OF A BIBLE
SEPTEMBER 7, 1864

In taking the various steps which have led to my present position in relation to the war, the public interest and my private interest have been perfectly parallel, because in no other way could I serve myself so well as by truly serving the Union.

LETTER TO ISAAC M. SCHERMERHORN
SEPTEMBER 12, 1864

The recent Inaugural Address . . . I expect . . . to wear as well as—perhaps better than—anything I have produced; but I believe it is not immediately popular. Men are not flattered by being shown that there has been a difference of purpose between the Almighty and them. To deny it, however, in this case is to deny that there is a God governing the world. It is a truth which I thought needed to be told; and as whatever of humiliation there is in it falls most directly on myself, I thought others might afford for me to tell it.

LETTER TO THURLOW WEED
MARCH 15, 1865

As a general rule, I abstain from reading the reports of attacks upon myself, wishing not to be provoked by that to which I cannot properly offer an answer.

LAST PUBLIC SPEECH
APRIL 11, 1865

## Lincoln, Abraham: Autobiography

Born, February 12, 1809, in Hardin County, Kentucky.
Education defective.
Profession, a lawyer.
Have been a captain of volunteers in Black Hawk war.
Postmaster at a very small office.
Four times a member of the Illinois legislature, and was a member of the lower house of Congress.

AUTOBIOGRAPHY SUPPLIED FOR DICTIONARY OF CONGRESS
JUNE 1858

I was born Feb. 12, 1809, in Hardin County, Kentucky. My parents were both born in Virginia of undistinguished families— second families, perhaps I should say. My mother, who died in my tenth year, was of a family of the name of Hanks, some of whom now reside in Adams, and others in Macon counties, Illinois. My paternal grandfather, Abraham Lincoln, emigrated from Rockingham County, Virginia, to Kentucky, about 1781 or 2, where, a year or two later, he was killed by Indians, not in battle, but by stealth when he was laboring to open a farm in the forest. His ancestors, who were Quakers, went to Virginia from Berks County, Pennsylvania. An effort to identify them with the New England family of the same name ended in nothing more definite than a similarity of Christian names in both families, such as Enoch, Levi, Mordecai, Solomon, Abraham and the like.

My father, at the death of his father, was but six years of age; and he grew up, literally without education. He removed from Kentucky to what is now Spencer county, Indiana, in my eighth year. We reached our new home about the same time the state came into the Union. It was a wild region with many bears and other wild animals still in the woods. There I grew up. There were some schools, so called; but no qualification was ever required of a teacher beyond *"readin, writin and cipherin,"* to the Rule of Three. If a straggler supposed to understand Latin happened to sojourn in the neighborhood, he was looked upon as a wizard. There was absolutely nothing to excite ambition for education. Of course when I came of age I did not know much. Still somehow, I could read, write and cipher to the Rule of Three; but that was all. I have not been to school since. The little advance I now have upon this store of education I have picked up from time to time under the pressure of necessity.

I was raised to farm work, which I continued till I was twenty-two. At twenty-one I came to Illinois, and passed the first year in Illinois—Macon county. Then I got to New Salem (at that time in Sangamon, now in Menard county) where I remained a year as a sort of clerk in a store. Then came the Black Hawk War; and I was elected a Captain of Volunteers—a success which gave me more pleasure than any I have had since. I went the campaign, was elated, ran for the Legislature the same year (1832) and was beaten—the only time I have been beaten by the people. The next, and three succeeding biennial elections, I was elected to the Legislature. I was not a candidate afterwards. During this Legislative period I had studied law, and removed to Springfield to practice it. In 1846 I was once elected to the lower House of Congress. Was not a candidate for re-election. From 1849 to 1854, both inclusive, practiced law more assiduously than ever before. Always a Whig in politics, and generally on the Whig electoral tickets, making active canvasses. I was losing interest in politics, when the repeal of the Missouri Compromise aroused me again. What I have done since then is pretty well known.

If any personal description of me is thought desirable, it may be said, I am, in height, six feet, four inches, nearly; lean in flesh, weighing, on an average, one hundred and eighty pounds; dark complexion, with coarse black hair, and gray eyes—no other marks or brands recollected.

LETTER TO JESSE W. FELL
DECEMBER 20, 1859

Abraham Lincoln was born Feb. 12, 1809, then in Hardin, now in the more recently formed county of Larue, Kentucky. His father, Thomas, and grandfather, Abraham, were born in Rockingham county, Virginia, whither their ancestors had come from Berks county, Pennsylvania. His lineage has been traced no farther back than this. The family were originally Quakers, though in later times they have fallen away from the peculiar habits of that people. The grandfather, Abraham, had four brothers—Isaac, Jacob, John and Thomas. So far as known, the descendants of Jacob and John are still in Virginia. Isaac went to a place near where Virginia, North Carolina and Tennessee, join; and his descendants are in that region. Thomas came to Kentucky and after many years died there, whence his descendants went to Missouri. Abraham, grandfather of the subject of this sketch, came to Kentucky, and was killed by Indians about the year 1784. He left a widow, three sons and two daughters. The eldest son, Mordecai, remained in Kentucky till late in life, when he removed to Hancock county, Illinois, where soon after he died, and where several of his descendants still reside. The second son, Josiah, removed at an early day to a place on Blue River, now within Harrison county, Indiana; but no recent information of him, or his family, has been obtained. The eldest sister, Mary, married Ralph Crume and some of her descendants are now known to be in Breckenridge county, Kentucky. The second sister, Nancy, married William Brumfield, and her family are not known to have left Kentucky, but there is no recent information from them. Thomas, the youngest son and father of the present subject, by the early death of his father and very narrow circumstances of his mother, even in childhood was a wandering laboring boy and grew up literally without education. He never did more in the way of writing than to bunglingly sign his own name. Before he was grown, he passed one year as a hired hand with his uncle Isaac on Watauga, a branch of the Holsteen River. Getting back into Kentucky, and having reached his 28th year, he married Nancy Hanks—mother of the present subject—in the year 1806. She also was born in Virginia; and relatives of hers of the name of Hanks, and of other names, now reside in Coles, in Macon and in Adams counties, Illinois, and also in Iowa. The present subject has no brother or sister of the whole or half blood. He had a sister, older than himself, who was grown and married, but died many years ago, leaving no child. Also a brother, younger than himself, who died in infancy. Before leaving Kentucky he and his sister were sent for short periods to A.B.C. schools, the first kept by Zachariah Riney, and the second by Caleb Hazel.

At this time his father resided on Knob Creek, on the road from Bardstown, Ky., to Nashville, Tenn., at a point three or three and a half miles south or southwest of Atherton's ferry on the Rolling Fork. From this place he removed to what is now Spencer county, Indiana, in the autumn of 1816, A. then being in his eighth year. This removal was partly on account of slavery; but chiefly on account of the difficulty in land titles in Ky. He settled in an unbroken forest; and the clearing away of surplus wood was the great task ahead. A., though very young, was large of his age, and had an ax put into his hands at once; and from that till within his twenty-third year he was almost constantly handling that most powerful instrument—less, of course, in plowing and harvesting seasons. At this place A. took an early start as a hunter, which was never much improved afterwards. (A few days before the completion of his eighth year, in the absence of his father, a flock of wild turkeys approached the new log cabin, and A. with a rifle gun, standing inside, shot through a crack and killed one of them. He has never since pulled a trigger on any larger game.) In the autumn of 1818 his mother died; and a year afterwards his father married Mrs. Sally Johnston—at Elizabethtown, Ky.—a widow, with three children of her first marriage. She proved a good and kind mother to A. and is still living in Coles county, Illinois. A. now thinks that the aggregate of all his schooling did not amount to one year. He was never in a college or academy as a student; and never inside of a college or academy building till since he had a law license. What he has in the way of education, he has picked up. After he was twenty-three, and had separated from his father, he studied English grammar, imperfectly of course, but so as to speak and write as well as he now does. He studied and nearly mastered the six books of Euclid since he was a member of Congress. He regrets his want of education, and does what he can to supply the want. In his tenth year he was kicked by a horse and apparently killed for a time. When he was nineteen, still residing in Indiana, he made his first trip upon a flatboat to New Orleans. He was a hired hand merely; and he and a son of the owner, without other assistance, made the trip. The nature of part of the cargo-load—as it was called—made it necessary for them to linger and trade along the Sugar coast and one night they were attacked by seven Negroes with intent to kill and rob them. They were hurt some in the melee, but succeeded in driving the Negroes from the boat and then "cut cable," "weighed anchor" and left.

March 1st 1830—A. having just completed his 21st year, his father and family, with the families of the two daughters and sons-in-law, of his step-mother, left the old homestead in Indiana, and came to Illinois. Their mode of conveyance was wagons drawn by ox teams, and A. drove one of the teams. They reached the county of Macon, and stopped there some time within the same month of March. His father and family settled a new place on the north side of the Sangamon river, at the junction of the timberland and prairie, about ten miles westerly from Decatur. Here they built a log cabin, into which they removed, and made sufficient of rails to fence ten acres of ground, fenced and broke the ground, and raised a crop of sown corn upon it the same year. These are, or are supposed to be, the rails about which so much is being said just now, though they are far from being the first or only rails ever made by A.

The sons-in-law were temporarily settled at other places in the county. In the autumn all hands were greatly afflicted with ague and fever to which they had not been used and by which they were greatly discouraged—so much so that they determined on leaving the county. They remained, however, through the succeeding winter, which was the winter of the very celebrated "deep snow" in Illinois. During that winter, A. together with his stepmother's son, John D. Johnston, and John Hanks, yet residing in Macon county, hired themselves to one Denton Offutt to take a flatboat from Beardstown, Illinois, to New Orleans, and for that purpose, were to join him—Offutt—at Springfield, Ill., so soon as the snow should go off. When it did go off—which was about the 1st of March 1831—the county was so flooded as to make traveling by land impracticable; to obviate which difficulty they purchased a large canoe and came down the Sangamon river in it. This is the time and the manner of A's first entrance into Sangamon County. They found Offutt at Springfield, but learned from him that he had failed in getting a boat at Beardstown. This lead to their hiring themselves to him at $12 per month each and getting the timber out of the trees and building a boat at old Sangamon Town on the Sangamon river, seven miles N.W. of Springfield, which boat they took to New Orleans, substantially upon the old contract. It was in connection with this boat that occurred the ludicrous incident of sewing up the hogs' eyes. Offutt bought thirty-odd large fat live hogs, but found difficulty in driving them from where he purchased them to the boat, and thereupon conceived the whim that he could sew up their eyes and drive them where he pleased. No sooner thought of than decided, he put his hands, including A., at the job which they completed—all but the driving. In their blind condition they could not be driven out of the lot or field they were in. This expedient failing, they were tied and hauled on carts to the boat. It was near the Sangamon River, within what is now Menard county.

During this boat enterprise acquaintance with Offutt, who was previously an entire stranger, he conceived a liking for A. and believing he could turn him to account, he contracted with him to act as clerk for him on his return from New Orleans in charge of a store and mill at New Salem, then in Sangamon, now in Menard county. Hanks had not gone to New Orleans, but having a family and being likely to be detained from home longer than at first expected had turned back from St. Louis. He is the same John Hanks who now engineers the "rail enterprise" at Decatur, and is a first cousin to A's mother. A's father with his own family and others mentioned had, in pursuance of their intention, re-

moved from Macon to Coles county. John D. Johnston, the step-
mother's son, went to them; and A. stopped indefinitely and, for
the first time as it were, by himself at New Salem, before mentioned. This was in July 1831. Here he rapidly made acquaint-
ances and friends. In less than a year Offutt's business was fail-
ing—had almost failed—when the Black Hawk War of 1832 broke
out. A. joined a volunteer company and to his own surprise was
elected captain of it. He says he has not since had any success in
life which gave him so much satisfaction. He went the campaign,
served near three months, met the ordinary hardships of such an
expedition, but was in no battle. He now owns in Iowa the land
upon which his own warrants for this service were located. Returning from the campaign, and encouraged by his great popularity among his immediate neighbors, he, the same year, ran
for the Legislature and was beaten—his own precinct, however,
casting its votes 277 for and 7 against him. And this too while he
was an avowed Clay man, and the precinct the autumn afterwards, giving a majority of 115 to Genl. Jackson over Mr. Clay.
This was the only time A. was ever beaten on a direct vote of
the people. He was now without means and out of business, but
was anxious to remain with his friends who had treated him with
so much generosity, especially as he had nothing elsewhere to go
to. He studied what he should do—thought of learning the black-
smith trade—thought of trying to study law—rather thought he
could not succeed at that without a better education. Before long,
strangely enough, a man offered to sell and did sell, to A. and
another, as poor as himself, an old stock of goods upon credit.
They opened as merchants; and he says that was *the* store. Of
course they did nothing but get deeper and deeper in debt. He
was appointed Postmaster at New Salem—the office being too insignificant to make his politics an objection. The store winked
out. The Surveyor of Sangamon offered to depute to A. that portion of his work which was within his part of the county. He
accepted, procured a compass and chain, studied Flint and
Gibson a little, and went at it. This procured bread and kept
soul and body together. The election of 1834 came, and he was
then elected to the Legislature by the highest vote cast for any
candidate. Major John T. Stuart, then in full practice of the law,
was also elected. During the canvass, in a private conversation he

encouraged A. to study law. After the election he borrowed books of Stuart, took them home with him, and went at it in good earnest. He studied with nobody. He still mixed in the surveying to pay board and clothing bills. When the Legislature met, the law books were dropped but were taken up again at the end of the session. He was re-elected in 1836, 1838 and 1840. In the autumn of 1836 he obtained a law license, and on April 15, 1837, removed to Springfield and commenced the practice, his old friend Stuart taking him into partnership. March 3rd, 1837, by a protest entered upon the Illinois House Journal of that date, at pages 817, 818, A. with Dan Stone, another representative of Sangamon, briefly defined his position on the slavery question; and so far as it goes, it was then the same that it is now. . . . In 1838 and 1840 Mr. L's party in the Legislature voted for him as Speaker, but being in the minority he was not elected. After 1840 he declined a re-election to the Legislature. He was on the Harrison electoral ticket in 1840, and on that of Clay in 1844, and spent much time and labor in both those canvasses. In Nov. 1842, he was married to Mary, daughter of Robert S. Todd, of Lexington, Kentucky. They have three living children, all sons—one born in 1843, one in 1850, and one in 1853. They lost one, who was born in 1846. In 1846, he was elected to the lower House of Congress and served one term only, commencing in Dec. 1847 and ending with the inauguration of Gen. Taylor in March 1849. All the battles of the Mexican War had been fought before Mr. L. took his seat in Congress, but the American army was still in Mexico, and the treaty of peace was not fully and formally ratified till the June afterwards. Much has been said of his course in Congress in regard to this war. A careful examination of the Journals and Congressional Globe shows that he voted for all the supply measures which came up and for all the measures in any way favorable to the officers, soldiers and their families who conducted the war through; with this exception, that some of these measures passed without yeas or nays, leaving no record as to how particular men voted. The Journals and Globe also show him voting that the war was unnecessarily and unconstitutionally begun by the President of the United States. This is the language of Mr. Ashmun's amendment, for which Mr. L. and nearly or quite all other Whigs of the House of Representatives voted.

Mr. L's reasons for the opinion expressed by this vote were briefly that the President had sent Genl. Taylor into an inhabited part of the country belonging to Mexico and not to the U.S. and thereby had provoked the first act of hostility—in fact the commencement of the war—that the place, being the country bordering on the east bank of the Rio Grande, was inhabited by native Mexicans born there under the Mexican government, and had never submitted to, nor been conquered by, Texas or the U.S. nor transferred to either by treaty—that although Texas claimed the Rio Grande as her boundary, Mexico had never recognized it, the people on the ground had never recognized it, and neither Texas nor the U.S. had ever enforced it—that there was a broad desert between that, and the country over which Texas had actual control—that the country where hostilities commenced, having once belonged to Mexico, must remain so until it was somehow legally transferred, which had never been done.

Mr. L. thought the act of sending an armed force among the Mexicans was *unnecessary* inasmuch as Mexico was in no way molesting or menacing the U.S. or the people thereof; and that it was *unconstitutional* because the power of levying war is vested in Congress and not in the President. He thought the principal motive for the act was to divert public attention from the surrender of "Fifty-four, forty, or fight" to Great Britain on the Oregon boundary question.

Mr. L. was not a candidate for re-election. This was determined upon and declared before he went to Washington, in accordance with an understanding among Whig friends, by which Col. Hardin and Col. Baker had each previously served a single term in the same District.

In 1848, during his term in Congress, he advocated Gen. Taylor's nomination for the Presidency, in opposition to all others, and also took an active part for his election; after his nomination —speaking a few times in Maryland, near Washington, several times in Massachusetts, and canvassing quite fully his own district in Illinois, which was followed by a majority in the district of over 1,500 for Gen. Taylor.

Upon his return from Congress he went to the practice of the law with greater earnestness than ever before. In 1852 he was upon the Scott electoral ticket and did something in the way of canvassing, but owing to the hopelessness of the cause in Illinois he did less than in previous presidential canvasses.

In 1854, his profession had almost superseded the thought of politics in his mind, when the repeal of the Missouri Compromise aroused him as he had never been before.

In the autumn of that year he took the stump with no broader practical aim or object than to secure, if possible, the re-election of Hon. Richard Yates to Congress. His speeches at once attracted a more marked attention than they had ever before done. As the canvass proceeded, he was drawn to different parts of the state outside of Mr. Yates' district. He did not abandon the law, but gave his attention, by turns, to that and politics. The state agricultural fair was at Springfield that year, and Douglas was announced to speak there.

In the canvass of 1856, Mr. L. made over fifty speeches, no one of which, so far as he remembers, was put in print. One of them was made at Galena, but Mr. L. has no recollection of any part of it being printed; nor does he remember whether in that speech he said anything about a Supreme Court decision. He may have spoken upon that subject, and some of the newspapers may have reported him as saying what is now ascribed to him, but he thinks he could not have expressed himself as represented.

AUTOBIOGRAPHY WRITTEN FOR JOHN L. SCRIPPS
JUNE 1860 (?)

## Lincoln, Robert T.

Please read and answer this letter as though I was not President, but only a friend. My son, now in his twenty-second year, having graduated at Harvard, wishes to see something of the war before it ends. I do not wish to put him in the ranks, nor yet to give him a commission to which those who have already served long are better entitled and better qualified to hold. Could he, without embarrassment to you or detriment to the service go into your military family with some nominal rank, I, and not the public, furnishing his necessary means? If no, say so without the least hesitation, because I am anxious and as deeply interested that you shall not be encumbered as you can be yourself.*

LETTER TO ULYSSES S. GRANT
JANUARY 19, 1865

## Lincoln, Thomas ("Tad")

Think you better put "Tad's" pistol away. I had an ugly dream about him.

TELEGRAM TO MARY TODD LINCOLN
JUNE 9, 1863

## Liquor

The practice of drinking is just as old as the world itself.

SPEECH TO WASHINGTON TEMPERANCE SOCIETY,
SPRINGFIELD, ILLINOIS
FEBRUARY 22, 1842

Whether or not the world would be vastly benefited by a total and final banishment from it of all intoxicating drinks seems to me not *now* to be an open question. Three fourths of mankind confess the affirmative with their *tongues* and, I believe, all the rest acknowledge it in their *hearts*.

SPEECH TO WASHINGTON TEMPERANCE SOCIETY,
SPRINGFIELD, ILLINOIS
FEBRUARY 22, 1842

The demon of intemperance ever seems to have delighted in sucking the blood of genius and of generosity.

SPEECH TO WASHINGTON TEMPERANCE SOCIETY,
SPRINGFIELD, ILLINOIS
FEBRUARY 22, 1842

* Robert T. Lincoln was appointed captain and assistant adjutant general of volunteers on February 11, 1865, and resigned on June 10, 1865.

## Logic

My understanding is, when a common job is done or a common enterprise prosecuted, if I put in five dollars to your one I have a right to take out five dollars to your one.

SPEECH AT SPRINGFIELD, ILLINOIS
JULY 17, 1858

A specious and fantastic arrangement of words by which a man can prove a horse chestnut to be a chestnut horse.

FIRST DEBATE WITH STEPHEN A. DOUGLAS,
OTTAWA, ILLINOIS
AUGUST 21, 1858

If you have ever studied geometry, you remember that by a course of reasoning Euclid proves that all the angles in a triangle are equal to two right angles. Euclid has shown you how to work it out. Now, if you undertake to disprove that proposition and to show that it is erroneous, would you prove it to be false by calling Euclid a liar?

FOURTH DEBATE WITH STEPHEN A. DOUGLAS,
CHARLESTON, ILLINOIS
SEPTEMBER 18, 1858

## Loyalty

Many free countries have lost their liberty, and *ours may* lose hers; but if she shall, be it my proudest plume, not that I was the *last* to desert, but that I *never* deserted her.

SPEECH ON THE SUB-TREASURY
DECEMBER 26, 1839

I think any officer who has been dismissed on suspicion of disloyalty, but does not go over to the enemy, continuing to protest his loyalty, entitles himself to a hearing.

MEMORANDUM TO SIMON CAMERON, SECRETARY OF WAR
NOVEMBER 2, 1861

The man who stands by and says nothing when the peril of his government is discussed cannot be misunderstood. If not hindered, he is sure to help the enemy. Much more, if he talks ambiguously—talks for his country with "buts" and "ifs" and "ands."

LETTER TO ERASTUS CORNING AND OTHERS
JUNE 12, 1863

In this struggle for the nation's life, I cannot so confidently rely on those whose elections may have depended upon disloyal votes. Such men, when elected, may prove true; but such votes are given them in the expectation that they will prove false.

LETTER TO AUGUST W. BRADFORD
NOVEMBER 2, 1863

## Loyalty Oaths

I have found that men who have not even been suspected of disloyalty are very averse to taking an oath of any sort as a condition to exercising an ordinary right of citizenship.

LETTER TO WILLIAM S. ROSECRANS
APRIL 4, 1864

## Magnanimity

It is always magnanimous to recant whatever we may have said in passion.

LETTER TO WILLIAM BUTLER
FEBRUARY 1, 1839

## Majority Rule

If the minority will not acquiesce, the majority must or the government must cease. There is no other alternative; for continuing the government is acquiescence on one side or the other. If a minority in such case will secede rather than acquiesce, they make a precedent which, in turn, will divide and ruin them; for a minority of their own will secede from them, whenever a majority refuses to be controlled by such minority.

FIRST INAUGURAL ADDRESS
MARCH 4, 1861

In a great national crisis like ours, unanimity of action among those seeking a common end is very desirable—almost indispensable. And yet no approach to such unanimity is attainable unless some deference shall be paid to the will of the majority, simply because it is the will of the majority.

ANNUAL MESSAGE TO CONGRESS
DECEMBER 6, 1864

## Man

All creation is a mine, and every man a miner. The whole earth, and all *within* it, *upon* it and *round about* it, including *himself*, in his physical, moral and intellectual nature, and his susceptibilities, are the infinitely various "leads" from which man, from the first, was to dig out his destiny.

FIRST LECTURE ON DISCOVERIES AND INVENTIONS,
BLOOMINGTON, ILLINOIS
APRIL 6, 1858

Man is not the only animal who labors; but he is the only one who *improves* his workmanship. This improvement he effects by *discoveries* and *inventions*.

FIRST LECTURE ON DISCOVERIES AND INVENTIONS,
BLOOMINGTON, ILLINOIS
APRIL 6, 1858

## Marriage

Whatever woman may cast her lot with mine, should any ever do so, it is my intention to do all in my power to make her happy and contented; and there is nothing I can imagine that would make me more unhappy than to fail in that effort.

LETTER TO MARY S. OWENS
MAY 7, 1837

I have now come to the conclusion never again to think of marrying, and for this reason: I can never be satisfied with any-one who would be blockhead enough to have me.

LETTER TO MRS. ORVILLE H. BROWNING
APRIL 1, 1838

My old father used to have a saying that "If you made a bad bargain, *hug* it the tighter."

LETTER TO JOSHUA F. SPEED
FEBRUARY 25, 1842

Nothing new here, except my marrying, which to me is matter of profound wonder.

LETTER TO SAMUEL D. MARSHALL
NOVEMBER 11, 1842

With pleasure I write my name in your album. Ere long some younger man will be more happy to confer *his* name upon *you*.

Don't allow it, Mary, until fully assured that he is worthy of the happiness.

INSCRIPTION IN THE AUTOGRAPH ALBUM OF MARY DELAHAY
DECEMBER 7, 1859

I would not offer . . . any wife a temptation to a permanent separation from her husband.

"TO WHOM IT MAY CONCERN" LETTER
GIVEN TO MRS. SALLIE WARD HUNT
APRIL 11, 1864

## Martial Law

Nothing justifies the suspending of the civil by the military authority but military necessity; and, of the existence of that necessity, the military commander and not a popular vote is to decide.

LETTER TO BENJAMIN F. BUTLER
AUGUST 9, 1864

## McClellan, George B.

*He is a brave and able man.*

SPEECH AT WASHINGTON, D.C.
AUGUST 6, 1862

## Memories

My childhood home I see again,
    And gladden with the view;
And still as mem'ries crowd my brain,
    There's sadness in it too.

O memory! thou midway world
    'Twixt Earth and Paradise,
Where things decayed, and love ones lost
    In dreamy shadows rise.

And freed from all that's gross or vile,
    Seem hallowed, pure and bright,
Like scenes in some enchanted isle,
    All bathed in liquid light.

As distant mountains please the eye,
    When twilight chases day—
As bugle tones, that, passing by,
    In distance die away—

As leaving some grand waterfall
    We ling'ring list its roar,
So memory will hallow all
    We've known, but know no more.

STANZAS FROM A POEM
FEBRUARY 1846

## Mexican War

In a final treaty of peace we shall probably be under a sort
of necessity of taking some territory; but it is my desire that we
shall not acquire any extending so far south as to enlarge and
aggravate the distracting question of slavery.

SUGGESTIONS ON WHAT ZACHARY TAYLOR SHOULD SAY
IF SELECTED AS WHIG CANDIDATE FOR PRESIDENT
MARCH 1848 (?)

All the battles of the Mexican War had been fought before Mr.
L. took his seat in Congress, but the American army was still in
Mexico, and the treaty of peace was not fully and formally rati-
fied till the June afterwards. Much has been said of his course in

Congress in regard to this war. A careful examination of the Journals and Congressional Globe shows that he voted for all the supply measures which came up and for all the measures in any way favorable to the officers, soldiers and their families who conducted the war through; with this exception, that some of these measures passed without yeas or nays, leaving no record as to how particular men voted. The Journals and Globe also show him voting that the war was unnecessarily and unconstitutionally begun by the President of the United States. . . .

Mr. L's reasons for the opinion expressed by this vote were briefly that the President had sent Genl. Taylor into an inhabited part of the country belonging to Mexico and not to the U.S. and thereby had provoked the first act of hostility—in fact the commencement of the war—that the place, being the country bordering on the east bank of the Rio Grande, was inhabited by native Mexicans born there under the Mexican government, and had never submitted to, nor been conquered by, Texas or the U.S. nor transferred to either by treaty—that although Texas claimed the Rio Grande as her boundary, Mexico had never recognized it, the people on the ground had never recognized it, and neither Texas nor the U.S. had ever enforced it—that there was a broad desert between that, and the country over which Texas had actual control—that the country where hostilities commenced, having once belonged to Mexico, must remain so until it was somehow legally transferred, which had never been done.

Mr. L. thought the act of sending an armed force among the Mexicans was *unnecessary* inasmuch as Mexico was in no way molesting or menacing the U.S. or the people thereof; and that it was *unconstitutional* because the power of levying war is vested in Congress and not in the President. He thought the principal motive for the act was to divert public attention from the surrender of "Fifty-four, forty, or fight" to Great Britain on the Oregon Boundary question.

AUTOBIOGRAPHY WRITTEN FOR JOHN L. SCRIPPS
JUNE 1860 (?)

## Military Arrests

The public safety renders it necessary that the grounds of these arrests should at present be withheld, but at the proper time they will be made public.

STATEMENT ON ARRESTS IN MARYLAND
SEPTEMBER 15, 1861

## Miscegenation

There is a natural disgust in the minds of nearly all white people to the idea of an indiscriminate amalgamation of the white and black races.

SPEECH AT SPRINGFIELD, ILLINOIS
JUNE 26, 1857

Slavery is the greatest source of amalgamation; and, next to it, not the elevation but the degeneration of the free blacks.

SPEECH AT SPRINGFIELD, ILLINOIS
JUNE 26, 1857

A separation of the races is the only perfect preventive of amalgamation, but as an immediate separation is impossible the next best thing is to *keep* them apart *where* they are not already together. If white and black people never get together in Kansas, they will never mix blood in Kansas.

SPEECH AT SPRINGFIELD, ILLINOIS
JUNE 26, 1857

I protest against that counterfeit logic which concludes that, because I do not want a black woman for a *slave*, I must necessarily want her for a *wife*. I need not have her for either; I can just leave her alone.

SPEECH AT SPRINGFIELD, ILLINOIS
JUNE 26, 1857

I protest, now and forever, against that counterfeit logic which presumes that because I do not want a Negro woman for a slave, I do necessarily want her for a wife. My understanding is that I need not have her for either; but as God made us separate, we can leave one another alone and do one another much good thereby. There are white men enough to marry all the white women, and enough black men to marry all the black women; and in God's name let them be so married.

SPEECH AT CHICAGO, ILLINOIS
JULY 10, 1858

I do not understand that because I do not want a Negro woman for a slave I must necessarily want her for a wife. My understanding is that I can just let her alone. I am now in my fiftieth year and I certainly never have had a black woman for either a slave or a wife. So it seems to me quite possible for us to get along without making either slaves or wives of Negroes.

FOURTH DEBATE WITH STEPHEN A. DOUGLAS,
CHARLESTON, ILLINOIS
SEPTEMBER 18, 1858

I have never had the least apprehension that I or my friends would marry Negroes if there was no law to keep them from it, but as Judge Douglas and his friends seem to be in great apprehension that they might, if there were no law to keep them from it, I give him the most solemn pledge that I will to the very last stand by the law of this state, which forbids the marrying of white people with Negroes.

FOURTH DEBATE WITH STEPHEN A. DOUGLAS,
CHARLESTON, ILLINOIS
SEPTEMBER 18, 1858

Judge Douglas will have it that I want a Negro wife. He never can be brought to understood that there is any middle ground on this subject. I have lived until my fiftieth year and have never had a Negro woman either for a slave or a wife, and I think I can

live fifty centuries, for that matter, without having had one for
either.

SIXTH DEBATE WITH STEPHEN A. DOUGLAS,
QUINCY, ILLINOIS
OCTOBER 13, 1858

## Misery

I am now the most miserable man living. If what I feel were
equally distributed to the whole human family, there would not
be one cheerful face on the earth.

LETTER TO JOHN T. STUART
JANUARY 23, 1841

## Misrepresentation

When a man hears himself somewhat misrepresented, it pro-
vokes him—at least, I find it so with myself. But when the misrep-
resentation becomes very gross and palpable, it is more apt to
amuse him.

FIRST DEBATE WITH STEPHEN A. DOUGLAS,
OTTAWA, ILLINOIS
AUGUST 21, 1858

## Missouri Compromise

Repeal of the Missouri Compromise . . . is wrong: wrong in its
direct effect, letting slavery into Kansas and Nebraska—and
wrong in its prospective principle, allowing it to spread to every
other part of the wide world where men can be found inclined to
take it. This *declared* indifference, but as I must think, covert
*real* zeal for the spread of slavery, I cannot but hate. I hate it
because of the monstrous injustice of slavery itself. I hate it

because it deprives our republican example of its just influence in the world; enables the enemies of free institutions, with plausibility, to taunt us as hypocrites; causes the real friends of freedom to doubt our sincerity; and especially because it forces so many really good men amongst ourselves into an open war with the very fundamental principles of civil liberty—criticizing the Declaration of Independence and insisting that there is no right principle of action but *self-interest.*

SPEECH AT PEORIA, ILLINOIS
OCTOBER 16, 1854

## Mistakes

I claim not to be more free from errors than others—perhaps scarcely so much.

SPEECH AT SPRINGFIELD, ILLINOIS
JULY 17, 1858

If I had made any mistake I was willing to be corrected.

SPEECH AT SPRINGFIELD, ILLINOIS
JULY 17, 1858

I frequently make mistakes myself, in the many things I am compelled to do hastily.

LETTER TO WILLIAM S. ROSECRANS
MAY 20, 1863

Everything I say, you know, goes into print. If I make a mistake it doesn't merely affect me nor you but the country. I, therefore, ought at least try not to make mistakes.

RESPONSE TO A SERENADE
APRIL 10, 1865

## Mob Rule

Whenever the vicious portion of the population shall be permitted to gather in bands of hundreds and thousands and burn churches, ravage and rob provision stores, throw printing presses into rivers, shoot editors, and hang and burn obnoxious persons at pleasure and with impunity, depend on it, this Government cannot last.

SPEECH TO YOUNG MEN'S LYCEUM,
SPRINGFIELD, ILLINOIS
JANUARY 27, 1838

The innocent, those who have ever set their faces against violations of law in every shape, alike with the guilty fall victims to the ravages of mob law.

SPEECH TO YOUNG MEN'S LYCEUM,
SPRINGFIELD, ILLINOIS
JANUARY 27, 1838

By the operation of this mobocratic spirit . . . the strongest bulwark of any Government, and particularly of those constituted like ours, may effectually be broken down and destroyed.

SPEECH TO YOUNG MEN'S LYCEUM,
SPRINGFIELD, ILLINOIS
JANUARY 27, 1838

There is no grievance that is a fit object of redress by mob law.

SPEECH TO YOUNG MEN'S LYCEUM,
SPRINGFIELD, ILLINOIS
JANUARY 27, 1838

When men take it in their heads today to hang gamblers or burn murderers, they should recollect that in the confusion usually attending such transactions they will be as likely to hang or burn someone who is neither a gambler nor a murderer as one who is; and that, acting upon the example they set, the mob of tomorrow may, and probably will, hang or burn some of them by the very same mistake.

SPEECH TO YOUNG MEN'S LYCEUM,
SPRINGFIELD, ILLINOIS
JANUARY 27, 1838

## Modesty

Considering the great degree of modesty which should always attend youth, it is probable that I have already been more presuming than becomes me.

COMMUNICATION TO THE PEOPLE OF
SANGAMON COUNTY, ILLINOIS
MARCH 9, 1832

Sound your own horn, for behold if you sound not your own horn your horn shall not be sounded.

SPEECH AT CLINTON, ILLINOIS
JULY 27, 1858

Gratefully accepting the proffered honor [to inscribe your new legal work to me], I give the leave, begging only that the inscription may be in modest terms, not representing me as a man of great learning or a very extraordinary man in any respect.

LETTER TO WILLIAM D. KELLEY
OCTOBER 13, 1860

Most heartily do I thank you for this magnificent reception, and while I cannot take to myself any share of the compliment thus paid, more than that which pertains to a mere instrument—an accidental instrument, perhaps I should say—of a great cause, I yet must look upon it as a most magnificent reception and, as such, most heartily do I thank you for it.

REPLY TO GOVERNOR OLIVER P. MORTON,
INDIANAPOLIS, INDIANA
FEBRUARY 11, 1861

## Money

It is an old maxim and a very sound one that he that dances should always pay the fiddler. Now, sir, if any gentlemen whose money is a burden to them choose to lead off a dance, I am decidedly opposed to the people's money being used to pay the fiddler.

SPEECH IN ILLINOIS LEGISLATURE
JANUARY 11, 1837

Any person who will reflect that money is only valuable while in circulation will readily perceive that any device which will keep the government revenues in constant circulation instead of being locked up in idleness is no inconsiderable advantage.

SPEECH ON THE SUB-TREASURY
DECEMBER 26, 1839

As the Dutch justice said, when he married folks, "Now, vere ish my hundred tollars?"

LETTER TO ANDREW MCCALLEN
JULY 4, 1851

The plainest print cannot be read through a gold eagle.

SPEECH AT SPRINGFIELD, ILLINOIS
JUNE 26, 1857

I am the poorest hand living to get others to pay.

LETTER TO NORMAN B. JUDD
NOVEMBER 16, 1858

The slaveholder does not like to be considered a mean fellow for holding that species of property, and hence he has to struggle within himself and sets about arguing himself into the belief that slavery is right. The property influences his mind. The dissenting minister who argued some theological point with one of the established church was always met by the reply, "I can't see it so." He opened the Bible and pointed him to a passage, but the orthodox minister replied, "I can't see it so." Then he showed him a single word—"Can you see that?" "Yes, I see it," was the reply. The dissenter laid a guinea over the word and asked, "Do you see it now?" . . . Whether the owners of this species of property do really see it as it is, it is not for me to say; but if they do, they see it as it is through 2,000,000,000 of dollars, and that is a pretty thick coating.

SPEECH AT NEW HAVEN, CONNECTICUT
MARCH 6, 1860

As to your kind wishes for myself, allow me to say I cannot enter the ring on the money basis—first, because in the main it is wrong; and secondly, I have not and cannot get the money. I say in the main the use of money is wrong; but for certain objects, in a political contest, the use of some is both right and indispensable.

LETTER TO MARK W. DELAHAY
MARCH 16, 1860

I could not raise ten thousand dollars if it would save me from the fate of John Brown. Nor have my friends, so far as I know, yet reached the point of staking any money on my chances of success.

LETTER TO E. STAFFORD
MARCH 17, 1860

I can and will pay it if it is right; but I do not wish to be "diddled"!

LETTER TO WILLIAM M. DICKSON
JUNE 7, 1860

I never keep anybody's money which I collect an hour longer than I can find a chance to turn it over to him.

LETTER TO MRS. DEZIAH VANCE
JUNE 9, 1860

There is powerful temptation in money.

LETTER TO WILLIAM S. ROSECRANS
MARCH 17, 1863

## Morality

God did not place good and evil before man, telling him to make his choice. On the contrary, he did tell him there was one tree of the fruit of which he should not eat upon pain of certain death.

SPEECH AT PEORIA, ILLINOIS
OCTOBER 16, 1854

Will springs from the two elements of moral sense and self-interest.

SPEECH AT SPRINGFIELD, ILLINOIS
JUNE 26, 1857

## Motive

Why build a cage if they expect to catch no birds?

SPEECH ON THE SUB-TREASURY
DECEMBER 26, 1839

## National Debt

Time alone relieves a debtor nation, so long as its population increases faster than unpaid interest accumulates on its debt.

ANNUAL MESSAGE TO CONGRESS
DECEMBER 1, 1862

# Navy

The naval force of the United States consists at this time of five hundred and eighty-eight vessels completed and in the course of completion, and of these seventy-five are ironclad or armored steamers . . . believed to exceed in number those of any other power. But while these may be relied upon for harbor defense and coast service, others of greater strength and capacity will be necessary for cruising purposes and to maintain our rightful position on the ocean.

ANNUAL MESSAGE TO CONGRESS
DECEMBER 8, 1863

The duties devolving on the naval branch of the service during the year, and throughout the whole of this unhappy contest, have been discharged with fidelity and eminent success.

ANNUAL MESSAGE TO CONGRESS
DECEMBER 8, 1863

Satisfactory and important as have been the performances of the heroic men of the navy at this interesting period, they are scarcely more wonderful than the success of our mechanics and artisans in the production of war vessels which has created a new form of naval power. Our country has advantages superior to any other nation in our resources of iron and timber, with inexhaustible quantities of fuel in the immediate vicinity of both, and all available and in close proximity to navigable waters. Without the advantage of public works, the resources of the nation have been developed and its power displayed in the construction of a navy of such magnitude which has, at the very period of its creation, rendered signal service to the Union.

ANNUAL MESSAGE TO CONGRESS
DECEMBER 8, 1863

The increase of the number of seamen in the public service—from seven thousand five hundred men in the spring of 1861, to about thirty-four thousand at the present time—has been accomplished without special legislation or extraordinary bounties to promote that increase.

ANNUAL MESSAGE TO CONGRESS
DECEMBER 8, 1863

## Necessity

It may be argued that there are certain conditions that make necessities and impose them upon us, and to the extent that a necessity is imposed upon a man he must submit to it.

SPEECH AT CHICAGO, ILLINOIS
JULY 10, 1858

## Negroes

Equal justice to the South, it is said, requires us to consent to the extending of slavery to new countries. That is to say, inasmuch as you do not object to my taking my hog to Nebraska, therefore I must not object to you taking your slave. Now, I admit this is perfectly logical, if there is no difference between hogs and Negroes.

SPEECH AT PEORIA, ILLINOIS
OCTOBER 16, 1854

It is your sense of justice and human sympathy continually telling you that the poor Negro has some natural right to himself —that those who deny it, and make mere merchandise of him, deserve kickings, contempt and death.

SPEECH AT PEORIA, ILLINOIS
OCTOBER 16, 1854

I confess I hate to see the poor creatures hunted down and caught and carried back to their stripes and unrewarded toils; but I bite my lips and keep quiet.

LETTER TO JOSHUA F. SPEED
AUGUST 24, 1855

[The assumption] that the public estimate of the black man is more favorable *now* than it was in the days of the Revolution . . . is a mistake. In some trifling particulars, the condition of that race has been ameliorated; but, as a whole, in this country, the change between then and now is decidedly the other way, and their ultimate destiny has never appeared so hopeless.

SPEECH AT SPRINGFIELD, ILLINOIS
JUNE 26, 1857

Our Declaration of Independence was held sacred by all and thought to include all; but now, to aid in making the bondage of the Negro universal and eternal, it is assailed and sneered at and construed and hawked at and torn till, if its framers could rise from their graves, they could not at all recognize it. All the powers of earth seem rapidly combining against him. Mammon is after him; ambition follows and philosophy follows and the theology of the day is fast joining the cry. They have him in his prison house, they have searched his person and left no prying instrument with him. One after another they have closed the heavy iron doors upon him and now they have him, as it were, bolted in with a lock of a hundred keys, which can never be unlocked without the concurrence of every key; the keys in the hands of a hundred different men, and they scattered to a hundred different and distant places; and they stand musing as to what invention, in all the dominions of mind and matter, can be produced to make the impossibility of his escape more complete than it is.

SPEECH AT SPRINGFIELD, ILLINOIS
JUNE 26, 1857

It is grossly incorrect to say or assume that the public estimate of the Negro is more favorable now than it was at the origin of the government.

SPEECH AT SPRINGFIELD, ILLINOIS
JUNE 26, 1857

All I ask for the Negro is that if you do not like him, let him alone. If God gave him but little, that little let him enjoy.

SPEECH AT SPRINGFIELD, ILLINOIS
JULY 17, 1858

Now, when by all these means you have succeeded in dehumanizing the Negro; when you have put him down and made it forever impossible for him to be but as the beast of the fields; when you have extinguished his soul and placed him where the ray of hope is blown out in darkness like that which broods over the spirits of the damned; are you quite sure the demon which you have roused *will not turn and rend you?*

SPEECH AT EDWARDSVILLE, ILLINOIS
SEPTEMBER 11, 1858

I will say then that I am not, nor ever have been, in favor of bringing about in any way the social and political equality of the white and black races; that I am not, nor ever have been, in favor of making voters or jurors of Negroes, nor of qualifying them to hold office, nor to intermarry with white people; and I will say in addition to this that there is a physical difference between the white and black races which I believe will forever forbid the two races living together on terms of social and political equality. And inasmuch as they cannot so live, while they do remain together there must be the position of superior and inferior, and I as much as any other man am in favor of having the superior position assigned to the white race. . . . I do not perceive that because the white man is to have the superior position the Negro should be denied everything. . . . I will add to this that I have never seen to my knowledge a man, woman or child who was in favor of producing a perfect equality, social and political, between Negroes and white men. . . . I do not understand there is any place where an alteration of the social and political relations of the Negro and the white man can be made except in the state legislature—not in the Congress of the United States—and as I do not really apprehend the approach of any such thing myself, and as Judge Douglas seems to be in constant horror that some such danger is rapidly approaching, I propose as the best means to prevent it that the Judge be kept at home and placed in the state legislature to fight the measure.

FOURTH DEBATE WITH STEPHEN A. DOUGLAS,
CHARLESTON, ILLINOIS
SEPTEMBER 18, 1858

Suppose it is true that the Negro is inferior to the white in the gifts of nature; is it not the exact reverse of justice that the white should, for that reason, take from the Negro any part of the little which has been given him? *"Give* to him that is needy" is the Christian rule of charity; but "Take from him that is needy" is the rule of slavery.

FRAGMENT ON PROSLAVERY THEOLOGY
OCTOBER 1858 (?)

Negro equality! Fudge!! How long, in the government of a God great enough to make and maintain this Universe, shall there continue knaves to vend, and fools to gulp, so low a piece of demagogism as this?

NOTES FOR SPEECHES
SEPTEMBER 1859 (?)

Now let me call your attention to one thing that has really happened which shows this gradual and steady debauching of public opinion. . . . Did you ever, five years ago, hear of anybody in the world saying that the Negro had no share in the Declaration of National Independence; that it did not mean Negroes at all; and when "all men" were spoken of, Negroes were not included? I am satisfied that five years ago that proposition was not put upon paper by any living being anywhere.

SPEECH AT COLUMBUS, OHIO
SEPTEMBER 16, 1859

But for your race among us there could not be war, although many men engaged on either side do not care for you one way or the other. Nevertheless, I repeat, without the institution of slavery and the colored race as a basis, the war could not have an existence.

SPEECH ON COLONIZATION TO A DEPUTATION OF NEGROES
AUGUST 14, 1862

I do not know how much attachment you may have toward our race. It does not strike me that you have the greatest reason to love them. But still you are attached to them at all events.

SPEECH ON COLONIZATION TO A DEPUTATION OF NEGROES
AUGUST 14, 1862

Negroes, like other people, act upon motives. Why should they do anything for us, if we will do nothing for them? If they stake their lives for us, they must be prompted by the strongest motive—even the promise of freedom. And the promise, being made, must be kept.

LETTER TO JAMES C. CONKLING
AUGUST 26, 1863

You say you will not fight to free Negroes. Some of them seem willing to fight for you; but, no matter. Fight you, then, exclusively to save the Union. . . . Whenever you shall have conquered all resistance to the Union, if I shall urge you to continue fighting, it will be an apt time then for you to declare you will not fight to free Negroes.

LETTER TO JAMES C. CONKLING
AUGUST 26, 1863

How to better the condition of the colored race has long been a study which has attracted my serious and careful attention; hence I think I am clear and decided as to what course I shall pursue in the premises, regarding it a religious duty as the nation's guardian of these people who have so heroically vindicated their manhood on the battlefield where, in assisting to save the life of the Republic, they have demonstrated in blood their right to the ballot, which is but the humane protection of the flag they have so fearlessly defended.

LETTER TO JAMES S. WADSWORTH
JANUARY 1864 (?)

You are about to have a convention which, among other things, will probably define the elective franchise [in Louisiana]. I barely suggest, for your private consideration, whether some of the colored people may not be let in—as, for instance, the very intelligent and especially those who have fought gallantly in our ranks. They would probably help in some trying time to come to keep the jewel of liberty within the family of freedom.

LETTER TO GOVERNOR MICHAEL HAHN OF LOUISIANA
MARCH 13, 1864

You must not force Negroes any more than white men.

TELEGRAM TO JOHN GLENN
FEBRUARY 7, 1865

The colored man . . . in seeing all united for him is inspired with vigilance and energy and daring. . . . Grant that he desires the elective franchise, will he not attain it sooner by saving the already advanced steps toward it than by running backward over them?

LAST PUBLIC SPEECH
APRIL 11, 1865

## Negroes: Colonization

Pharaoh's country was cursed with plagues and his hosts were drowned in the Red Sea for striving to retain a captive people who had already served them more than four hundred years. May like disasters never befall us! If, as the friends of colonization hope, the present and coming generations of our countrymen shall by any means succeed in freeing our land from the dangerous presence of slavery and, at the same time, in restoring a captive people to their long-lost fatherland, with bright prospects for the future—and this, too, so gradually that neither races nor individuals shall have suffered by the change—it will indeed be a glorious consummation.

EULOGY ON HENRY CLAY
JULY 6, 1852

It is morally right and at the same time favorable to, or at least not against, our interest to transfer the African to his native clime, and we shall find a way to do it however great the task may be. The children of Israel, to such numbers as to include four hundred thousand fighting men, went out of Egyptian bondage in a body.

SPEECH AT SPRINGFIELD, ILLINOIS
JUNE 26, 1857

The proposed contract . . . may . . . be the introduction to . . . an equally desirable measure to secure the removal of Negroes from this country.

LETTER TO CALEB B. SMITH
OCTOBER 23, 1861 (?)

To carry out the plan of colonization may involve the acquiring of territory and also the appropriation of money beyond that to be expended in the territorial acquisition. Having practiced the acquisition of territory for nearly sixty years, the question of constitutional power to do so is no longer an open one to us. . . . If it be said that the only legitimate object of acquiring territory is to furnish homes for white men, this measure effects that object; for the emigration of colored men leaves additional room for white men remaining or coming here.

ANNUAL MESSAGE TO CONGRESS
DECEMBER 3, 1861

I do not speak of emancipation *at once*, but of a *decision* at once to emancipate *gradually*. Room in South America for colonization can be obtained cheaply, and in abundance; and when numbers shall be large enough to be company and encouragement for one another, the freed people will not be so reluctant to go.

APPEAL TO BORDER STATE REPRESENTATIVES
TO FAVOR COMPENSATED EMANCIPATION
JULY 12, 1862

I think your race suffer very greatly, many of them by living among us; while ours suffer from your presence. In a word we suffer on each side. If this is admitted, it affords a reason at least why we should be separated.

SPEECH ON COLONIZATION TO A DEPUTATION OF NEGROES
AUGUST 14, 1862

There is an unwillingness on the part of our people, harsh as it may be, for you free colored people to remain with us. Now, if you could give a start to the white people, you would open a wide door for many to be made free. If we deal with those who are not free at the beginning, and whose intellects are clouded by slavery, we have very poor materials to start with. If intelligent colored men, such as are before me, would move in this matter, much might be accomplished. It is exceedingly important that we have men at the beginning capable of thinking as white men, and not those who have been systematically oppressed.

SPEECH ON COLONIZATION TO A DEPUTATION OF NEGROES
AUGUST 14, 1862

I suppose one of the principal difficulties in the way of colonization is that the free colored man cannot see that his comfort would be advanced by it. . . . Gen. Washington himself endured greater physical hardships than if he had remained a British subject. Yet he was a happy man because he was engaged in benefiting his race. . . . The place I am thinking about having for a colony is in Central America. It is nearer to us than Liberia. . . . This particular place has all the advantages for a colony . . . harbors among the finest in the world . . . rich coal mines. . . . Coal land is the best thing I know of with which to commence an enterprise. . . . The political affairs in Central America are not in quite as satisfactory condition as I wish. There are contending factions in that quarter; but it is true that all the factions are agreed alike on the subject of colonization and want it and are more generous than we are here. To your colored race they have no objection. Besides, I would endeavor to have you . . . made the equals of the best.

SPEECH ON COLONIZATION TO A DEPUTATION OF NEGROES
AUGUST 14, 1862

Liberia and Haiti are, as yet, the only countries to which colonists of African descent from here could go with certainty of being received and adopted as citizens; and I regret to say such persons, contemplating colonization, do not seem so willing to migrate to those countries as to some others, nor so willing as I think their interest demands. I believe, however, opinion among them in this respect is improving and that, ere long, there will be an augmented and considerable migration to both these countries from the United States.

ANNUAL MESSAGE TO CONGRESS
DECEMBER 1, 1862

I cannot make it better known than it already is that I strongly favor colonization.

ANNUAL MESSAGE TO CONGRESS
DECEMBER 1, 1862

With deportation, even to a limited extent, enhanced wages to white labor is mathematically certain. Labor is like any other commodity in the market—increase the demand for it, and you increase the price of it. Reduce the supply of black labor by colonizing the black laborer out of the country, and by precisely so much you increase the demand for, and wages of, white labor.

ANNUAL MESSAGE TO CONGRESS
DECEMBER 1, 1862

## Negroes: Troops

The colored population is the great *available* and yet *unavailed* of force for restoring the Union. The bare sight of fifty thousand armed and drilled black soldiers on the banks of the Mississippi would end the rebellion at once.

LETTER TO ANDREW JOHNSON
MARCH 26, 1863

I see the enemy are driving at them fiercely, as is to be expected. It is important to the enemy that such a force shall *not* take shape and grow and thrive in the South; and in precisely the same proportion, it is important to us that it *shall*. Hence the utmost caution and vigilance is necessary on our part. The enemy will make extra efforts to destroy them; and we should do the same to preserve and increase them.

LETTER TO DAVID HUNTER
APRIL 1, 1863

In relation to . . . the raising of colored troops in the North, . . . I have to say . . . that being raised, say to the number of ten thousand, I would very cheerfully send them to the field under Gen. [John C.] Frémont, assigning him a department with such white force also as I might be able to put in. . . .

LETTER TO CHARLES SUMNER
JUNE 1, 1863

I desire that a renewed and vigorous effort be made to raise colored forces along the shores of the Mississippi.

LETTER TO EDWIN M. STANTON
JULY 21, 1863

I believe it is a resource which, if vigorously applied now, will soon close the contest. It works doubly, weakening the enemy and strengthening us. We were not fully ripe for it until the river was opened. Now I think at least a hundred thousand can and ought to be rapidly organized along its shores, relieving all the white troops to serve elsewhere.

LETTER TO ULYSSES S. GRANT
AUGUST 9, 1863

I know, as fully as one can know the opinions of others, that some of the commanders of our armies in the field who have given us our most important successes believe the emancipation policy and the use of colored troops constitute the heaviest blow yet dealt to the rebellion, and that at least one of those important successes could not have been achieved when it was but for the aid of black soldiers. Among the commanders holding these views are some who have never had any affinity with what is called abolitionism or with Republican party politics, but who hold them as purely military opinions.

LETTER TO JAMES C. CONKLING
AUGUST 26, 1863

I thought that whatever Negroes can be got to do as soldiers leaves just so much less for white soldiers to do in saving the Union.

LETTER TO JAMES C. CONKLING
AUGUST 26, 1863

The raising of colored troops I think will greatly help in every way.

LETTER TO ANDREW JOHNSON
SEPTEMBER 11, 1863

A delegation is here saying that our armed colored troops are at many if not all the landings on the Patuxent River, and by their presence, with arms in their hands, are frightening quiet people and producing great confusion.

LETTER TO ROBERT C. SCHENCK
OCTOBER 21, 1863

I personally wish Jacob R. Freese of New Jersey to be appointed a Colonel for a colored regiment—and this regardless of whether he can tell the exact shade of Julius Caesar's hair.

LETTER TO EDWIN M. STANTON
NOVEMBER 11, 1863

If I were to judge from [your] letter, without any external knowledge, I should suppose that all the colored people south of Washington were struggling to get to Massachusetts; that Massachusetts was anxious to receive and retain the whole of them as permanent citizens; and that the United States Government here was interposing and preventing this. But I suppose these are neither really the facts, nor meant to be asserted as true by you. Coming down to what I suppose to be the real facts, you are engaged in trying to raise colored troops for the U.S. and wish to take recruits from Virginia, through Washington, to Massachusetts for that object; and the loyal Governor of Virginia, also trying to raise troops for us, objects to your taking his material away; while we, having to care for all and being responsible alike to all, have to do as much for him as we would have to do for you if he was, by our authority, taking men from Massachusetts to fill up Virginia regiments. No more than this has been intended by me; nor, as I think, by the Secretary of War. There may have been some abuses of this as a rule which, if known, should be prevented in future. If, however, it be really true that Massachusetts wishes to afford a permanent home within her borders for all or even a large number of colored persons who will come to her, I shall be only too glad to know it. It would give relief in a very difficult point; and I would not for a moment hinder from going any person who is free by the terms of the proclamation or any of the acts of Congress.

LETTER TO GOVERNOR JOHN A. ANDREW OF MASSACHUSETTS
FEBRUARY 18, 1864

Military emancipation, and arming the blacks . . . shows a gain of quite a hundred and thirty thousand soldiers, seamen and laborers. . . . We have the men; and we could not have had them without the measure. And now let any Union man who complains of the measure test himself by writing down in one line that he is for subduing the rebellion by force of arms and in the next that he is for taking these hundred and thirty thousand men from the Union side and placing them where they would be but for the measure he condemns. If he cannot face his case so stated, it is only because he cannot face the truth.

LETTER TO ALBERT G. HODGES
APRIL 4, 1864

There is a witness in every white man's bosom that he would rather go to the war having the Negro help him, than to help the enemy against him.

LETTER TO CHARLES D. ROBINSON
AUGUST 17, 1864

There are but few aspects of this great war on which I have not already expressed my views by speaking or writing. There is one—the recent efforts of our erring brethren, sometimes so called, to employ the slaves in their armies. The great question with them has been, "Will the Negro fight for them?" They ought to know better than we; and, doubtless, do know better than we. . . . There is one thing about the Negroes fighting for the rebels which we can know as well as they can; and that is that they cannot at the same time fight in their armies and stay at home and make bread for them. And this being known and remembered we can have but little concern whether they become soldiers or not. I am rather in favor of the measure and would at any time, if I could, have loaned them a vote to carry it. We have to reach the bottom of the insurgent resources; and that they employ, or seriously think of employing, the slaves as soldiers gives us glimpses of the bottom.

SPEECH TO 140TH INDIANA REGIMENT
MARCH 17, 1865

## Neutral Rights

A civil war occurring in a country where foreigners reside and carry on trade under treaty stipulations is necessarily fruitful of complaints of the violation of neutral rights. All such collisions tend to excite misapprehensions, and possibly to produce mutual reclamations between nations which have a common interest in preserving peace and friendship.

ANNUAL MESSAGE TO CONGRESS
DECEMBER 1, 1862

## New England

Up here in New England you have a soil that scarcely sprouts black-eyed beans, and yet where will you find wealthy men so wealthy and poverty so rarely in extremity? There is not another such place on earth!

SPEECH AT NEW HAVEN, CONNECTICUT
MARCH 6, 1860

## News

Good news, from a reliable source, is always welcome.

LETTER TO SIMON CAMERON
AUGUST 6, 1860

I have a good deal of news from New York; but, of course, it is from *friends* and is one-sided.

LETTER TO JOHN PETTIT
SEPTEMBER 14, 1860

## Newspapers

Please pardon me for suggesting that if the papers like yours [Missouri *Republican*], which heretofore have persistently garbled and misrepresented what I have said, will now fully and fairly place it before their readers, there can be no further misunderstanding.

LETTER TO NATHANIEL P. PASCHALL
NOVEMBER 16, 1860

I write this to assure you that the administration will not discriminate against the [New York] *Herald*, especially while it sustains us so generously and the cause of the country so ably as it has been doing.

LETTER TO JAMES GORDON BENNETT
SEPTEMBER 28, 1861

It is important to humor the *Herald*.

MEMORANDUM ON THE NEW YORK *Herald*
DECEMBER 1862 OR FEBRUARY 1863 (?)

I wish you would allow the [*National*] *Republican* (my paper, as you jokingly call it) to be paid for advertising. The nonpayment is a source of trouble to me.

MEMORANDUM TO EDWIN M. STANTON
JULY 2, 1863

At your instance I directed a part of the advertising for this [War] Department to be done in the St. Joseph *Tribune*. I have just been informed that the *Tribune* openly avows its determination that in no event will it support the re-election of the President. As you probably know, please inform me whether this is true. The President's wish is that no objection shall be made to any paper respectfully expressing its preference for the *nomination* of any candidate; but that the patronage of the government shall be given to none which engages in cultivating a sentiment to oppose the *election* of any when he shall have been fairly nominated by the regular Union National Convention.

LETTER TO BENJAMIN F. LOAN*
FEBRUARY 22, 1864

## Niagara Falls

Niagara Falls! By what mysterious power is it that millions and millions are drawn from all parts of the world to gaze upon Niagara Falls?

FRAGMENT
SEPTEMBER 1848

Its power to excite reflection and emotion is its great charm.

FRAGMENT
SEPTEMBER 1848

It calls up the indefinite past. When Columbus first sought this continent—when Christ suffered on the cross—when Moses led Israel though the Red Sea—nay, even, when Adam first came from the hand of his Maker—then as now, Niagara was roaring here. The eyes of that species of extinct giants whose bones fill the mounds of America have gazed on Niagara as ours do now. Contemporary with the whole race of men, and older than the first man, Niagara is strong and fresh today as ten thousand years ago.

FRAGMENT
SEPTEMBER 1848

## Oaths

On principle I dislike an oath which requires a man to swear he *has* not done wrong. It rejects the Christian principle of for-

* Lincoln presumably drafted this letter for Edwin M. Stanton to sign.

giveness on terms of repentance. I think it is enough if the man does no wrong *hereafter.*

LETTER TO EDWIN M. STANTON
FEBRUARY 5, 1864

## Obedience

When differences of opinion arise between officers of the Government, the ranking officer must be obeyed.

LETTER TO SAMUEL W. MOULTON
JULY 31, 1863

## Obesity

I knew she was over-size, but she now appeared a fair match for Falstaff.

LETTER TO MRS. ORVILLE H. BROWNING
APRIL 1, 1838

## Obfuscation

When birds and animals are looked at through a fog they are seen to disadvantage.

REMARKS AT JERSEY CITY, NEW JERSEY
JUNE 24, 1862

## Obscurity

Many men of good judgment live and die unnoticed.

EULOGY ON HENRY CLAY
JULY 6, 1852

## Optimism

Like a rejected lover making merry at the wedding of his rival.

SPEECH AT CHICAGO, ILLINOIS
DECEMBER 10, 1856

## Patents

I am for the government having the best articles in spite of patent controversies.

LETTER TO GEORGE D. RAMSAY
MARCH 10, 1864

## Patriotism

The American people are *much* attached to their Government. I know they would suffer *much* for its sake; I know they would endure evils long and patiently before they would ever think of exchanging it for another.

ADDRESS TO YOUNG MEN'S LYCEUM,
SPRINGFIELD, ILLINOIS
JANUARY 27, 1838

"The Pioneer Fire Company." May they extinguish all the bad flames, but keep the flame of patriotism ever burning brightly in the hearts of the ladies.

TOAST TO THE PIONEER FIRE COMPANY,
SPRINGFIELD, ILLINOIS
JULY 5, 1858

Patriotic devotion . . . is . . . the foundation of all else that is valuable in this great national trial.

LETTER TO EDWIN M. STANTON
MARCH 28, 1864

Gold is good in its place; but living, brave, patriotic men are better than gold.

RESPONSE TO A SERENADE
NOVEMBER 10, 1864

## Patronage

No commercial object of government patronage can be so exclusively *general* as to not be of some peculiar *local* advantage; but, on the other hand, nothing is so *local* as to not be of some general advantage.

SPEECH ON INTERNAL IMPROVEMENTS
IN HOUSE OF REPRESENTATIVES
JUNE 20, 1848

When an office or a job is not already in Democratic hands . . . it should be given to a Whig. Even at this, full half the government patronage will still be in the hands of our opponents at the end of four years; and if still *less* than this is done for our friends, I think they will have just cause to complain, and I verily believe the administration cannot be sustained.

LETTER TO WILLIAM B. PRESTON, SECRETARY OF THE NAVY
APRIL 20, 1849

If anything be given the state [of Illinois], it should be so given as to gratify our friends and to stimulate them to future exertions.

LETTER TO JOSIAH M. LUCAS
APRIL 25, 1849

All the anxious politicians of his [Stephen A. Douglas's] party, or who have been of his party for years past, have been looking upon him as certainly, at no distant day, to be the President of the United States. They have seen in his round, jolly, fruitful face post offices, land offices, marshalships and cabinet appointments, chargeships and foreign missions, bursting and sprouting out in wonderful exuberance ready to be laid hold of by their greedy hands. And as they have been gazing upon this attractive picture so long they cannot, in the little distraction that has taken place in the party, bring themselves to give up the charming hope; but with greedier anxiety they rush about him, sustain him and give him marches, triumphal entries and receptions beyond what even in the days of his highest prosperity they could have brought about in his favor.

SPEECH AT SPRINGFIELD, ILLINOIS
JULY 17, 1858

Nobody has ever expected me to be President. In my poor, lean, lank face, nobody has ever seen that any cabbages were sprouting out.

SPEECH AT SPRINGFIELD, ILLINOIS
JULY 17, 1858

In regard to the patronage sought with so much eagerness and jealousy, I have prescribed for myself the maxim, "Justice to all."

LETTER TO WILLIAM H. SEWARD
DECEMBER 8, 1860

As to the matter of dispensing patronage, it perhaps will surprise you to learn that I have information that *you* claim to have my authority to arrange that matter in N.Y. I do not believe you have so claimed; but still so some men say. On that subject you know all I have said to you is "Justice to all," and I beg you to believe I have said nothing more particular to any one.

LETTER TO THURLOW WEED
FEBRUARY 4, 1861

The great point in his [Christopher Adams's] favor is that Thurlow Weed and Horace Greeley join in recommending him. I suppose the like never happened before, and never will again; so that it is now or never.

LETTER TO SALMON P. CHASE
MAY 8, 1861

It is difficult for you to understand what is nevertheless true, that the bare reading of a letter of that length requires more than any one person's share of my time. And when read, what is it but an evidence that you intend to importune me for one thing, and another, and another, until in self-defense I must drop all and devote myself to find a place, even though I remove somebody else to do it, and thereby turn him and his friends upon me for indefinite future importunity and hindrance from the legitimate duties for which I am supposed to be placed here?

LETTER TO MRS. L. H. PHIPPS
MARCH 9, 1863

## Peace

I shall do all that may be in my power to promote a peaceful settlement of all our difficulties. The man does not live who is more devoted to peace than I am. None who would do more to preserve it. But it may be necessary to put the foot down firmly. . . .

SPEECH AT TRENTON, NEW JERSEY
FEBRUARY 21, 1861

But . . . let us not think only of whipping rebels, or of those who seem to think only of whipping Negroes, but of those pleasant days which it is to be hoped are in store for us when, seated behind a good pair of horses, we can crack our whips and drive through a peaceful, happy and prosperous land.

SPEECH TO A MASSACHUSETTS DELEGATION
MARCH 13, 1862

Engaged, as I am, in a great war, I fear it will be difficult for the world to understand how fully I appreciate the principles of peace.

LETTER TO SAMUEL B. TOBEY
MARCH 19, 1862

Peace does not appear so distant as it did. I hope it will come soon, and come to stay; and so come as to be worth the keeping in all future time. It will then have been proved that, among free men, there can be no successful appeal from the ballot to the bullet, and they who take such appeal are sure to lose their case and pay the cost. And then there will be some black men who can remember that—with silent tongue, and clenched teeth, and steady eye, and well-poised bayonet—they have helped mankind on to this great consummation; while, I fear, there will be some white ones unable to forget that—with malignant heart, and deceitful speech—they have strove to hinder it.

LETTER TO JAMES C. CONKLING
AUGUST 26, 1863

Any proposition which embraces the restoration of peace, the integrity of the whole Union, and the abandonment of slavery, and which comes by and with an authority that can control the armies now at war against the United States will be received and considered by the Executive government of the United States, and will be met by liberal terms on other substantial and collateral points; and the bearer, or bearers, thereof shall have safe conduct both ways.

DOCUMENT ADDRESSED "TO WHOM IT MAY CONCERN"
JULY 18, 1864

To me it seems plain that saying reunion and abandonment of slavery would be considered, if offered, is not saying that nothing *else* or *less* would be considered if offered [but] . . . I am sure you would not desire me to say, or to leave an inference, that I am ready, whenever convenient, to join in re-enslaving those who shall have served us in consideration of our promise. As matter of morals, could such treachery by any possibility escape the curses of Heaven, or of any good man? As matter of policy, to *announce* such a purpose would ruin the Union cause itself. All recruiting of colored men would instantly cease, and all colored men now in our service would instantly desert us. And rightfully, too. Why should they give their lives for us with full notice of our purpose to betray them? . . . Allow me to remind you that no one having control of the rebel armies or, in fact, having any influence whatever in the rebellion, has offered or intimated a willingness to a restoration of the Union in any event or on any condition whatever. . . . Shall we be weak enough to allow the enemy to distract us with an abstract question which he himself refuses to present as a practical one? . . . If Jefferson Davis wishes, for himself or for the benefit of his friends at the North, to know what I would do if he were to offer peace and re-union, saying nothing about slavery, let him try me.

LETTER TO CHARLES D. ROBINSON
AUGUST 17, 1864

You will proceed forthwith and obtain, if possible, a conference for peace with Hon. Jefferson Davis, or any person by him authorized for that purpose. You will address him in entirely respectful terms, at all events, and in any that may be indispensable to secure the conference. At said conference you will propose, on behalf this government, that upon the restoration of the Union and the national authority, the war shall cease at once, all remaining questions to be left for adjustment by peaceful modes. If this be accepted, hostilities to cease at once. If it be not accepted, you will then request to be informed what terms, if any, embracing the restoration of the Union would be accepted. If any such be presented you in answer, you will forthwith report the same to this government, and await further instructions. If the presentation of any terms embracing the restoration of the Union be declined, you will then request to be informed what terms of peace would be accepted; and on receiving any answer, report the same to this government, and await further instructions.

LETTER TO HENRY J. RAYMOND
AUGUST 24, 1864

The public purpose to re-establish and maintain the national authority is unchanged and, as we believe, unchangeable. The manner of continuing the effort remains to choose. On careful consideration of all the evidence accessible it seems to me that no attempt at negotiation with the insurgent leader could result in any good. He would accept nothing short of severance of the Union—precisely what we will not and cannot give. His declarations to this effect are explicit and oft-repeated. He does not attempt to deceive us. He affords us no excuse to deceive ourselves. He cannot voluntarily reaccept the Union; we cannot voluntarily yield it. Between him and us the issue is distinct, simple and inflexible. It is an issue which can only be tried by war and decided by victory. If we yield, we are beaten; if the Southern people fail him, he is beaten. Either way, it would be the victory and defeat following war. What is true, however, of him who heads the insurgent cause is not necessarily true of those who follow. Although he cannot reaccept the Union, they can. Some of them, we know, already desire peace and reunion. The number of such may increase. They can, at any moment, have peace simply by laying down their arms and submitting to the national authority under the Constitution. After so much, the government could not, if it would, maintain war against them. The loyal people would not sustain or allow it. . . . In stating a single condition of peace, I mean simply to say that the war will cease on the part of the government whenever it shall have ceased on the part of those who began it.

ANNUAL MESSAGE TO CONGRESS
DECEMBER 6, 1864

You may say to [Jefferson Davis] that I have constantly been, am now and shall continue ready to receive any agent whom he or any other influential person now resisting the national authority may informally send to me, with the view of securing peace to the people of our one common country.

LETTER TO FRANCIS P. BLAIR, SR.
JANUARY 18, 1865

With malice toward none; with charity for all; with firmness in the right, as God gives us to see the right, let us strive on to finish the work we are in; to bind up the nation's wounds; to care for him who shall have borne the battle, and for his widow, and his orphan—to do all which may achieve and cherish a just, and a lasting peace, among ourselves, and with all nations.

SECOND INAUGURAL ADDRESS
MARCH 4, 1865

## Perseverance

As you ask my advice, it is that if you are doing well you better stick to it. If you have a good start there and should give it up, you might not get it again, here or elsewhere.

LETTER TO JOHN T. HANKS
SEPTEMBER 24, 1860

Your good mother tells me you are feeling very badly in your new situation. Allow me to assure you it is a perfect certainty that you will very soon feel better—quite happy—if you only stick to the resolution you have taken to procure a military education. I am older than you, have felt badly myself, and *know* what I tell you is true. Adhere to your purpose and you will soon feel as well as you ever did. On the contrary, if you falter and give up you will lose the power of keeping any resolution, and will regret it all your life. Take the advice of a friend who, though he never saw you, deeply sympathizes with you, and stick to your purpose.

LETTER TO QUINTIN CAMPBELL
JUNE 28, 1862

## Persuasion

When the conduct of men is designed to be influenced, *persuasion*, kind, unassuming persuasion, should ever be adopted.

ADDRESS TO WASHINGTON TEMPERANCE SOCIETY,
SPRINGFIELD, ILLINOIS
FEBRUARY 22, 1842

## Pierce, Franklin

I think it is well that P. is away from the N.H. people. He will do less harm anywhere else; and, by *when* he has gone, his neighbors will understand him better.

LETTER TO SIMON CAMERON
SEPTEMBER 1861

## Planning

If we could first know *where* we are and *whither* we are tending, we could then better judge *what* to do and *how* to do it.

"A HOUSE DIVIDED" SPEECH, SPRINGFIELD, ILLINOIS
JUNE 16, 1858

## Political Campaigns

In accordance with established custom and the principles of true republicanism, it becomes my duty to make known to you —the people whom I propose to represent—my sentiments with regard to local affairs.

COMMUNICATION TO THE PEOPLE OF
SANGAMON COUNTY, ILLINOIS
MARCH 9, 1832

If elected, I shall consider the whole people of Sangamon my constituents, as well those that oppose as those that support me.

LETTER TO THE *Sangamo* (ILLINOIS) *Journal*
JUNE 13, 1836

I have this moment been shown a handbill signed "Truth Teller," in which my name is done up in large capitals. . . . All

I have to say is that the author is a *liar* and a *scoundrel,* and that if he will avow the authorship to me, I promise to give his proboscis a good wringing.

HANDBILL ADDRESSED TO THE PEOPLE OF
SANGAMON COUNTY, ILLINOIS
NOVEMBER 1836 (?)

I would rejoice to be spared the labor of a contest; but "being in" I shall go it thoroughly and to the bottom.

LETTER TO BENJAMIN F. JAMES
JANUARY 14, 1846

I made the declaration that I would not be a candidate again more from a wish to deal fairly with others, to keep peace among our friends and to keep the district from going to the enemy, than for any cause personal to myself; so that, if it should so happen that nobody else wishes to be elected, I could not refuse the people the right of sending me again.

LETTER TO WILLIAM H. HERNDON
JANUARY 8, 1848

I can say, as Mr. [Henry] Clay said of the annexation of Texas, that "personally I would not object" to a re-election, although I thought at the time, and still think, it would be quite as well for me to return to the law at the end of a single term.

LETTER TO WILLIAM H. HERNDON
JANUARY 8, 1848

I neither seek, expect or desire a nomination for a seat in the next Congress; . . . I prefer my name should not be brought forward in that connection; and . . . I would now peremptorily forbid the use of it, could I feel entirely at liberty to do so.

LETTER TO THE *Illinois Journal*
JUNE 5, 1850

Auxiliary to [the] main points . . . are their thunderings of cannon, their marching and music, their fizzlegigs and fireworks; but I will not waste time with them. They are but the little trappings of the campaign.

SPEECH AT SPRINGFIELD, ILLINOIS
JULY 17, 1858

While pretending no indifference to earthly honors, I *do claim* to be actuated in this contest [for the Senate] by something higher than an anxiety for office.

SPEECH AT LEWISTOWN, ILLINOIS
AUGUST 21, 1858

I stand here surrounded by friends—*some political, all personal* friends, I trust— . . . I have borne a laborious and, in some respects to myself, a painful part in the contest. Through all, I have neither assailed nor wrestled with any part of the Constitution. The legal rights of the Southern people to reclaim their fugitives I have constantly admitted. The legal right of Congress to interfere with their institution in the states, I have constantly denied. In resisting the spread of slavery to new territory, and with that what appears to me to be a tendency to subvert the first principle of free government itself, my whole effort has consisted. To the best of my judgment I have labored *for* and not *against* the Union. As I have not felt, so I have not expressed any harsh sentiment toward our Southern brethren. I have constantly declared, as I really believed, the only difference between them and us is the difference of circumstances. I have meant to assail the motives of no party, or individual; and if I have in any instance (of which I am not conscious) departed from my purpose, I regret it. . . .

SPEECH AT SPRINGFIELD, ILLINOIS
OCTOBER 30, 1858

I am glad I made the late race. It gave me a hearing on the great and durable question of the age which I could have had in no other way; and though I now sink out of view and shall be forgotten, I believe I have made some remarks which will tell for the cause of civil liberty long after I am gone.

LETTER TO ANSON G. HENRY
NOVEMBER 19, 1858

I wish no explanation made to our enemies. What they want is a squabble and a fuss; and that they can have if we explain, and they cannot have if we don't.

LETTER TO CORNELIUS F. MCNEILL
APRIL 6, 1860

I have not permitted myself, gentlemen, to conclude that I am the best man in the country; but I am reminded, in this connection, of a story of an old Dutch farmer who remarked to a companion once that "it was not best to swap horses when crossing streams."

REPLY TO DELEGATION FROM NATIONAL UNION LEAGUE
JUNE 9, 1864

I earnestly believe that the consequences of this day's work . . . will be to the lasting advantage, if not to the very salvation, of the country. I cannot at this hour say what has been the result of the election; but, whatever it may be, I have no desire to modify this opinion—that all who have labored today in behalf of the Union organization have wrought for the best interests of their country and the world, not only for the present but for all future ages.

RESPONSE TO A SERENADE
NOVEMBER 8, 1864

## Political Conventions

The point of danger is the temptation in different localities to "*platform*" for something which will be popular just there but which, nevertheless, will be a firebrand elsewhere, and especially in a national convention. . . . What gets very rife outside of conventions is very likely to find its way into them.

LETTER TO SCHUYLER COLFAX
JULY 6, 1859

Wish not to interfere about V.P. Cannot interfere about platform. Convention must judge for itself.

NOTE ON A LETTER FROM JOHN G. NICOLAY TO JOHN HAY
JUNE 6, 1864

## Political Parties

A free people, in times of peace and quiet—when pressed by no common danger—naturally divide into parties. At such times, the man who is of neither party is not—cannot be—of any consequence.

EULOGY ON HENRY CLAY
JULY 6, 1852

I know how painful it must be to an honest, sincere man to be urged by his party to the support of a measure which on his conscience he believes to be wrong.

LETTER TO JOHN M. PALMER
SEPTEMBER 7, 1854

I suppose my opposition to the principle of slavery is as strong as that of any member of the Republican party; but I had also supposed that the *extent* to which I feel authorized to carry that opposition, practically, was not at all satisfactory to that party.

LETTER TO ICHABOD CODDING
NOVEMBER 27, 1854

Upon those men who are, in sentiment, opposed to the spread and nationalization of slavery rests the task of preventing it.

FRAGMENT ON THE FORMATION OF THE REPUBLICAN PARTY
FEBRUARY 1857

The Republicans inculcate, with whatever of ability they can, that the Negro is a man; that his bondage is cruelly wrong; and that the field of his oppression ought not to be enlarged. The Democrats deny his manhood; deny, or dwarf to insignificance, the wrong of his bondage; so far as possible, crush all sympathy for him, and cultivate and excite hatred and disgust against him; compliment themselves as Union-savers for doing so; and call the indefinite outspreading of his bondage "a sacred right of self-government."

SPEECH AT SPRINGFIELD, ILLINOIS
JUNE 26, 1857

The Republicans of the nation mustered . . . under the single impulse of resistance to a common danger with every external circumstance against us. Of *strange, discordant* and even *hostile* elements, we gathered from the four winds and *formed* and fought the battle through, under the constant hot fire of a disciplined, proud and pampered enemy.

"A HOUSE DIVIDED" SPEECH, SPRINGFIELD, ILLINOIS
JUNE 16, 1858

The Republican party is made up of those who, as far as they can peaceably, will oppose the extension of slavery and who will hope for its ultimate extinction.

SPEECH AT CHICAGO, ILLINOIS
JULY 10, 1858

I am, in a certain sense, made the standard-bearer in behalf of the Republicans. I was made so merely because there had to be someone so placed—I being in no wise preferable to any other one of the twenty-five, perhaps a hundred, we have in the Republican ranks.

SPEECH AT SPRINGFIELD, ILLINOIS
JULY 17, 1858

I do not understand the Republican party to be committed to the proposition "No more slave states." I think they are not so committed. Most certainly they prefer there should be no more; but I know there are many of them who think we are under obligation to admit slave states from Texas,* if such shall be presented for admission; but I think the party as such is not committed either way.

LETTER TO HENRY E. DUMMER
AUGUST 5, 1858

As to politics, I am doing what I can for the cause.

LETTER TO ALBERT PARKER
AUGUST 10, 1858

The difference between the Republican and the Democratic parties on the leading issue of this contest, as I understand it, is that the former consider slavery a moral, social and political wrong, while the latter *do not* consider it either a moral, social or political wrong. . . . I will not allege that the Democratic party consider slavery morally, socially and politically *right;* though their tendency to that view has, in my opinion, been constant and unmistakable for the past five years.

SPEECH AT EDWARDSVILLE, ILLINOIS
SEPTEMBER 11, 1858

The Judge [Stephen A. Douglas] has also detained us awhile in regard to the distinction between his party and our party. . . . He assumes that our party is altogether sectional—that the party to which he adheres is national; and the argument is that no party can be a rightful party—can be based upon rightful principles—unless it can announce its principles everywhere. I presume Judge Douglas could not go into Russia and announce the doctrine of our national democracy; he could not denounce the doctrine of kings and emperors and monarchies in Russia; and it may be true of this country that in some places we may not be able to proclaim a doctrine as clearly true as the truth of democracy, because there is a section so directly opposed to

* The resolution of annexation by which Texas was admitted to the Union provided that new states in addition to Texas, not exceeding four, might be formed out of the territory with the consent of Texas.

it that they will not tolerate us in doing so. Is it the true test of the soundness of a doctrine that in some places people won't let you proclaim it?

FIFTH DEBATE WITH STEPHEN A. DOUGLAS,
GALESBURG, ILLINOIS
OCTOBER 7, 1858

Remembering . . . that the Jefferson party were formed upon their supposed superior devotion to the *personal* rights of men, holding the rights of *property* to be secondary only and greatly inferior, and then assuming that the so-called Democracy of today are the Jefferson, and their opponents the anti-Jefferson, parties, . . . note how completely the two have changed hands as to the principle upon which they were originally supposed to be divided. The Democracy of today hold the *liberty* of one man to be absolutely nothing, when in conflict with another man's right of *property*. Republicans, on the contrary, are for both the *man* and the *dollar;* but in cases of conflict, the man *before* the dollar. I remember once being much amused at seeing two partially intoxicated men engage in a fight with their great-coats on, which fight, after a long and rather harmless contest, ended in each having fought himself *out* of his own coat and *into* that of the other. If the two leading parties of this day are really identical with the two in the days of Jefferson and Adams, they have performed about the same feat as the two drunken men.

LETTER TO HENRY L. PIERCE AND OTHERS
APRIL 6, 1859

I assume that Republicans throughout the nation believe they are right and are earnest and determined in their cause. Let them, then, keep constantly in view that that chief object of their organization is to prevent the *spread* and *nationalization* of slavery.

NOTES FOR SPEECHES AT COLUMBUS AND CINCINNATI, OHIO
SEPTEMBER 16, 17, 1859

I think the chances were more than equal that we could have beaten the Democracy united. Divided, as it is, its chance appears indeed very slim. But great is Democracy in resources; and it may yet give its fortunes a turn.

LETTER TO ANSON G. HENRY

JULY 4, 1860

The point you press—the importance of thorough organization—is felt and appreciated by our friends everywhere. And yet it involves so much more of dry and irksome labor that most of them shrink from it—preferring parades and shows and monster meetings. I know not how this can be helped. I do what I can in my position for organization; but it does not amount to as much as it should.

LETTER TO HENRY WILSON

SEPTEMBER 1, 1860

I gave my opinion that we, as Republicans, would ultimately beat them as Democrats. . . . I also told them how I expected they would be treated after they should have been beaten; and I now wish to recall their attention to what I then said upon that subject. I then said: "When we do, as we say, beat you, you perhaps want to know what we will do with you. I will tell you, so far as I am authorized to speak for the opposition, what we mean to do with you. We mean to treat you, as near as we possibly can, as Washington, Jefferson and Madison treated you. We mean to leave you alone and in no way to interfere with your institution; to abide by all and every compromise of the Constitution. . . . We mean to remember that you are as good as we; that there is no difference between us other than the difference of circumstances. We mean to recognize and bear in mind always that you have as good hearts in your bosoms as other people, or as we claim to have, and treat you accordingly."

SPEECH AT CINCINNATI, OHIO

FEBRUARY 12, 1861

Almost all men in this country, and in any country where freedom of thought is tolerated, attach themselves to political parties. It is but ordinary charity to attribute this to the fact that in so attaching himself to the party which his judgment prefers, the citizen believes he thereby promotes the best interests of the whole country; and when an election is passed, it is altogether befitting a free people that until the next election they should be as one people.

REPLY TO GOVERNOR EDWIN D. MORGAN AT
ALBANY, NEW YORK
FEBRUARY 18, 1861

I certainly know that if the war fails, the administration fails, and that I *will* be blamed for it whether I deserve it or not. And I ought to be blamed, if I could do better. You think I could do better; therefore you blame me already. I think I could not do better; therefore I blame you for blaming me. I understand you *now* to be willing to accept the help of men who are not Republicans, provided they have "heart in it." Agreed. I want no others. But who is to be the judge of hearts, or of "heart in it"? If I must discard my own judgment and take yours, I must also take that of others; and by the time I should reject all I should be advised to reject, I should have none left, Republicans or others—not even yourself. For, be assured . . . there are men who have "heart in it" that think you are performing your part as poorly as you think I am performing mine.

LETTER TO CARL SCHURZ
NOVEMBER 24, 1862

## Political Platforms

I have supposed myself, since the organization of the Republican party at Bloomington in May 1856, bound as a party man by the platforms of the party, then and since.

SECOND DEBATE WITH STEPHEN A. DOUGLAS,
FREEPORT, ILLINOIS
AUGUST 27, 1858

I have declared my approval of the platform and accepted the nomination. Now, if I were to *publicly* shift this position by adding or subtracting anything, the convention would have the right, and probably would be inclined, to displace me as their candidate. And I feel confident that you, on reflection, would not wish me to give *private* assurances to be seen by some and kept secret from others.

LETTER TO G. YOKE TAMS
SEPTEMBER 22, 1860

I see you have erected a very fine and handsome platform here for me, and I presume you expected me to speak from it. If I should go upon it you would imagine that I was about to deliver you a much longer speech than I am. I wish you to understand that I mean no discourtesy to you by thus declining. I intend discourtesy to no one. But I wish you to understand that though I am unwilling to go upon this platform, you are not at liberty to draw any inferences concerning any other platform with which my name has been or is connected.

REMARKS AT SYRACUSE, NEW YORK
FEBRUARY 18, 1861

In this time of national peril I would have preferred to meet you upon a level one step higher than any party platform; because I am sure that from such more elevated position we could do better battle for the country we all love than we possibly can from these lower ones where, from force of habit, the prejudices of the past, and selfish hopes of the future, we are sure to expend much of our ingenuity and strength in finding fault with and aiming blows at each other.

LETTER TO ERASTUS CORNING AND OTHERS
JUNE 12, 1863

I know no reason to doubt that I shall accept the nomination tendered; and yet, perhaps I should not declare definitely before reading and considering what is called the platform.

REPLY TO COMMITTEE NOTIFYING HIM OF RENOMINATION
JUNE 9, 1864

## Politicians

A set of men who have interests aside from the interests of the people and who, to say the most of them, are, taken as a mass, at least one long step removed from honest men. I say this with the greater freedom because, being a politician myself, none can regard it as personal.

SPEECH IN ILLINOIS LEGISLATURE
JANUARY 11, 1837

These political fiends are not half sick enough yet. "Party malice" and not "public good" possesses them entirely.

LETTER TO HENRY J. RAYMOND
NOVEMBER 28, 1860

If the politicians and leaders of parties were as true as the PEOPLE, there would be little fear that the peace of the country would be disturbed.

REMARKS AT LAWRENCEBURG, INDIANA
FEBRUARY 12, 1861

## Polk, James

His mind, tasked beyond its power, is running hither and thither like some tortured creature on a burning surface, finding no position on which it can settle down and be at ease.

SPEECH IN HOUSE OF REPRESENTATIVES
JANUARY 12, 1848

## Polygamy

There is nothing in the United States Constitution or law against polygamy.

SPEECH AT SPRINGFIELD, ILLINOIS
JUNE 26, 1857

## Popular Sovereignty

What is Popular Sovereignty? Is it the right of the people to have slavery or not have it, as they see fit, in the territories? I will state—and I have an able man to watch me—my understanding is that Popular Sovereignty, as now applied to the question of slavery, does allow the people of a territory to have slavery if they want to, but does not allow them *not* to have it if they *do not* want it.

FIRST DEBATE WITH STEPHEN A. DOUGLAS,
OTTAWA, ILLINOIS
AUGUST 21, 1858

Has [Douglas's Popular Sovereignty] not got down as thin as the homeopathic soup that was made by boiling the shadow of a pigeon that had starved to death?

SIXTH DEBATE WITH STEPHEN A. DOUGLAS,
QUINCY, ILLINOIS
OCTOBER 13, 1858

I believe there is a genuine popular sovereignty. I think a definition of genuine popular sovereignty in the abstract would be about this: That each man shall do precisely as he pleases with himself and with all those things which exclusively concern him. Applied to government, this principle would be that a general government shall do all those things which pertain to it and all the local governments shall do precisely as they please in respect to those matters which exclusively concern them. I understand that this government of the United States under which we live is based upon this principle; and I am misunderstood if it is supposed that I have any war to make upon that principle.

SPEECH AT COLUMBUS, OHIO
SEPTEMBER 16, 1859

The people of these United States are the rightful masters of both Congresses and courts not to overthrow the Constitution, but to overthrow the men who pervert that Constitution.

SPEECH AT CINCINNATI, OHIO
SEPTEMBER 17, 1859

An effort has been made for a policy that shall treat [slavery] as neither right nor wrong. It is based upon utter indifference. . . . It holds that it makes no more difference to us whether the territories become free or slave states than whether my neighbor stocks his farm with horned cattle or puts it into tobacco. All recognize this policy, the plausible, sugar-coated name of which is *"popular sovereignty."* . . . Now such a policy may have a temporary run; it may spring up as necessary to the political prospects of some gentleman; but it is utterly baseless; the people are not indifferent.

SPEECH AT NEW HAVEN, CONNECTICUT
MARCH 6, 1860

## Posterity

Posterity has done nothing for us, and theorize on it as we may, practically we shall do very little for it unless we are made to think we are at the same time doing something for ourselves.

ADDRESS TO WASHINGTON TEMPERANCE SOCIETY,
SPRINGFIELD, ILLINOIS
FEBRUARY 22, 1842

Few can be induced to labor exclusively for posterity, and none will do it enthusiastically.

ADDRESS TO WASHINGTON TEMPERANCE SOCIETY,
SPRINGFIELD, ILLINOIS
FEBRUARY 22, 1842

In all the trying positions in which I shall be placed, and doubtless I shall be placed in many trying ones, my reliance will be placed upon you and the people of the United States—

and I wish you to remember now and forever that . . . if the Union of these states and the liberties of this peoples shall be lost, it is but little to any one man of fifty-two years of age, but a great deal to the thirty millions of people who inhabit these United States and to their posterity in all coming time. It is your business to rise up and preserve the Union and liberty, for yourselves and not for me.

REPLY TO GOVERNOR OLIVER P. MORTON,
INDIANAPOLIS, INDIANA
FEBRUARY 11, 1861

May our children and our children's children to a thousand generations continue to enjoy the benefits conferred upon us by a united country, and have cause yet to rejoice under those glorious institutions bequeathed us by Washington and his compeers.

SPEECH AT FREDERICK, MARYLAND
OCTOBER 4, 1862

A nation may be said to consist of its territory, its people, and its laws. The territory is the only part which is of certain durability.

ANNUAL MESSAGE TO CONGRESS
DECEMBER 1, 1862

*Poverty*

In this country one can scarcely be so poor but that, if he *will*, he *can* acquire sufficient education to get through the world respectably.

EULOGY ON HENRY CLAY
JULY 6, 1852

It is bad to be poor. I shall go to the wall for bread and meat if I neglect my business this year as well as last.

LETTER TO HAWKINS TAYLOR
SEPTEMBER 6, 1859

## Prayer

The rebel soldiers are praying with a good deal more earnestness, I fear, than our own troops, and expecting God to favor their side; for one of our own soldiers, who had been taken prisoner, told Senator [Henry] Wilson, a few days since, that he met with nothing so discouraging as the evident sincerity of those he was among in their prayers.

REPLY TO EMANCIPATION MEMORIAL PRESENTED BY
CHICAGO CHRISTIANS OF ALL DENOMINATIONS
SEPTEMBER 13, 1862

## Preparedness

The most we can do now is to watch events and be as well prepared as possible for any turn things may take.

LETTER TO DAVID HUNTER
DECEMBER 22, 1860

I think the necessity of being *ready* increases. Look to it.

LETTER TO ANDREW G. CURTIN
APRIL 8, 1861

## Presidency

Allow the President to invade a neighboring nation whenever *he* shall deem it necessary to repel an invasion, and you allow him to do so *whenever he may choose to say* he deems it necessary for such purpose—and you allow him to make war at pleasure.

LETTER TO WILLIAM H. HERNDON
FEBRUARY 15, 1848

We prefer a candidate who . . . will allow the people to have their own way, regardless of his private opinions.

SPEECH IN HOUSE OF REPRESENTATIVES
JULY 27, 1848

The Presidency, even to the most experienced politicians, is no bed of roses.

EULOGY ON ZACHARY TAYLOR
JULY 25, 1850

No human being can fill that station and escape censure.

EULOGY ON ZACHARY TAYLOR
JULY 25, 1850

Upon the death of . . . any President, we are naturally led to consider what will be its effect, politically, upon the country.

EULOGY ON ZACHARY TAYLOR
JULY 25, 1850

Whoever does not get the State of New York will not be elected President.

SPEECH TO SCOTT CLUB, SPRINGFIELD, ILLINOIS
AUGUST 26, 1852

As to the Presidential nomination, claiming no greater exemption from selfishness than is common, I still feel that my whole aspiration should be, and therefore must be, to be placed anywhere or nowhere as may appear most likely to advance our cause.

LETTER TO JAMES F. BABCOCK
APRIL 14, 1860

As you request, I will be entirely frank. The taste *is* in my mouth a little; and this, no doubt, disqualifies me to some extent to form correct opinions. You may confidently rely, however, that by no advice or consent of mine shall my pretensions be pressed to the point of endangering our common cause.

LETTER TO LYMAN TRUMBULL
APRIL 29, 1860

No man can be elected President without some opponents, as well as supporters; and if, when elected, he cannot be installed till he first appeases his enemies by breaking his pledges and betraying his friends, this government and all popular government is already at an end. Demands for such surrender, once recognized and yielded to, are without limit as to nature, extent or repetition. They break the only bond of faith between public and public servant; and they distinctly set the minority over the majority. Such demands acquiesced in would not merely be the ruin of a man or a party; but as a precedent they would ruin the government itself.

FRAGMENT OF SPEECH INTENDED FOR KENTUCKIANS
FEBRUARY 1861

I have been selected to fill an important office for a brief period, and am now, in your eyes, invested with an influence which will soon pass away; but should my administration prove to be a very wicked one or, what is more probable, a very foolish one, if you the PEOPLE are but true to yourselves and to the Constitution, there is but little harm I can do, *thank God!*

REMARKS AT LAWRENCEBURG, INDIANA
FEBRUARY 12, 1861

Very great responsibility rests upon me in the position to which the votes of the American people have called me. I am deeply sensible of that weighty responsibility. I cannot but know what you all know, that without a name, perhaps without a reason why I should have a name, there has fallen upon me a task such as did not rest even upon the Father of his Country, and so feeling I cannot but turn and look for the support without which it will be impossible for me to perform that great task. I turn, then, and look to the American people and to that God who has never forsaken them.

ADDRESS TO OHIO LEGISLATURE, COLUMBUS, OHIO
FEBRUARY 13, 1861

If any of the other candidates had been elected, I think it would have been altogether becoming and proper for all to have joined in showing honor, quite as well to the office and the country as to the man.

SPEECH AT COLUMBUS, OHIO
FEBRUARY 13, 1861

By your Constitution you have another chance in four years. No great harm can be done by us in that time—in that time there can be nobody hurt. If anything goes wrong, however, and you find you have made a mistake, elect a better man next time. There are plenty of them.

SPEECH AT STEUBENVILLE, OHIO
FEBRUARY 14, 1861

By the Constitution, the Executive may recommend measures which he may think proper; and he may veto those he thinks improper; and it is supposed he may add to these certain indirect influences to affect the action of Congress. My political education strongly inclines me against a very free use of any of these means by the Executive to control the legislation of the country. As a rule, I think it better that Congress should originate as well as perfect its measures without external bias.

SPEECH AT PITTSBURGH, PENNSYLVANIA
FEBRUARY 15, 1861

*Standing as I do, with my hand upon this staff, and under the folds of the American flag,* I ASK YOU TO STAND BY ME AS LONG AS I STAND BY IT.

REMARKS AT DUNKIRK, NEW YORK
FEBRUARY 16, 1861

I am unwilling, on any occasion, that I should be so meanly thought of as to have it supposed for a moment that I regard these demonstrations as tendered to me personally. They should be tendered to no individual man. They are tendered to the country, to the institutions of the country and to the perpetuity of the liberties of the country for which those institutions were made and created.

SPEECH AT BUFFALO, NEW YORK<br>FEBRUARY 16, 1861

I am sure I bring a heart true to the work. For the ability to perform it, I must trust in that Supreme Being who has never forsaken this favored land through the instrumentality of this great and intelligent people. Without that assistance, I shall surely fail. With it I cannot fail.

SPEECH AT BUFFALO, NEW YORK<br>FEBRUARY 16, 1861

It is true that while I hold myself, without mock modesty, the humblest of all individuals that have ever been elevated to the Presidency, I have a more difficult task to perform than any of them.

REMARKS AT FONDA, NEW YORK<br>FEBRUARY 18, 1861

When I came . . . to preside in the government of the United States, . . . one duty paramount to all others was before me, namely, to maintain and preserve at once the Constitution and the integrity of the federal republic. A conscientious purpose to perform this duty is a key to all the measures of administration which have been and to all which will hereafter be pursued. Under our form of government and my official oath, I could not depart from this purpose if I would.

LETTER TO THE WORKINGMEN OF MANCHESTER, ENGLAND<br>JANUARY 19, 1863

The courts, and not the President, must decide questions of land titles. . . . Mere vague assertions that the decisions of the courts are fraudulent, with appeals to me to reverse them, cannot be entertained.

LETTER TO WILLIAM T. OTTO<br>JUNE 1, 1863

In my administration I might have committed some errors. It would be, indeed, remarkable if I had not. I have acted according to my best judgment in every case. . . . As a pilot, I have used my best exertions to keep afloat our ship of state and shall be glad to resign my trust at the appointed time to another pilot more skillful and successful than I may prove. In every case, and at all hazards, the government must be perpetuated.

REPLY TO MEMBERS OF PRESBYTERIAN GENERAL ASSEMBLY
JUNE 2, 1863

I freely acknowledge myself the servant of the people according to the bond of service—the United States Constitution; and that, as such, I am responsible to them.

LETTER TO JAMES C. CONKLING
AUGUST 26, 1863

I think the Constitution invests its commander-in-chief with the law of war in time of war.

LETTER TO JAMES C. CONKLING
AUGUST 26, 1863

A second term would be a great honor and a great labor, which together perhaps I would not decline if tendered.

LETTER TO ELIHU B. WASHBURNE
OCTOBER 26, 1863

Mr. [Daniel] Webster once stated the proposition that a President could not be so applauded and ministered unto when his term of office, and with it his power to confer favors, drew near to its close as he had been in the heyday of his inauguration. . . . This may be a general truth; but, to my personal knowledge, it is not particularly true in Baltimore. For instance, on the 22nd or 23rd of February, 1861 . . . I passed through Baltimore, rich with honorable and fat offices soon to be dispensed, and not one hand reached forth to greet me, not one voice broke the stillness to cheer me. Now, three years having past, and offices having passed away, Baltimore marks my coming and cheers me when I come. . . . I take it to be unquestionable that what happened here three years ago, and what happens here now, was contempt of office then, and is purely appreciation of merit now.

DRAFT OF ADDRESS TO SANITARY FAIR,
BALTIMORE, MARYLAND
APRIL 1864

I felt that measures otherwise unconstitutional might become lawful by becoming indispensable to the preservation of the nation. Right or wrong, I assumed this ground and now avow it.

LETTER TO ALBERT G. HODGES
APRIL 4, 1864

I am naturally antislavery. If slavery is not wrong, nothing is wrong. I cannot remember when I did not so think, and feel. And yet I have never understood that the Presidency conferred upon me an unrestricted right to act officially upon this judgment and feeling. . . . I aver that, to this day, I have done no official act in mere deference to my abstract judgment and feeling on slavery.

LETTER TO ALBERT G. HODGES
APRIL 4, 1864

This morning, as for some days past, it seems exceedingly probable that this Administration will not be re-elected. Then it will be my duty to so co-operate with the President-elect, as to save the Union between the election and the inauguration; as he will have secured his election on such ground that he cannot possibly save it afterwards.

MEMORANDUM ON PROBABLE FAILURE OF RE-ELECTION
AUGUST 23, 1864

Having served four years in the depths of a great, and yet unended, national peril, I can view this call to a second term in no wise more flatteringly to myself than as an expression of the public judgment that I may better finish a difficult work in which I have labored from the first than could any one less severely schooled to the task. In this view, and with assured reliance on that Almighty Ruler who has so graciously sustained us thus far and with increased gratitude to the generous people for their continued confidence, I accept the renewed trust, with its yet onerous and perplexing duties and responsibilities.

REPLY TO NOTIFICATION COMMITTEE
MARCH 1, 1865

## Principle

The *probability* that we may fall in the struggle *ought not* to deter us from the support of a cause we believe to be just.

SPEECH ON THE SUB-TREASURY
DECEMBER 26, 1839

I cannot reasonably hope to convince you that we have any principles. The most I can expect is to assure you that we think we have, and are quite contented with them.

SPEECH IN HOUSE OF REPRESENTATIVES
JULY 27, 1848

Stand with anybody that stands RIGHT. Stand with him while he is right and PART with him when he goes wrong.

SPEECH AT PEORIA, ILLINOIS
OCTOBER 16, 1854

I have no objection to "fuse" with anybody provided I can fuse on ground which I think is right.

LETTER TO OWEN LOVEJOY
AUGUST 11, 1855

Moral principle is all, or nearly all, that unites us of the North.

FRAGMENT ON SECTIONALISM
JULY 1856

Those who feel that our position is right should stand firm, and be active, when action is needed.

LETTER TO W. H. GRAY
JUNE 4, 1858

*We* have to fight this battle on principle, and upon principle alone.

SPEECH AT SPRINGFIELD, ILLINOIS
JULY 17, 1858

I have meant to assail the motives of no party or individual; and if I have in any instance (of which I am not conscious) departed from my purpose, I regret it.

SPEECH AT SPRINGFIELD, ILLINOIS
OCTOBER 30, 1858

Important principles may, and must, be inflexible.

LAST PUBLIC SPEECH
APRIL 11, 1865

## Prisoners

The Marshal of the United States in the vicinity of forts where political prisoners are held will supply decent lodging and subsistence for such prisoners unless they shall prefer to provide those respects for themselves, in which cases they will be allowed to do so by the commanding officers in charge.

COMMUNICATION TO UNITED STATES MARSHALS
JULY 31, 1861

## Prisoners of War

I would desire that in any arrangements for a general exchange of prisoners (now about being made, as I understand), loyal men now prisoners in our hands should not be indiscriminately turned back into the power of the enemy.

MEMORANDUM TO EDWIN M. STANTON
JULY 18, 1862

It is the duty of every government to give protection to its citizens of whatever class, color or condition, and especially to those who are duly organized as soldiers in the public service. The law of nations and the usages and customs of war as carried on by civilized powers permit no distinction as to color in the treatment of prisoners of war as public enemies. To sell or enslave any captured person on account of his color, and for no offense against the laws of war, is a relapse into barbarism and a crime against the civilization of the age. The government of the United States will give the same protection to all its soldiers, and if the enemy shall sell or enslave anyone because of his color, the offense shall be punished by retaliation upon the enemy's prisoners in our possession. It is therefore ordered that for every soldier of the United States killed in violation of the laws of war, a rebel soldier shall be executed; and for every one enslaved by the enemy or sold into slavery, a rebel soldier shall be placed at hard labor on the public works and continued at such labor until the other shall be released and receive the treatment due to a prisoner of war.

ORDER OF RETALIATION ISSUED BY THE
ADJUTANT GENERAL'S OFFICE
JULY 30, 1863

I am so pressed in regard to prisoners of war in our custody whose homes are within our lines and who wish to not be exchanged, but to take the oath and be discharged, that I hope you will pardon me for again calling up the subject. My impression is that we will not ever force the exchange of any of this class; that, taking the oath and being discharged, none of them will again go to the rebellion, but the rebellion again coming to them, a considerable percentage of them, probably not a majority, would rejoin it; that by a cautious discrimination the number so discharged would not be large enough to do any considerable mischief in any event, would relieve distress in at least some meritorious cases, and would give me some relief from an intolerable pressure. . . . In using the strong hand, as now compelled to do, the government has a difficult duty to perform. At the very best, it will by turns do both too little and too much. It can properly have no motive of revenge, no purpose to punish merely for punishment's sake. While we must, by all available means, prevent the overthrow of the government, we should avoid planting and cultivating too many thorns in the bosom of society.

LETTER TO EDWIN M. STANTON
MARCH 18, 1864

## Procrastination

Leave nothing for tomorrow which can be done today.

NOTES FOR A LAW LECTURE
JULY 1850 (?)

Whatever piece of business you have in hand, before stopping do all the labor pertaining to it which can then be done.

NOTES FOR A LAW LECTURE
JULY 1850 (?)

It is better . . . to save the work while it is begun. You have done the labor; maintain it—keep it.

SPEECH AT CHICAGO, ILLINOIS
JULY 10, 1858

Delay is ruining us.

LETTER TO DON C. BUELL
JANUARY 7, 1862

## Profiteering

Few things are so troublesome to the government as the fierceness with which the profits of trading in cotton are sought.

The temptation is so great that nearly everybody wishes to be in it; and when in, the question of profit controls all, regardless of whether the cotton seller is loyal or rebel, or whether he is paid in corn meal or gunpowder. The officers of the army, in numerous instances, are believed to connive and share the profits, and thus the army itself is diverted from fighting the rebels to speculating in cotton.

LETTER TO WILLIAM KELLOGG

JUNE 29, 1863

## Promises

There is something so ludicrous in *promises* of good or *threats* of evil a great way off as to render the whole subject with which they are connected easily turned into ridicule.

ADDRESS TO WASHINGTON TEMPERANCE SOCIETY,

SPRINGFIELD, ILLINOIS

FEBRUARY 22, 1842

## Property

"No person," under the shadow of the Constitution, "shall be deprived of life, liberty, or property without due process of law." Against whom does this guaranty protect the rights of property? Not against Congress alone, but against the world.

NOTES FOR SPEECHES

SEPTEMBER 1858 (?)

Public opinion is founded to a great extent on a property basis. What lessens the value of property is opposed, what enhances its value is favored.

SPEECH AT HARTFORD, CONNECTICUT

MARCH 5, 1860

Property is the fruit of labor—property is desirable—is a positive good in the world.

REPLY TO NEW YORK WORKINGMEN'S DEMOCRATIC
REPUBLICAN ASSOCIATION
MARCH 21, 1864

## Prudence

It is . . . more unusual nowadays to find a man who can hold his tongue than to find one who cannot.

REMARKS AT PITTSBURGH, PENNSYLVANIA
FEBRUARY 14, 1861

The Union must be preserved, and hence all indispensable means must be employed. We should not be in haste to determine that radical and extreme measures, which may reach the loyal as well as the disloyal, are indispensable.

ANNUAL MESSAGE TO CONGRESS
DECEMBER 3, 1861

I hope to "stand firm" enough not to go backward, and yet not go forward fast enough to wreck the country's cause.

LETTER TO ZACHARIAH CHANDLER
NOVEMBER 20, 1863

We shall sooner have the fowl by hatching the egg than by smashing it.

LAST PUBLIC SPEECH
APRIL 11, 1865

## Public Opinion

The universal *sense* of mankind on any subject is an argument, or at least an *influence*, not easily overcome. The success of the argument in favor of the existence of an overruling Providence mainly depends upon that sense; and men ought not, in justice, to be denounced for yielding to it, in any case, or for giving it up slowly, *especially* where they are backed by interest, fixed habits or burning appetites.

ADDRESS TO WASHINGTON TEMPERANCE SOCIETY,
SPRINGFIELD, ILLINOIS
FEBRURY 22, 1842

*Wisdom* and *patriotism* in a public office, under institutions like ours, are wholly inefficient and worthless unless they are sustained by the confidence and devotion of the people.

EULOGY ON ZACHARY TAYLOR
JULY 25, 1850

A universal feeling, whether well- or ill-founded, cannot be safely disregarded.

SPEECH AT PEORIA, ILLINOIS
OCTOBER 16, 1854

Our government rests in public opinion. Whoever can change public opinion can change the government.

SPEECH AT CHICAGO, ILLINOIS
DECEMBER 10, 1856

Public sentiment is everything. With public sentiment, nothing can fail; without it, nothing can succeed. Consequently he who moulds public sentiment goes deeper than he who enacts statutes or pronounces decisions. He makes statutes and decisions possible or impossible to be executed.

FIRST DEBATE WITH STEPHEN A. DOUGLAS,
OTTAWA, ILLINOIS
AUGUST 21, 1858

Public opinion in this country is everything.

SPEECH AT COLUMBUS, OHIO
SEPTEMBER 16, 1859

The enthusiastic uprising of the people in our cause is our great reliance; and we cannot safely give it any check, even though it overflows and runs in channels not laid down in any chart.

LETTER TO EDWIN D. MORGAN
MAY 20, 1861

## Punishment

I do not like this punishment of withholding pay—it falls so very hard upon poor families.

LETTER TO EDWIN M. STANTON
MARCH 1, 1864

## Quarrels

Let minor differences and personal preferences, if there be such, go to the winds.

NOTES FOR SPEECH AT CHICAGO, ILLINOIS
FEBRUARY 28, 1857

I don't care about a quibble in regard to words.

SPEECH AT CHICAGO, ILLINOIS
JULY 10, 1858

I have too many *family* controversies (so to speak) already on my hands to voluntarily, or so long as I can avoid it, take up another.

LETTER TO JOHN A. MCCLERNAND
JANUARY 22, 1863

The advice of a father to his son, "Beware of entrance to a quarrel but, being in, bear it that the opposed may beware of thee," is good; and yet not the best. Quarrel not at all. No man resolved to make the most of himself can spare time for personal contention. Still less can he afford to take all the consequences, including the vitiating of his temper and the loss of self-control. Yield larger things to which you can show no more than equal right; and yield lesser ones, though clearly your own. Better give your path to a dog than be bitten by him in contesting for the right. Even killing the dog would not cure the bite.

> LETTER TO JAMES M. CUTTS
> OCTOBER 26, 1863

## Raffles

The President has no authority as to whether you may raffle for the benevolent object you mention. If there is no objection in the Iowa laws, there is none here.

> LETTER TO MOTHER MARY GONYEAG
> DECEMBER 15, 1863

## Railroads

No other improvement that reason will justify us in hoping for can equal in utility the railroad. It is a never-failing source of communication between places of business remotely situated from each other. Upon the railroad the regular progress of commercial intercourse is not interrupted by either high or low water, or freezing weather, which are the principal difficulties that render our future hopes of water communication precarious and uncertain.

> COMMUNICATION TO THE PEOPLE OF
> SANGAMON COUNTY, ILLINOIS
> MARCH 9, 1832

Dear Sir:
Says Tom to John: "Here's your old rotten wheelbarrow. I've broke it usin' on it. I wish *you* would mend it, case I shall want to borrow it this arter-noon."

Acting on this as a precedent, I say, "Here's your old 'chalked hat.'* I wish you would take it and send me a new one, case I shall want to use it the first of March."

LETTER TO RICHARD P. MORGAN,
SUPERINTENDENT OF THE ACTON RAILROAD
FEBRUARY 13, 1856

## Reconstruction

Let the reconstruction be the work of such men only as can be trusted for the Union. Exclude all others.

LETTER TO ANDREW JOHNSON
SEPTEMBER 11, 1863

It is suggested as proper that in constructing a loyal state government in any state, the name of the state, the boundary, the subdivisions, the Constitution and general code of laws, as before the rebellion, be maintained.

MEMORANDUM ON CONSTRUCTING LOYAL STATE GOVERNMENTS
DECEMBER 1863 (?)

You desire to know—in the event of our complete success in the field, the same being followed by a loyal and cheerful submission on the part of the South—if universal amnesty should not be accompanied with universal suffrage. . . . If our success should thus be realized, followed by such desired results, I cannot see, if universal amnesty is granted, how, under the circumstances, I can avoid exacting in return universal suffrage or at least suffrage on the basis of intelligence and military service. . . . The restoration of the rebel states to the Union must rest upon the principle of civil and political equality of both races; and it must be sealed by general amnesty.

LETTER TO JAMES S. WADSWORTH
JANUARY 1864 (?)

* "Chalked hat" refers to a railway pass, a white check being placed in the hat band of the person travelling on a pass.

The reinauguration of the national authority—reconstruction—
. . . is fraught with great difficulty. Unlike the case of a war between independent nations, there is no authorized organ for us
to treat with. No one man has authority to give up the rebellion
for any other man. We simply must begin with, and mould from,
disorganized and discordant elements. Nor is it a small additional
embarrassment that we, the loyal people, differ among ourselves
as to the mode, manner and means of reconstruction. . . . We
all agree that the seceded states, so-called, are out of their proper
practical relation with the Union and that the sole object of the
government, civil and military, in regard to those states is to
again get them into that proper practical relation. I believe it is
not only possible but, in fact, easier to do this without deciding,
or even considering, whether these states have even been out of
the Union, than with it. Finding themselves safely at home, it
would be utterly immaterial whether they had ever been abroad.
Let us all join in doing the acts necessary to restoring the proper
practical relations between these states and the Union; and each
forever after innocently indulge his own opinion whether, in doing the acts, he brought the states from without into the Union,
or only gave them proper assistance, they never having been out
of it.

LAST PUBLIC SPEECH
APRIL 11, 1865

## Recreation

Constituted as man is, he has positive need of occasional rec-
reation; and whatever can give him this, associated with virtue
and advantage and free from vice and disadvantage, is a positive
good.

SPEECH AT MILWAUKEE, WISCONSIN
SEPTEMBER 30, 1859

## Religion

I do not think I could myself be brought to support a man for office whom I knew to be an open enemy of and scoffer at religion.

HANDBILL TO VOTERS OF SEVENTH CONGRESSIONAL
DISTRICT OF ILLINOIS
JULY 31, 1846

In early life I was inclined to believe in what I understand is called the "Doctrine of Necessity"—that is, that the human mind is impelled to action or held in rest by some power over which the mind itself has no control.

HANDBILL TO VOTERS OF SEVENTH CONGRESSIONAL
DISTRICT OF ILLINOIS
JULY 31, 1846

That I am not a member of any Christian church is true; but I have never denied the truth of the Scriptures, and I have never spoken with intentional disrespect of religion in general, or of any denomination of Christians in particular.

HANDBILL TO VOTERS OF SEVENTH CONGRESSIONAL
DISTRICT OF ILLINOIS
JULY 31, 1846

I have often wished that I were a more devout man than I am.

REMARKS TO BALTIMORE PRESBYTERIAN SYNOD
OCTOBER 24, 1863

I have never interfered, nor thought of interfering, as to who shall or shall not preach in any church; nor have I knowingly, or believingly, tolerated anyone else to so interfere by my authority. . . . I will not have control of any church on any side.

LETTER TO OLIVER D. FILLEY
DECEMBER 22, 1863

THE PRESIDENT'S LAST, SHORTEST AND BEST SPEECH*

On Thursday of last week two ladies from Tennessee came before the President asking the release of their husbands held as prisoners of war at Johnson's Island. They were put off till Friday, when they came again; and were again put off to Saturday. At each of the interviews one of the ladies urged that her husband was a religious man. On Saturday the President ordered the release of the prisoners and then said to this lady, "You say your husband is a religious man; tell him when you meet him that I say I am not much of a judge of religion, but that, in my opinion, the religion that sets men to rebel and fight against their government because, as they think, that government does not sufficiently help *some* men to eat their bread on the sweat of *other* men's faces is not the sort of religion upon which people can get to heaven!"

STORY WRITTEN FOR NOAH BROOKS
DECEMBER 1864

## Repentance

I am a patient man—always willing to forgive on the Christian terms of repentance; and also to give ample *time* for repentance.

LETTER TO REVERDY JOHNSON
JULY 26, 1862

## Repetition

Those who will not read, or heed, what I have already publicly said would not read, or heed, a repetition of it.

LETTER TO WILLIAM S. SPEER
OCTOBER 23, 1860

First, I could say nothing which I have not already said and which is in print and open for the inspection of all. To press a

* Title to this story given by Lincoln.

repetition of this upon those who *have* listened is useless; to press it upon those who have *refused* to listen and still refuse would be wanting in self-respect and would have the appearance of sycophancy and timidity, which would excite the contempt of good men, and encourage bad ones to clamor the more loudly.

LETTER TO TRUMAN SMITH
NOVEMBER 10, 1860

## Resolution

Although I was fixed "firm as the surge-repelling rock" in my resolution, I found I was continually repenting the rashness which had led me to make it.

LETTER TO MRS. ORVILLE H. BROWNING
APRIL 1, 1838

## Responsibility

It is an old maxim and a very sound one that he that dances should always pay the fiddler.

SPEECH IN ILLINOIS LEGISLATURE
JANUARY 11, 1837

If we do not triumph, the fault will be our own.

LETTER TO ELIHU B. WASHBURNE
APRIL 26, 1858

If there ever could be a proper time for mere catch arguments, that time surely is not now. In times like the present, men should utter nothing for which they would not willingly be responsible through time and in eternity.

ANNUAL MESSAGE TO CONGRESS
DECEMBER 1, 1862

## Revolution

It is a quality of revolution not to go by *old* lines or *old* laws, but to break up both and make new ones.

SPEECH IN HOUSE OF REPRESENTATIVES<br>JANUARY 12, 1848

Any people anywhere, being inclined and having the power, have the *right* to rise up and shake off the existing government and form a new one that suits them better. This is a most valuable, a most sacred right—a right which we hope and believe is to liberate the world. Nor is the right confined to cases in which the whole people of an existing government may choose to exercise it. Any portion of such people that *can, may* revolutionize and make their *own* of so much of the territory as they inhabit. More than this, a *majority* of any portion of such people may revolutionize, putting down a *minority* intermingling with or near about them who may oppose their movement.

SPEECH IN HOUSE OF REPRESENTATIVES<br>JANUARY 12, 1848

This country, with its institutions, belongs to the people who inhabit it. Whenever they shall grow weary of the existing government, they can exercise their *constitutional* right of amending it or their *revolutionary* right to dismember or overthrow it.

FIRST INAUGURAL ADDRESS<br>MARCH 4, 1861

## Ridicule

I have endured a great deal of ridicule without much malice; and have received a great deal of kindness, not quite free from ridicule.

LETTER TO JAMES H. HACKETT<br>NOVEMBER 2, 1863

## Russia

[A] country where they make no pretense of loving liberty
. . . where despotism can be taken pure and without the base
alloy of hypocrisy.

LETTER TO JOSHUA F. SPEED
AUGUST 24, 1855

I think a good lecture or two on "Serfs, Serfdom and Emancipation in Russia" would be both interesting and valuable.

LETTER TO BAYARD TAYLOR
DECEMBER 25, 1863

## Salesmanship

If you would win a man to your cause, *first* convince him that
you are his sincere friend.

ADDRESS TO THE WASHINGTON TEMPERANCE SOCIETY,
SPRINGFIELD, ILLINOIS
FEBRUARY 22, 1842

## Secession

The people of the South have too much of good sense and
good temper to attempt the ruin of the government rather than
see it administered as it was administered by the men who made
it.

LETTER TO JOHN B. FRY
AUGUST 15, 1860

A writer unknown to me [says] the officers of the Army at
Fort Kearney have determined, in case of Republican success at

the approaching Presidential election, to take themselves and the arms at that point South for the purpose of resistance to the government.

LETTER TO DAVID HUNTER
OCTOBER 26, 1860

Disunionists *per se* are now in hot haste to get out of the Union precisely because they perceive they cannot much longer maintain apprehension among the Southern people that their homes and firesides and lives are to be endangered by the action of the Federal Government. With such, "*Now, or never*" is the maxim. I am rather glad of this military preparation in the South. It will enable the people the more easily to suppress any uprisings there, which their misrepresentations of purposes may have encouraged.

PASSAGE WRITTEN FOR A SPEECH BY LYMAN TRUMBULL,
SPRINGFIELD, ILLINOIS
NOVEMBER 20, 1860

I believe you can pretend to find but little, if anything, in my speeches about secession; but my opinion is that no state can in any way lawfully get out of the Union without the consent of the others, and that it is the duty of the President and other government functionaries to run the machine as it is.

LETTER TO THURLOW WEED
DECEMBER 17, 1860

I will suffer death before I will consent or will advise my friends to consent to any concession or compromise which looks like buying the privilege of taking possession of this government to which we have a constitutional right; because, whatever I might think of the merit of the various propositions before Congress, I should regard any concession in the face of menace the destruction of the government itself.

REMARKS ON CONCESSION TO SECESSION
JANUARY 1861

My intention is to give this subject all the consideration which I possibly can before I speak fully and definitely in regard to it—so that, when I do speak, I may be as nearly right as possible. And when I do speak, fellow citizens, I hope to say nothing in opposition to the spirit of the Constitution, contrary to the integrity of the Union, or which will in any way prove inimical to the liberties of the people or to the peace of the whole country.

SPEECH AT PITTSBURGH, PENNSYLVANIA
FEBRUARY 15, 1861

It follows . . . that no state, upon its own mere motion, can lawfully get out of the Union; that *resolves* and *ordinances* to that effect are legally void; and that acts of violence within any state or states against the authority of the United States are insurrectionary or revolutionary.

FIRST INAUGURAL ADDRESS
MARCH 4, 1861

I therefore consider that in view of the Constitution and the laws, the Union is unbroken; and, to the extent of my ability, I shall take care, as the Constitution itself expressly enjoins upon me, that the laws of the Union be faithfully executed in all the states.

FIRST INAUGURAL ADDRESS
MARCH 4, 1861

Plainly, the central idea of secession is the essence of anarchy. A majority, held in restraint by constitutional checks and limitations and always changing easily with deliberate changes of popular opinions and sentiments, is the only true sovereign of a free people. Whoever rejects it does of necessity fly to anarchy or despotism. Unanimity is impossible; the rule of a minority, as a permanent arrangement, is wholly inadmissible; so that, rejecting the majority principle, anarchy or despotism in some form is all that is left.

FIRST INAUGURAL ADDRESS
MARCH 4, 1861

Physically speaking, we cannot separate. We cannot remove our respective sections from each other nor build an impassable wall between them. A husband and wife may be divorced and go out of the presence and beyond the reach of each other; but the different parts of our country cannot do this. They cannot but remain face to face; and intercourse, either amicable or hostile, must continue between them. . . . Can aliens make treaties easier than friends can make laws? Can treaties be more faithfully enforced between aliens than laws can among friends?

FIRST INAUGURAL ADDRESS
MARCH 4, 1861

The nation purchased with money the countries out of which several of these states were formed. Is it just that they shall go off without leave and without refunding? . . . Is it just, either, that creditors shall go unpaid or the remaining states pay the whole? . . . Again, if one state may secede, so may another; and when all shall have seceded, none is left to pay the debts. Is this quite just to creditors? Did we notify them of this sage view of ours when we borrowed their money?

MESSAGE TO CONGRESS IN SPECIAL SESSION
JULY 4, 1861

The principle itself is one of disintegration, and upon which no government can possibly endure.

MESSAGE TO CONGRESS IN SPECIAL SESSION
JULY 4, 1861

If all the states, save one, should assert the power to *drive* that one out of the Union, it is presumed the whole class of seceder politicians would at once deny the power and the act as the greatest outrage upon state rights. But suppose that precisely the same act, instead of being called "driving the one out," should be called "the seceding of the others from that one," it would be exactly what the seceders claim to do; unless, indeed, they make the point that the one, because it is a minority, may rightfully do what the others, because they are a majority, may not rightfully do. These politicians are subtle and profound on the rights of minorities. They are not partial to that power which made the

Constitution and speaks from the preamble, calling itself "We, the People."

MESSAGE TO CONGRESS IN SPECIAL SESSION
JULY 4, 1861

It is said that the admission of West Virginia is secession and tolerated only because it is our secession. Well, if we call it by that name, there is still difference enough between secession against the Constitution and secession in favor of the Constitution.

OPINION ON ADMISSION OF WEST VIRGINIA INTO THE UNION
DECEMBER 31, 1862

I have always thought the act of secession is legally nothing and needs no repealing.

LETTER TO BENJAMIN F. FLANDERS
NOVEMBER 9, 1863

I have never had a theory that secession could absolve states or people from their obligations.

LETTER TO WILLIAM CROSBY AND HENRY P. NICHOLS
JANUARY 16, 1864

## Secrecy

Does not every merchant have his secret mark? And who is ever silly enough to complain about it?

SPEECH IN ILLINOIS LEGISLATURE
JANUARY 11, 1837

## Segregation

What I would most desire would be the separation of the white and black races.

SPEECH AT SPRINGFIELD, ILLINOIS
JULY 17, 1858

The aspiration of men is to enjoy equality with the best when free, but on this broad continent not a single man of your race is made the equal of a single man of ours. Go where you are treated the best and the ban is still upon you.

SPEECH ON COLONIZATION TO A DEPUTATION OF NEGROES
AUGUST 14, 1862

## Self-Government

The doctrine of self-government is right—absolutely and eternally right.

SPEECH AT PEORIA, ILLINOIS
OCTOBER 16, 1854

I trust I understand and truly estimate the right of self-government. My faith in the proposition that each man should do precisely as he pleases with all which is exclusively his own lies at the foundation of the sense of justice there is in me. I extend the principles to communities of men as well as to individuals. I so extend it because it is politically wise, as well as naturally just.

SPEECH AT PEORIA, ILLINOIS
OCTOBER 16, 1854

According to our ancient faith, the just powers of governments are derived from the consent of the governed. Now the relation of masters and slaves is, PRO TANTO, a total violation of this principle. The master not only governs the slave without his consent, but he governs him by a set of rules altogether different from those which he prescribes for himself. Allow ALL the governed an equal voice in government and that, and that only, is self-government.

SPEECH AT PEORIA, ILLINOIS
OCTOBER 16, 1854

If the Negro *is* a man, is it not to that extent a total destruction of self-government to say that he too shall not govern *himself?*

SPEECH AT PEORIA, ILLINOIS
OCTOBER 16, 1854

I . . . believe in self-government as I understand it; but I do not understand that the privilege one man takes of making a slave of another, or holding him as such, is any part of "self-government." To call it so is, to my mind, simply absurd and ridiculous. I am for the people of the whole nation doing just as they please in all matters which concern no other part, and for each individual doing just as he chooses in all matters which concern nobody else.

FRAGMENT OF A SPEECH
MAY 1858

The deceitful cloak of "self-government," wherewith "the sum of all villainies" seeks to protect and adorn itself, must be torn from its hateful carcass. That burlesque upon judicial decisions, and slander and profanation upon the honored names and sacred history of republican America must be overruled and expunged from the books of authority. To give the victory to the right, not *bloody bullets*, but *peaceful ballots* only, are necessary. Thanks to our good old Constitution, and organization under it, these alone are necessary. It only needs that every right-thinking man shall go to the polls and, without fear or prejudice, *vote* as he *thinks*.

FRAGMENT OF A SPEECH
MAY 1858

## Self-Sufficiency

All we can do is to take care of ourselves as we best may.

LETTER TO JOSEPH GILLESPIE
FEBRUARY 11, 1854

## Shakespeare

Some of Shakespeare's plays I have never read; while others I have gone over perhaps as frequently as any unprofessional reader. Among the latter are Lear, Richard Third, Henry Eighth,

Hamlet, and especially Macbeth. I think nothing equals Macbeth. It is wonderful. . . . I think the soliloquy in Hamlet commencing "O, my offense is rank" surpasses that commencing "To be, or not to be."

LETTER TO JAMES H. HACKETT
AUGUST 17, 1863

## Ships

I know but little about ships.

LETTER TO GIDEON WELLES
MAY 14, 1861

## Simplicity

As plain as the adding up of the weights of three small hogs.

LETTER TO SUPPORTERS OF MILLARD FILLMORE
SEPTEMBER 8, 1856

## Slavery

The institution of slavery is founded on both injustice and bad policy.

PROTEST IN ILLINOIS LEGISLATURE
MARCH 3, 1837

Perpetual slavery—where the lash of the master is proverbially more ruthless and unrelenting than any other where.

LETTER TO MARY SPEED
SEPTEMBER 27, 1841

I hold it to be a paramount duty of us in the free states, due to the Union of the states and perhaps to liberty itself (paradox though it may seem), to let slavery of the other states alone; while, on the other hand, I hold it to be equally clear that we should never knowingly lend ourselves directly or indirectly to prevent that slavery from dying a natural death—to find new places for it to live in when it can no longer exist in the old.

LETTER TO WILLIAMSON DURLEY
OCTOBER 3, 1845

I am a Northern man, or rather a Western free state man, with a constituency I believe to be, and with personal feelings I know to be, against the extension of slavery.

SPEECH IN HOUSE OF REPRESENTATIVES
JULY 27, 1848

That unfortunate source of discord—Negro slavery.

EULOGY ON HENRY CLAY
JULY 6, 1852

No wise man has perceived how it can be at *once* eradicated without producing a greater evil, even to the cause of human liberty itself.

EULOGY ON HENRY CLAY
JULY 6, 1852

The ant who has toiled and dragged a crumb to his nest will furiously defend the fruit of his labor against whatever robber assails him. So plain, that the most dumb and stupid slave that ever toiled for a master does constantly *know* that he is wronged. So plain that no one, high or low, ever does mistake it except in a plainly *selfish* way. For although volume upon volume is written to prove slavery a very good thing, we never hear of the man who wishes to take the good of it *by being a slave himself*.

FRAGMENT
JULY 1854 (?)

If A. can prove, however conclusively, that he may of right enslave B.—why may not B. snatch the same argument and prove equally that he may enslave A.? You say A. is white and B. is black. It is *color*, then; the lighter having the right to enslave the darker. Take care. By this rule you are to be slave to the first man you meet with a fairer skin than your own. You do not mean *color* exactly?—You mean the whites are *intellectually* the superiors of the blacks and, therefore, have the right to enslave them? Take care again. By this rule you are to be slave to the first man you meet with an intellect superior to your own. But, say you, it is a question of *interest*; and, if you can make it your *interest*, you have the right to enslave another. Very well. And if he can make it his interest, he has the right to enslave you.

FRAGMENT<br>JULY 1854 (?)

When Southern people tell us they are no more responsible for the origin of slavery than we, I acknowledge the fact. When it is said that the institution exists and that it is very difficult to get rid of it in any satisfactory way, I can understand and appreciate the saying. I surely will not blame them for not doing what I should not know how to do myself. If all earthly power were given me, I should not know what to do as to the existing institution. My first impulse would be to free all the slaves and send them to Liberia—to their own native land. But a moment's reflection would convince me that whatever of high hope (as I think there is) there may be in this in the long run, its sudden execution is impossible. If they were all landed there in a day, they would all perish in the next ten days. What then? Free them all, and keep them among us as underlings? Is it quite certain that this betters their condition? I think I would not hold one in slavery at any rate, yet the point is not clear enough for me to denounce people upon. What next? Free them, and make them politically and socially our equals? My own feelings will not admit to this; and if mine would, we well know that those of the great mass of white people will not. Whether this feeling accords with justice and sound judgment is not the sole question, if indeed it is any part of it. A universal feeling, whether well- or ill-founded, cannot be safely disregarded. We cannot, then, make them equals. It does seem to me that systems of gradual emancipation might be adopted; but for their tardiness in this I will not undertake to judge our brethren of the South. When they remind us of their constitutional rights, I acknowledge them, not grudgingly, but fully and fairly; and I would give them any legislation for the reclaiming of their fugitives which should not, in its stringency, be more likely to carry a free man into slavery than our ordinary criminal laws are to hang an innocent one. But all this, to my judgment, furnishes no more excuse for permitting slavery to go into our own free territory than it would for reviving the African slave trade by law. The law which forbids the bringing of slaves *from* Africa and that which has so long forbid the taking them *to* Nebraska can hardly be distinguished on any moral principle; and the repeal of the former could find as plausible excuses as that of the latter.

SPEECH AT PEORIA, ILLINOIS
OCTOBER 16, 1854


I have no prejudice against the Southern people. They are just what we would be in their situation. If slavery did not now exist among them, they would not introduce it. If it did now exist amongst us, we should not instantly give it up. This I believe of the masses north and south. Doubtless there are individuals, on both sides, who would not hold slaves under any circumstances; and others who would gladly introduce slavery anew if it were out of existence. We know that some Southern men do free their slaves, go north, and become tiptop abolitionists; while some Northern men go south and become most cruel slavemasters.

SPEECH AT PEORIA, ILLINOIS
OCTOBER 16, 1854


The Yankees who are opposed to it may be more numerous; but in military phrase, the battlefield is too far from *their* base of operations.

SPEECH AT PEORIA, ILLINOIS
OCTOBER 16, 1854

Wherever slavery is, it has been first introduced without law. The oldest laws we find concerning it are not laws introducing it, but *regulating* it as an already existing thing.

SPEECH AT PEORIA, ILLINOIS
OCTOBER 16, 1854

The opening of new countries to slavery tends to the perpetuation of the institution, and so does KEEP men in slavery who otherwise would be free.

SPEECH AT PEORIA, ILLINOIS
OCTOBER 16, 1854

In 1820 you joined the North, almost unanimously, in declaring the African slave trade piracy and in annexing to it the punishment of death. Why did you do this? If you did not feel that it was wrong, why did you join in providing that men should be hung for it? The practice was no more than bringing wild Negroes from Africa to sell to such as would buy them. But you never thought of hanging men for catching and selling wild horses, wild buffaloes or wild bears.

SPEECH AT PEORIA, ILLINOIS
OCTOBER 16, 1854

There can be no moral right in connection with one man's making a slave of another.

SPEECH AT PEORIA, ILLINOIS
OCTOBER 16, 1854

The great mass of mankind . . . consider slavery a great moral wrong, and their feelings against it is not evanescent but eternal. It lies at the very foundation of their sense of justice, and it cannot be trifled with. It is a great and durable element of popular action and, I think, no statesman can safely disregard it.

SPEECH AT PEORIA, ILLINOIS
OCTOBER 16, 1854

The spirit which desired the peaceful extinction of slavery has itself become extinct with the *occasion* and the *men* of the Revolution.

LETTER TO GEORGE ROBERTSON

AUGUST 15, 1855

The condition of the Negro slave in America, scarcely less terrible to the contemplation of a free mind, is now as fixed and hopeless of change for the better as that of the lost souls of the finally impenitent. The Autocrat of all the Russias will resign his crown and proclaim his subjects free republicans sooner than will our American masters voluntarily give up their slaves.

LETTER TO GEORGE ROBERTSON

AUGUST 15, 1855

I dislike slavery.

LETTER TO JOSHUA F. SPEED

AUGUST 24, 1855

We have been in the habit of deploring the fact that slavery exists amongst us. We have ever deplored it. Our forefathers did, and they declared, as we have done in later years, the blame rested on the mother government of Great Britain. We constantly condemn Great Britain for not preventing slavery from coming amongst us. She would not interfere to prevent it, and so individuals were enabled to introduce the institution without opposition.

SPEECH AT KALAMAZOO, MICHIGAN

AUGUST 27, 1856

Slavery is wrong and . . . like every other wrong which some men commit if left alone, it ought to be prohibited by law.

FRAGMENT OF A SPEECH

MAY 1858

Congress ought to prohibit slavery wherever it can be done without violation of the Constitution or of good faith.

FRAGMENT OF A SPEECH<br>MAY 1858

Nearly everybody does care something about slavery—is either for it or against it.

FRAGMENT OF A SPEECH<br>MAY 1858

Welcome or unwelcome, agreeable or disagreeable, whether this shall be an entire slave nation *is* the issue before us. Every incident—every little shifting of scenes or of actors—only clears away the intervening trash, compacts and consolidates the opposing hosts and brings them more and more distinctly face to face. The conflict will be a severe one and it will be fought through by those who *do* care for the result and not by those who do not care—by those who are *for* and those who are against a legalized national slavery.

FRAGMENT OF A SPEECH<br>MAY 1858

The people should be *perfectly* free to form their constitution in their own way—as *perfectly* free from the *presence* of *slavery* amongst them as from every other improper influence.

LETTER TO JEDIAH F. ALEXANDER<br>MAY 15, 1858

We may, ere long, see . . . another Supreme Court decision declaring that the Constitution of the United States does not permit a *state* to exclude slavery from its limits. And this may especially be expected if the doctrine of "care not whether slavery be voted *down* or voted *up*" shall gain upon the public mind sufficiently to give promise that such a decision can be maintained when made. Such a decision is all that slavery now lacks of being alike lawful in all the states. Welcome or unwelcome, such decision *is* probably coming and will soon be upon us unless the power of the present political dynasty shall be met and overthrown.

"A HOUSE DIVIDED" SPEECH, SPRINGFIELD, ILLINOIS

JUNE 16, 1858

— ( Neither the general government, nor any other power outside of the slave states, can constitutionally or rightfully interfere with slaves or slavery where it already exists. ]

LETTER TO JOHN L. SCRIPPS

JUNE 23, 1858

I have always hated slavery.

SPEECH AT CHICAGO, ILLINOIS

JULY 10, 1858

— ( I believe there is no right, and ought to be no inclination in the people of the free states, to enter into the slave states and interfere with the question of slavery at all. )

SPEECH AT CHICAGO, ILLINOIS

JULY 10, 1858

— If I were in Congress and a vote should come up on a question whether slavery should be prohibited in a new territory . . . I would vote that it should.

SPEECH AT CHICAGO, ILLINOIS

JULY 10, 1858

It may be argued that there are certain conditions that make necessities and impose them upon us, and to the extent that a necessity is imposed upon a man he must submit to it. I think that was the condition in which we found ourselves when we established this government. We had slavery among us, we could not get our Constitution unless we permitted them to remain in slavery, we could not secure the good we did secure if we grasped for more, and having by necessity submitted to that much, it does not destroy the principle that is the charter of our liberties. Let that charter stand as our standard.

SPEECH AT CHICAGO, ILLINOIS
JULY 10, 1858

I have again and again said that I would not enter into any of the states to disturb the institution of slavery. Judge Douglas said . . . that I used language most able and ingenious for concealing what I really meant; and that while I had protested against entering into the slave states, I nevertheless did mean to go on the banks of the Ohio and throw missiles into Kentucky to disturb them in their domestic institutions.

SPEECH AT SPRINGFIELD, ILLINOIS
JULY 17, 1858

The institution of slavery ought to be placed in the very attitude where the framers of this government placed it, and left it. I do not understand that the framers of our Constitution left the people of the free states in the attitude of firing bombs or shells into the slave states.

SPEECH AT SPRINGFIELD, ILLINOIS
JULY 17, 1858

I do wish to see the spread of slavery arrested and to see it placed where the public mind shall rest in the belief that it is in course of ultimate extinction.

SPEECH AT SPRINGFIELD, ILLINOIS
JULY 17, 1858

Although I have ever been opposed to slavery, so far I rested in the hope and belief that it was in course of ultimate extinction.

SPEECH AT SPRINGFIELD, ILLINOIS
JULY 17, 1858

I have thought the public mind will never rest till the power of Congress to restrict the spread of it shall again be acknowledged and exercised on the one hand or, on the other, all resistance be entirely crushed out.

SPEECH AT SPRINGFIELD, ILLINOIS
JULY 17, 1858

Quite recently in Virginia, a man—owner of slaves—made a will providing that after his death certain of his slaves should have their freedom, if they should so choose, and go to Liberia rather than remain in slavery. They chose to be liberated. But the persons to whom they would descend as property claimed them as slaves. A suit was instituted which finally came to the Supreme Court of Virginia and was therein decided against the slaves upon the ground that a Negro cannot make a choice—that they had no legal power to choose—could not perform the condition upon which their freedom depended. I do not mention this with any purpose of criticizing, but to connect it with the arguments as affording additional evidence of the change of sentiment upon this question of slavery in the direction of making it perpetual and national. I argue now as I did before that there is such a tendency, and I am backed not merely by the facts but by the open confession in the slave states.

SPEECH AT SPRINGFIELD, ILLINOIS
JULY 17, 1858

How has the planting of slavery in new countries always been effected? It has now been decided that slavery cannot be kept out of our new territories by any legal means. In what do our new territories now differ in this respect from the old colonies when slavery was first planted within them? It was planted, as Mr. [Henry] Clay once declared and as history proves true, by individual men in spite of the wishes of the people, the mother government refusing to prohibit it and withholding from the people of the colonies the authority to prohibit it for themselves. Mr. Clay says this was one of the great and just causes of complaint against Great Britain by the colonies and the best apology we can now make for having the institution amongst us.

SPEECH AT SPRINGFIELD, ILLINOIS
JULY 17, 1858

When our government was established we had the institution of slavery among us. We were, in a certain sense, compelled to tolerate its existence. It was a sort of necessity. We had gone through our struggle and secured our own independence. The framers of the Constitution found the institution of slavery amongst their other institutions at the time. They found that by an effort to eradicate it, they might lose much of what they had already gained. They were obliged to bow to the necessity. They gave power to Congress to abolish the slave trade at the end of twenty years. They also prohibited it in the territories where it did not exist. They did what they could and yielded to the necessity for the rest. I also yield to all which follows from that necessity. What I would most desire would be the separation of the white and black races.

SPEECH AT SPRINGFIELD, ILLINOIS
JULY 17, 1858

I have no purpose directly or indirectly to interfere with the institution of slavery in the states where it exists. I believe I have no lawful right to do so, and I have no inclination to do so.

FIRST DEBATE WITH STEPHEN A. DOUGLAS,
OTTAWA, ILLINOIS
AUGUST 21, 1858

What is necessary to make the institution national? Not war. There is no danger that the people of Kentucky will shoulder their muskets and with a young nigger stuck on every bayonet march into Illinois and force them upon us. There is no danger of our going over there and making war upon them. Then what is necessary for the nationalization of slavery? It is simply the next Dred Scott decision. It is merely for the Supreme Court to decide that no *state* under the Constitution can exclude it, just as they have already decided that under the Constitution neither Congress nor the territorial legislature can do it. When that is decided and acquiesced in, the whole thing is done.

FIRST DEBATE WITH STEPHEN A. DOUGLAS,
OTTAWA, ILLINOIS
AUGUST 21, 1858

I am impliedly, if not expressly, pledged to a belief in the *right* and *duty* of Congress to prohibit slavery in all the United States territories.

SECOND DEBATE WITH STEPHEN A. DOUGLAS,
OTTAWA, ILLINOIS
AUGUST 27, 1858

I do not believe this government *can* endure permanently half slave and half free, yet I do not admit, nor does it at all follow, that the admission of a single slave state will permanently fix the character and establish this as a universal slave nation.

SECOND DEBATE WITH STEPHEN A. DOUGLAS,
OTTAWA, ILLINOIS
AUGUST 27, 1858

Slavery was originally planted on this continent without the aid of friendly legislation. History proves this. After it was actually in existence to a sufficient extent to become, in some sort, a public interest, it began to receive legislative attention, but not before. How futile, then, is the proposition that the people of a territory can exclude slavery by simply not legislating in its favor.

NOTES FOR SPEECHES
SEPTEMBER 1858 (?)

Suppose, now, a provision in a state constitution should . . . [declare] directly or substantially that "any person may be deprived of life, liberty, or property without due process of law," a direct contradiction—collision—would be pronounced between the United States Constitution and such state constitution. And can there be any doubt but that which is declared to be the supreme law would prevail over the other to the extent of the collision? There is no escape from this conclusion but in one way, and that is to deny that the Supreme court, in the Dred Scott case, properly applies this constitutional guaranty of property. The Constitution itself impliedly admits that a person may be deprived of property by "due process of law," and the Republicans hold that if there be a law of Congress or territorial legislature telling the slaveholder in advance that he shall not bring his slave into the territory upon pain of forfeiture, and he still will bring him in, he will be deprived of his property in such slave by "due process of law." And the same would be true in the case of taking a slave into a state against a state constitution or law prohibiting slavery.

NOTES FOR SPEECHES
SEPTEMBER 1858 (?)

I hold that the proposition that slavery cannot enter a new country without police regulations is historically false. . . . How came this Dred Scott decision to be made? It was made upon the case of a Negro being taken and actually held in slavery in Minnesota Territory, claiming his freedom because the act of Congress prohibited his being so held there, . . . held in slavery . . . not only without police regulations, but in the teeth of Congressional legislation supposed to be valid at the time. This shows that there is vigor enough in slavery to plant itself in a new country even against unfriendly legislation. It takes not only law but the *enforcement* of law to keep it out. That is the history of this country upon the subject.

THIRD DEBATE WITH STEPHEN A. DOUGLAS,
JONESBORO, ILLINOIS
SEPTEMBER 15, 1858

The sum of pro-slavery theology seems to be this: "Slavery is not universally *right*, nor yet universally *wrong*; it is better for *some* people to be slaves; and, in such cases, it is the will of God that they be such." . . . Slavery is good for some people!!! As a *good* thing, slavery is strikingly peculiar in this, that it is the only good thing which no man ever seeks the good of *for himself*.

FRAGMENT ON PROSLAVERY THEOLOGY
OCTOBER 1858 (?)

Perhaps that Democrat who says he is as much opposed to slavery as I am will tell me that I am wrong about this. . . .

You say it is wrong; but don't you constantly object to anybody else saying so? Do you not constantly argue that this is not the right place to oppose it? You say it must not be opposed in the free states, because slavery is not here; it must not be opposed in the slave states, because it is there; it must not be opposed in politics, because that will make a fuss; it must not be opposed in the pulpit, because it is not religion. Then where is the place to oppose it?

SIXTH DEBATE WITH STEPHEN A. DOUGLAS,
QUINCY, ILLINOIS
OCTOBER 13, 1858

If you will get everybody else to stop talking about it, I assure you I will quit before they have half done so.

SEVENTH DEBATE WITH STEPHEN A. DOUGLAS,
ALTON, ILLINOIS
OCTOBER 15, 1858

I do not wish to be misunderstood upon this subject of slavery in this country. I suppose it may long exist, and perhaps the best way for it to come to an end peaceably is for it to exist for a length of time. But I say that the spread and strengthening and perpetuation of it is an entirely different proposition. There we should in every way resist it as a wrong, treating it as a wrong, with the fixed idea that it must and will come to an end.

SPEECH AT CHICAGO, ILLINOIS
MARCH 1, 1859

Taking slaves into new territories and buying slaves in Africa are identical things—identical *rights* or identical *wrongs*—and the argument which establishes one will establish the other.

LETTER TO SAMUEL GALLOWAY
JULY 28, 1859

Free labor has the inspiration of hope; pure slavery has no hope.

FRAGMENT ON FREE LABOR
SEPTEMBER 1859 (?)

The only comparative peace we have had with slavery . . . was in the period from the Revolution to 1820—precisely the period through which we were closing out the African slave trade, abolishing slavery in several of the states, and restraining the spread of it into new ones . . . precisely the period in which the public mind had reason to rest, and did rest, in the belief that slavery was in course of ultimate extinction.

NOTES FOR SPEECHES AT COLUMBUS AND CINCINNATI, OHIO
SEPTEMBER 16, 17, 1859

We think the slaves, and free white laboring men, too, have more reason to be tired of *slavery* than masters have to be tired of *agitation* about it.

NOTES FOR SPEECHES AT COLUMBUS AND CINCINNATI, OHIO
SEPTEMBER 16, 17, 1859

Whoever would prevent slavery becoming national and perpetual yields all when he yields to a policy which treats it either as being *right* or as being a matter of indifference.

NOTES FOR SPEECHES AT COLUMBUS AND CINCINNATI, OHIO
SEPTEMBER 16, 17, 1859

The "equality of man" principle which actuated our forefathers in the establishment of the government is right; and . . . slavery, being directly opposed to this, is morally wrong. I think that if anything can be proved by natural theology, it is that slavery is morally wrong.

SPEECH AT HARTFORD, CONNECTICUT
MARCH 5, 1860

The proposition that there is a struggle between the white man and the Negro contains a falsehood. There is *no* struggle between them. It assumes that unless the white man enslaves the Negro, the Negro will enslave the white man. In that case, I think I would go for enslaving the black man, in preference to being enslaved myself. . . . There is, however, no such controversy here.

SPEECH AT HARTFORD, CONNECTICUT
MARCH 5, 1860

Slavery is *the* great political question of the nation.

SPEECH AT HARTFORD, CONNECTICUT
MARCH 5, 1860

In front of us sat an old gentleman with an enormous wen upon his neck. Everybody would say the wen was a great evil and would cause the man's death after a while—but you couldn't cut it out, for he'd bleed to death in a minute. But *would you engraft the seeds of that wen on the necks of sound and healthy men?* He must endure and be patient, hoping for possible relief. The wen represents slavery on the neck of this country.

SPEECH AT HARTFORD, CONNECTICUT
MARCH 5, 1860

If I find a venomous snake lying on the open prairie, I seize the first stick and kill him at once. But if that snake is in bed with my children, I must be more cautious—I shall, in striking the snake, also strike the children or arouse the reptile to bite the children. Slavery is the venomous snake in bed with the children. But if the question is whether to kill it on the prairie or *put it in bed with other children,* I think we'd *kill* it!

SPEECH AT HARTFORD, CONNECTICUT
MARCH 5, 1860

I don't mean that we ought to attack it where it exists. To me it seems that if we were to form a government anew, in view of the actual presence of slavery, we should find it necessary to frame just such a government as our fathers did, giving to the slaveholder the entire control where the system was established while we possessed the power to restrain it from going outside those limits. From the necessities of the case we should be compelled to form just such a government as our blessed fathers gave us; and, surely, if they have so made it, that adds another reason why we should let slavery alone where it exists.

SPEECH AT NEW HAVEN, CONNECTICUT
MARCH 6, 1860

The Constitution alludes to slavery three                    mentioning it once.

SPEECH AT NEW HAVEN, CONNECTICUT
MARCH 6, 1860

That the going many thousand miles, seizing a set of savages,
bringing them here and making slaves of them is a *necessity* imposed on *us* by *them* involves a species of logic to which my
mind will scarcely assent.

LETTER TO CHARLES H. FISHER
AUGUST 27, 1860

Let there be no compromise on the question of *extending*
slavery, If there be, all our labor is lost and, ere long, must be
done again. The dangerous ground—that into which some of our
friends have a hankering to run—is Pop. Sov. [Popular Sover-
eignty]. Have none of it. Stand firm. The tug has to come, and
better now than any time hereafter.

LETTER TO LYMAN TRUMBULL
DECEMBER 10, 1860

Entertain no proposition for a compromise in regard to the *extension* of slavery.

LETTER TO WILLIAM KELLOGG
DECEMBER 11, 1860

Prevent, as far as possible, any of our friends from demoraliz-
ing themselves and our cause by entertaining propositions for
compromise of any sort on *"slavery extension."* There is no possible compromise upon it but which puts us under again and
leaves all our work to do over again. Whether it be a Mo. line, or
Eli Thayer's Pop. Sov., it is all the same. Let either be done, and
immediately filibustering and extending slavery recommences.
On that point hold firm as with a chain of steel.

LETTER TO ELIHU B. WASHBURNE
DECEMBER 13, 1860

Mr. Lincoln is not pledged to the ultimate extinction of slavery; does not hold the black man to be the equal of the white . . . ; and never did stigmatize their white people as immoral and unchristian.

LETTER TO HENRY J. RAYMOND
DECEMBER 18, 1860

You think slavery is *right* and ought to be extended; while we think it is *wrong* and ought to be restricted. That I suppose is the rub.

LETTER TO ALEXANDER H. STEPHENS
DECEMBER 22, 1860

On the territorial question—that is, the question of extending slavery under the national auspices—I am inflexible. I am for no compromise which *assists* or *permits* the extension of the institution on soil owned by the nation. And any trick by which the nation is to acquire territory and then allow some local authority to spread slavery over it is as obnoxious as any other.

LETTER TO WILLIAM H. SEWARD
FEBRUARY 1, 1861

As to fugitive slaves, . . . slave trade among the slave states, and whatever springs of necessity from the fact that the institution is amongst us, I care but little, so that what is done be comely and not altogether outrageous.

LETTER TO WILLIAM H. SEWARD
FEBRUARY 1, 1861

Had slavery no existence among us and were the question asked, "Shall we adopt such an institution?" we should agree as to the reply which should be made. If there be any diversity in our views it is not as to whether we should receive slavery when free from it, but as to how we may best get rid of it already amongst us. Were an individual asked whether he would wish to have a wen on his neck, he could not hesitate as to the reply; but were it asked whether a man who has such a wen should at once be relieved of it by the application of the surgeon's knife, there might be diversity of opinion; perhaps the man might bleed to death as the result of such an operation.

REMARKS TO COMMITTEE OF REFORMED PRESBYTERIAN SYNOD
JULY 17, 1862

Among the friends of the Union there is great diversity of sentiment and of policy in regard to slavery and the African race amongst us. Some would perpetuate slavery; some would abolish it suddenly and without compensation; some would abolish it gradually and with compensation; some would remove the freed people from us, and some would retain them with us; and there are yet other minor diversities. Because of these diversities, we waste much strength in struggles among ourselves. By mutual concession we should harmonize and act together. This would be compromise; but it would be compromise among the friends and not with the enemies of the Union.

ANNUAL MESSAGE TO CONGRESS
DECEMBER 1, 1862

Whereas, while *heretofore* states and nations have tolerated slavery, *recently*, for the first in the world, an attempt has been made to construct a new nation upon the basis of and with the primary and fundamental object to maintain, enlarge and perpetuate human slavery; therefore,

Resolved, that no such embryo state should ever be recognized by, or admitted into, the family of Christian and civilized nations; and that all Christian and civilized men everywhere should, by all lawful means, resist to the utmost such recognition or admission.

RESOLUTION ON SLAVERY DRAFTED FOR
POSSIBLE ADOPTION IN GREAT BRITAIN
APRIL 15, 1863

I never knew a man who wished to be himself a slave. Consider, if you know, any *good* thing that no man desires for himself.

FROM AN AUTOGRAPH ALBUM
MARCH 22, 1864

I am naturally antislavery. If slavery is not wrong, nothing is wrong.

LETTER TO ALBERT G. HODGES

APRIL 4, 1864

The petition of persons under eighteen, praying that I would free all slave children, and the heading of which petition it appears you wrote, was handed me a few days since by Senator [Charles] Sumner. Please tell these little people I am very glad their young hearts are so full of just and generous sympathy and that, while I have not the power to grant all they ask, I trust they will remember that God has and that, as it seems, He wills to do it.

LETTER TO MRS. HORACE MANN

APRIL 5, 1864

I have always thought that all men should be free; but if any should be slaves it should be first those who desire it for *themselves*, and secondly those who *desire* it for *others*. Whenever I hear anyone arguing for the slavery I feel a strong impulse to see it tried on him personally.

SPEECH TO 140TH INDIANA REGIMENT

MARCH 17, 1865

## Slave Trade

I have not allowed myself to forget that the abolition of the slave trade by Great Britain was agitated a hundred years before it was a final success; that the measure had its open fire-eating opponents; its stealthy "don't care" opponents; its dollar-and-cent opponents; its inferior race opponents; its Negro equality opponents; and its religion and good-order opponents; that all these opponents got offices, and their adversaries got none. But I have also remembered that though they blazed like tallow candles for a century, at last they flickered in the socket, died out, stank in the dark for a brief session and were remembered no more, even by the smell.

FRAGMENT ON THE STRUGGLE AGAINST SLAVERY

JULY 1858 (?)

I do not stand pledged to the prohibition of the slave trade between the different states. . . . I am *pledged* to nothing about it. . . . I must say, however, that if Congress does possess the Constitutional power to abolish the slave trade among the different states, I should still not be in favor of the exercise of that power, unless upon some conservative principle, as I conceive it, akin to what I have said in relation to the abolition of slavery in the District of Columbia.

SECOND DEBATE WITH STEPHEN A. DOUGLAS,<br>FREEPORT, ILLINOIS<br>AUGUST 27, 1858

The supplemental treaty between the United States and Great Britain for the suppression of the African slave trade, made on the 17th day of February last, has been duly ratified and carried into execution. It is believed that, so far as American ports and American citizens are concerned, . . . inhuman and odious traffic has been brought to an end.

ANNUAL MESSAGE TO CONGRESS<br>DECEMBER 8, 1863

## Slave Traders

You have amongst you a sneaking individual of the class of native tyrants known as the "SLAVE DEALER." He watches your necessities and crawls up to buy your slave at a speculating price. If you cannot help it, you sell to him; but if you can help it, you drive him from your door. You despise him utterly. You do not recognize him as a friend or even as an honest man. Your children must not play with his; they may rollick freely with the little Negroes, but not with the slave dealer's children. If you are obliged to deal with him, you try to get through the job without so much as touching him. It is common with you to join hands with the men you meet; but with the slave dealer you avoid the ceremony—instinctively shrinking from the snaky contact. If he grows rich and retires from business, you still remember him and still keep up the ban of nonintercourse upon him and his family. Now why is this? You do not so treat the man who deals in corn, cattle or tobacco.

SPEECH AT PEORIA, ILLINOIS
OCTOBER 16, 1854

## Sorrow

I do not feel my own sorrows much more keenly than I do yours, when I know of them.

LETTER TO JOSHUA F. SPEED
FEBRUARY 3, 1842

In this sad world of ours, sorrow comes to all; and, to the young it comes with bitterest agony because it takes them unawares. The older have learned to ever expect it.

LETTER TO FANNY MCCULLOUGH
DECEMBER 23, 1862

## Speech-making

I find speaking here [House of Representatives] and elsewhere about the same thing. I was about as badly scared, and no worse, as I am when I speak in court.

LETTER TO WILLIAM H. HERNDON
JANUARY 8, 1848

Extemporaneous speaking should be practiced and cultivated.

NOTES FOR A LAW LECTURE
JULY 1850 (?)

I have made a great many poor speeches in my life, and I feel considerably relieved now to know that the dignity of the position in which I have been placed does not permit me to expose myself any longer.

REMARKS AT A REVIEW OF NEW YORK REGIMENTS
JULY 4, 1861

In my present position it is hardly proper for me to make speeches. . . . If I were as I have been most of my life, I might perhaps talk amusing to you for half an hour, and it wouldn't hurt anybody.

SPEECH AT FREDERICK, MARYLAND
OCTOBER 4, 1862

I am not accustomed to the use of language of eulogy.

REMARKS AT SANITARY FAIR, WASHINGTON, D.C.
MARCH 18, 1864

The hardest of all speeches I have to answer is a serenade.

RESPONSE TO A SERENADE
BY AN OHIO DELEGATION
JUNE 9, 1864

I believe I shall never be old enough to speak without embarrassment when I have nothing to talk about.

RESPONSE TO A SERENADE
DECEMBER 6, 1864

## Stanton, Edwin M.

He mixes no politics whatever with his duties.

LETTER TO JAMES G. BENNETT
MAY 21, 1862

## States' Rights

I declare that the maintenance inviolate of the rights of the states, and especially the right of each state to order and control its own domestic institutions according to its own judgment exclusively, is essential to that balance of powers on which the perfection and endurance of our political fabric depends.

LETTER TO DUFF GREEN
DECEMBER 28, 1860

What is the particular sacredness of a state? I speak not of that position which is given to a state in and by the Constitution of the United States, for that all of us agree to—we abide by; but that position assumed, that a state can carry with it out of the Union that which it holds in sacredness by virtue of its connection with the Union. I am speaking of that assumed right of a state, as a primary principle, that the Constitution should rule all that is less than itself and ruin all that is bigger than itself. But, I ask, wherein does consist that right? If a state in one instance, and a county in another, should be equal in extent of territory, and equal in the number of people, wherein is that state any better than the county? Can a change of name change the right? By what principle of original right is it that one fiftieth or one ninetieth of a great nation, by calling themselves a state, have the right to break up and ruin that nation as a matter of original principle?

SPEECH AT INDIANAPOLIS, INDIANA
FEBRUARY 11, 1861

The question is as to what the Constitution means—"What are their rights under the Constitution?" That is all. To decide that, who shall be the judge? Can you think of any other than the voice of the people? If the majority does not control, the minority must—would that be right? Though the majority may be wrong, and I will not undertake to say that they were not wrong in electing me, yet we must adhere to the principle that the majority shall rule.

SPEECH AT STEUBENVILLE, OHIO
FEBRUARY 14, 1861

I understand a proposed amendment to the Constitution—which amendment, however, I have not seen—has passed Congress, to the effect that the federal government shall never interfere with the domestic institutions of the states, including that of persons held in service. . . . I have no objection to its being made express and irrevocable.

FIRST INAUGURAL ADDRESS
MARCH 4, 1861

Our states have neither more nor less power than that reserved to them in the Union by the Constitution—no one of them ever having been a state *out* of the Union. . . . Having never been states, either in substance or in name, *outside* of the Union, whence this magical omnipotence of "state rights" . . . ? Much is said about the "sovereignty" of the states; but the word, even, is not in the national Constitution; nor, as is believed, in any of the state constitutions. . . . The states have their *status* IN the Union, and they have no other *legal status*.

MESSAGE TO CONGRESS IN SPECIAL SESSION
JULY 4, 1861

This relative matter of national power and state rights, as a principle, is no other than the principle of *generality* and *locality*. Whatever concerns the whole should be confided to the whole—to the general government; while whatever concerns *only* the state should be left exclusively to the state.

MESSAGE TO CONGRESS IN SPECIAL SESSION
JULY 4, 1861

*Statistics*

The point—the power to hurt—of all figures consists in the *truthfulness* of their application.

SPEECH IN HOUSE OF REPRESENTATIVES
JULY 27, 1848

*Stockholders*

They are men of wealth—of large capital—and consequently beyond the power of fortune or even the shafts of malice.

SPEECH IN ILLINOIS LEGISLATURE
JANUARY 11, 1837

*Strangers*

From the first appearance of man upon the earth down to very recent times, the words *"stranger"* and *"enemy"* were *quite* or *almost* synonymous. Long after civilized nations had defined robbery and murder as high crimes and had affixed severe punishments to them when practiced among and upon their own people respectively, it was deemed no offense, but even meritorious, to rob and murder and enslave *strangers* whether as nations or as individuals. Even yet, this has not totally disappeared. The man of the highest moral cultivation, in spite of all which abstract principle can do, likes him whom he *does* know much better than him whom he does *not* know. To correct the evils, great and small, which spring from want of sympathy and from positive enmity among *strangers*, as nations or as individuals, is one of the highest functions of civilization.

SPEECH AT MILWAUKEE, WISCONSIN
SEPTEMBER 30, 1859

## Success

But the game is caught; and . . . with the catching end the pleasures of the chase.

SPEECH TO YOUNG MEN'S LYCEUM,<br>SPRINGFIELD, ILLINOIS<br>JANUARY 27, 1838

Always bear in mind that your own resolution to succeed is more important than any other one thing.

LETTER TO ISHAM REAVIS<br>NOVEMBER 5, 1855

## Suffering

For some reason (perhaps because we are killed so quickly) we shall never be sensible of our suffering.

REPLY TO JAMES ADAMS<br>OCTOBER 18, 1837

## Suffrage

I go for admitting all whites to the right of suffrage who pay taxes or bear arms (by no means excluding females).

LETTER TO THE *Sangamo* (ILLINOIS) *Journal*<br>JUNE 13, 1836

The right of suffrage has often been assumed and exercised by aliens under pretenses of naturalization, which they have disavowed when drafted into the military service. I submit the expediency of such an amendment of the law as will make the fact of voting an estoppel against any plea of exemption from military service, or other civil obligation, on the ground of alienage.

ANNUAL MESSAGE TO CONGRESS
DECEMBER 8, 1863

I cannot see, if universal amnesty is granted, how, under the circumstances, I can avoid exacting in return universal suffrage or, at least, suffrage on the basis of intelligence and military service. . . . The restoration of the rebel states to the Union must rest upon the principle of civil and political equality of both races; and it must be sealed by general amnesty.

LETTER TO JAMES S. WADSWORTH
JANUARY 1864 (?)

## Superstition

I always was superstitious.

LETTER TO JOSHUA F. SPEED
JULY 4, 1842

I am superstitious.

LETTER TO JAMES W. GRIMES
JULY 12, 1856

## Supreme Court

The candid citizen must confess that if the policy of the government upon vital questions affecting the whole people is to be irrevocably fixed by decisions of the Supreme Court, the instant they are made in ordinary litigation between parties, in personal actions, the people will have ceased to be their own rulers, having to that extent practically resigned their government into the hands of that eminent tribunal. Nor is there, in this view, any assault upon the court or the judges. It is a duty, from which they may not shrink, to decide cases properly brought before them; and it is no fault of theirs if others seek to turn their decisions to political purposes.

FIRST INAUGURAL ADDRESS
MARCH 4, 1861

## *Suspicion*

Suspicion and jealousy never did help any man in any situation.

LETTER TO WILLIAM H. HERNDON
JULY 10, 1848

We need nothing so much as to get rid of unjust suspicions of one another.

LETTER TO CHARLES L. WILSON
JUNE 1, 1858

## *Sympathy*

I wish to disparage no one—certainly not those who sympathize with me; but I must say I need success more than I need sympathy.

LETTER TO CARL SCHURZ
NOVEMBER 24, 1862

## *Tariffs*

I suppose the true effect of duties upon prices to be as follows: If a certain duty be levied upon an article which by nature cannot be produced in this country, as three cents a pound upon coffee, the effect will be that the consumer will pay one cent more per pound than before, the producer will take one cent less, and the merchant one cent less in profits—in other words, the burden of the duty will be distributed over consumption, production and commerce, and not confined to either. But if a duty amounting to full protection be levied upon an article which can be produced here with as little labor as elsewhere, as iron, that article will ultimately, and at no distant day, in consequence of such duty, be sold to our people cheaper than before, at least by the amount of the cost of *carrying* it from abroad.

NOTES FOR A TARIFF DISCUSSION
DECEMBER 1847

It appears to me that the national debt created by the [Mexican] war renders a modification of the existing tariff indispensable; and when it shall be modified, I should be pleased to see it adjusted with a due reference to the protection of our home industry. The particulars, it appears to me, must and should be left to the untrammeled discretion of Congress.

SUGGESTIONS ON WHAT ZACHARY TAYLOR SHOULD SAY IF
SELECTED AS WHIG CANDIDATE FOR PRESIDENT
MARCH 1848 (?)

The tariff is to the government what a meal is to the family; but, while this is admitted, it still becomes necessary to modify and change its operations according to new interests and new circumstances. . . . I have long thought that if there be any article of necessity which can be produced at home with as little or nearly the same labor as abroad, it would be better to protect that article. Labor is the true standard of value.

SPEECH AT PITTSBURGH, PENNSYLVANIA
FEBRUARY 15, 1861

## Taylor, Zachary

Gen. Taylor's battles were not distinguished for brilliant military maneuvers; but, in all, he seems rather to have conquered by the exercise of a sober and steady judgment coupled with a dogged incapacity to understand that defeat was possible. His rarest military trait was a combination of negatives—absence of *excitement* and absence of *fear*. He could not be *flurried* and he could not be *scared*.

EULOGY ON ZACHARY TAYLOR
JULY 25, 1850

Terrible as he was to his country's enemies, no man was so little disposed to have difficulty with his friends.

EULOGY ON ZACHARY TAYLOR
JULY 25, 1850

None can be found to declare that he was ever a tyrant anywhere, in anything.

EULOGY ON ZACHARY TAYLOR
JULY 25, 1850

The American people, in electing Gen. Taylor to the Presidency, thereby showing their high appreciation of his sterling but unobtrusive qualities, did their *country* a service and *themselves* an imperishable honor.

EULOGY ON ZACHARY TAYLOR
JULY 25, 1850

It is *much* for the young to know that treading the hard path of duty, as he trod it, *will* be noticed and *will* lead to high places.

EULOGY ON ZACHARY TAYLOR
JULY 25, 1850

He is gone. The conqueror at last is conquered. The fruits of his labor, his name, his memory and example are all that is left us—his example verifying the great truth that "He that humbleth himself shall be exalted," teaching that to serve one's country with a singleness of purpose gives assurance of that country's gratitude, secures its best honors, and makes "a dying bed, soft as downy pillows are."

EULOGY ON ZACHARY TAYLOR
JULY 25, 1850

## Temper

If I do get up a little temper I have no sufficient time to keep it up.

LETTER TO FRANZ SIGEL
FEBRUARY 5, 1863

As I am trying to preserve my own temper, by avoiding irritants so far as practicable, I have declined to read the cross letter.

LETTER TO HAMILTON R. GAMBLE
JULY 23, 1863

## Temperance

The cause itself seems suddenly transformed from a cold abstract theory to a living, breathing, active and powerful chieftain, going forth "conquering and to conquer."

ADDRESS TO WASHINGTON TEMPERANCE SOCIETY,
SPRINGFIELD, ILLINOIS
FEBRUARY 22, 1842

The *preacher*, it is said, advocates temperance because he is a fanatic and desires a union of church and state; the *lawyer*, from his pride and vanity of hearing himself speak; and the *hired agent* for his salary.

ADDRESS TO WASHINGTON TEMPERANCE SOCIETY,
SPRINGFIELD, ILLINOIS
FEBRUARY 22, 1842

I think that the reasonable men of the world have long since agreed that intemperance is one of the greatest, if not the very greatest, of all evils amongst mankind. . . . The mode of cure is one about which there may be differences of opinion. You have suggested that in any army—our army—drunkenness is a great evil. . . . This undoubtedly is true and while it is, perhaps, rather a bad source to derive comfort from, nevertheless, in a hard struggle, I do not know but what it is some consolation to be aware that there is some intemperance on the other side, too.

REPLY TO SONS OF TEMPERANCE
SEPTEMBER 29, 1863

## Territories

On the admission of the states into the Union carved from the territory we owned before the Constitution, no question—or at most, no considerable question—arose about slavery, those which were within the limits of or owned by the old states following, respectively, the condition of the parent state, and those with the Northwest Territory following the previously made provision.

EULOGY ON HENRY CLAY
JULY 6, 1852

I am not generally opposed to honest acquisition of territory; and, in any given case, I would or would not oppose such acquisition accordingly as I might think such acquisition would or would not aggravate the slavery question among ourselves.

SECOND DEBATE WITH STEPHEN A. DOUGLAS,
FREEPORT, ILLINOIS
AUGUST 27, 1858

I do not stand pledged against the admission of a new state into the Union with such a constitution as the people of that state may see fit to make.

SECOND DEBATE WITH STEPHEN A. DOUGLAS,
FREEPORT, ILLINOIS
AUGUST 27, 1858

I do not now, nor ever did, stand pledged against the admission of any more slave states into the Union. . . . I should be exceedingly glad to know that there would never be another slave state admitted into the Union; but I must add that if slavery shall be kept out of the territories during the territorial existence of any one given territory, and the people shall, having a fair chance and a clear field when they come to adopt the Constitution, uninfluenced by the actual presence of the institution among them, I see no alternative, if we own the country, but to admit them into the Union.

SECOND DEBATE WITH STEPHEN A. DOUGLAS,
FREEPORT, ILLINOIS
AUGUST 27, 1858

Whatever motive a man or a set of men may have for making annexation of property or territory, it is very easy to assert, but much less easy to disprove, that it is necessary for the wants of the country.

FIFTH DEBATE WITH STEPHEN A. DOUGLAS,
GALESBURG, ILLINOIS
OCTOBER 7, 1858

Now irrespective of the moral aspect of this question as to whether there is a right or wrong in enslaving a Negro, I am still in favor of our new territories being in such a condition that white men may find a home—may find some spot where they can better their condition—where they can settle upon new soil and better their condition in life. I am in favor of this not merely . . . for our own people who are born amongst us, but as an outlet for *free white people everywhere*, the world over—in which Hans and Baptiste and Patrick, and all other men from all the world, may find new homes and better their conditions in life.

SEVENTH DEBATE WITH STEPHEN A. DOUGLAS,
ALTON, ILLINOIS
OCTOBER 15, 1858

## Thought

Intensity of thought . . . will sometimes wear the sweetest idea threadbare and turn it to the bitterness of death.

LETTER TO JOSHUA F. SPEED
JANUARY 3, 1842

## Treason

The Saviour of the world chose twelve disciples, and even one of that small number, selected by superhuman wisdom, turned out a traitor and a devil.

SPEECH ON THE SUB-TREASURY
DECEMBER 26, 1839

## Truth

Where a thing *is not*, it cannot be pointed out.

REPLY TO JAMES ADAMS
OCTOBER 18, 1837

We have made the statements we have because we know them to be true—and we choose to live or die by them.

REPLY TO JAMES ADAMS
OCTOBER 18, 1837

You are compelled to speak; and your only alternative is to tell the *truth* or tell a *lie*. I cannot doubt which you would do.

LETTER TO WILLIAM H. HERNDON
FEBRUARY 1, 1848

I planted myself upon the truth and the truth only, so far as I knew it or could be brought to know it.

SPEECH AT SPRINGFIELD, ILLINOIS
JULY 17, 1858

I only ask my friends and all who are eager for the truth, that when they hear me represented as saying or meaning anything strange, they will turn to my own words and examine for themselves.

SPEECH AT CLINTON, ILLINOIS
JULY 27, 1858

*Truth* is generally the best vindication against slander.

LETTER TO EDWIN M. STANTON
JULY 14, 1864

## Tyranny

Is it unreasonable . . . to expect that some man possessed of the loftiest genius, coupled with ambition sufficient to push it to its utmost stretch, will at some time spring up among us? And when such a one does, it will require the people to be united with each other, attached to the government and laws, and generally intelligent, to successfully frustrate his designs.

SPEECH TO YOUNG MEN'S LYCEUM,
SPRINGFIELD, ILLINOIS
JANUARY 27, 1838

Of all those who come into the world, only a small percentage are natural tyrants.

SPEECH AT PEORIA, ILLINOIS
OCTOBER 16, 1854

## Union

Much as I hate slavery, I would consent to the extension of it rather than see the Union dissolved, just as I would consent to any GREAT evil to avoid a GREATER one.

SPEECH AT PEORIA, ILLINOIS
OCTOBER 16, 1854

Our political problem now is, "Can we, as a nation, continue together *permanently—forever*—half slave and half free?" The problem is too mighty for me. May God in his mercy superintend the solution.

LETTER TO GEORGE ROBERTSON
AUGUST 15, 1855

The Union . . . won't be dissolved. We don't want to dissolve it, and if you attempt it, *we won't let you.* With the purse and sword, the army and navy and treasury, in our hands and at our command, you *couldn't do it.* This government would be very weak, indeed, if a majority, with a disciplined army and navy and a well-filled treasury, could not preserve itself when attacked by an unarmed, undisciplined, unorganized minority. All this talk about the dissolution of the Union is humbug—nothing but folly. *We* WON'T dissolve the Union, and *you* SHAN'T.

SPEECH AT GALENA, ILLINOIS
JULY 23, 1856

A majority will never dissolve the Union.

SPEECH AT KALAMAZOO, MICHIGAN
AUGUST 27, 1856

"A house divided against itself cannot stand." I believe this government cannot endure permanently half *slave* and half *free.* I do not expect the Union to be *dissolved*—I do not expect the house to *fall*—but I *do* expect it will cease to be divided. It will become *all* one thing or *all* the other. Either the *opponents* of slavery will arrest the further spread of it and place it where the public mind shall rest in the belief that it is in course of ultimate extinction; or its *advocates* will push it forward till it shall become alike lawful in *all* the states, *old* as well as *new—North* as well as *South.*

"A HOUSE DIVIDED" SPEECH, SPRINGFIELD, ILLINOIS<br>JUNE 16, 1858

I am quite aware this government has endured half slave and half free for eighty-two years. I understand that little bit of history.

SPEECH AT SPRINGFIELD, ILLINOIS<br>JULY 17, 1858

The great variety of the local institutions in the states, springing from differences in the soil, differences in the face of the country and in the climate, are bonds of union. They do not make "a house divided against itself," but they make a house united. If they produce in one section of the country what is called for by the wants of another section, and this other section can supply the wants of the first, they are not matters of discord but bonds of union, true bonds of union. But can this question of slavery be considered as among *these* varieties in the institutions of the country? I leave it to you to say whether, in the history of our government, this institution of slavery has not always failed to be a bond of union and, on the contrary, been an apple of discord and an element of division in the house. I ask you to consider whether, so long as the moral constitution of men's minds shall continue to be the same after this generation and assemblage shall sink into the grave and another race shall arise with the same moral and intellectual development we have—whether, if that institution is standing in the same irritating position in which it now is, it will not continue an element of division?

FIRST DEBATE WITH STEPHEN A. DOUGLAS,<br>OTTAWA, ILLINOIS<br>AUGUST 21, 1858

Has anything ever threatened the existence of this Union save and except this very institution of slavery? What is it that we hold most dear amongst us? Our own liberty and prosperity. What has ever threatened our liberty and prosperity save and except this institution of slavery? If this is true, how do you propose to improve the condition of things by enlarging slavery—by spreading it out and making it bigger?

SEVENTH DEBATE WITH STEPHEN A. DOUGLAS,
ALTON, ILLINOIS
OCTOBER 15, 1858

Does anything in any way endanger the perpetuity of this Union but that single thing, slavery? . . . What ever endangered this Union save and except slavery? Did any other thing ever cause a moment's fear? All men must agree that this thing alone has ever endangered the perpetuity of the Union. But if it was threatened by any other influence, would not all men say that the best thing that could be done, if we could not or ought not to destroy it, would be at least to keep it from growing any larger? Can any man believe that the way to save the Union is to extend and increase the only thing that threatens the Union, and to suffer it to grow bigger and bigger?

SPEECH AT NEW HAVEN, CONNECTICUT
MARCH 6, 1860

We have just carried an election on principles fairly stated to the people. Now we are told in advance the government shall be broken up unless we surrender to those we have beaten before we take the offices. In this they are either attempting to play upon us or they are in dead earnest. Either way, if we surrender, it is the end of us and of the government.

LETTER TO JAMES T. HALE
JANUARY 11, 1861

Still we are bound together, I trust, in Christianity, civilization and patriotism, and are attached to our country and our whole country. While some of us may differ in political opinions, still we are all united in one feeling for the Union. We all believe in the maintenance of the Union, of every star and every stripe of the glorious flag, and permit me to express the sentiment that upon the union of the states there shall be between us no difference.

SPEECH AT LAFAYETTE, INDIANA
FEBRUARY 11, 1861

When the people rise in masses in behalf of the Union and the liberties of their country, truly may it be said, "The gates of hell shall not prevail against them."

REPLY TO GOVERNOR OLIVER P. MORTON,
INDIANAPOLIS, INDIANA
FEBRUARY 11, 1861

If all do not join now to save the good old ship of the Union this voyage, nobody will have a chance to pilot her on another voyage.

SPEECH AT CLEVELAND, OHIO
FEBRUARY 15, 1861

But let me tell to those of you who did not vote for me an anecdote of a certain Irish friend that I met yesterday. He said he did not vote for me, but went for Douglas. "Now," said I to him, "I will tell you what you ought to do in that case. If we all turn in and keep the ship from sinking this voyage, there may be a chance for Douglas on the next; but if we let it go down now, neither he nor anybody else will have an opportunity of sailing in it again."

REMARKS AT RAVENNA, OHIO
FEBRUARY 15, 1861

There is nothing that can ever being me willingly to consent to the destruction of this Union under which . . . the whole country has acquired its greatness, unless it were to be that thing for which the Union itself was made. I understand a ship to be made for the carrying and preservation of cargo, and so long as the ship can be saved, with the cargo, it should never be abandoned. This Union should likewise never be abandoned unless it fails and the probability of its preservation shall cease to exist without throwing the passengers and cargo overboard. So long, then, as it is possible that the prosperity and the liberties of the people can be preserved in the Union, it shall be my purpose at all times to preserve it.

REPLY TO MAYOR FERNANDO WOOD,
NEW YORK CITY
FEBRUARY 20, 1861

I hold that in contemplation of universal law and of the Constitution, the Union of these states is perpetual. Perpetuity is implied, if not expressed, in the fundamental law of all national governments. It is safe to assert that no government proper ever had a provision in its organic law for its own termination. Continue to execute all the express provisions of our national Constitution, and the Union will endure forever—it being impossible to destroy it, except by some action not provided for in the instrument itself.

FIRST INAUGURAL ADDRESS
MARCH 4, 1861

The Constitution provides, and all the states have accepted the provision, that "The United States shall guarantee to every state in this Union a republican form of government." But, if a state may lawfully go out of the Union, having done so it may also discard the republican form of government; so that to prevent its going out is an indispensable *means* to the *end* of maintaining the guaranty mentioned; and when an end is lawful and obligatory, the indispensable means to it are also lawful and obligatory.

MESSAGE TO CONGRESS IN SPECIAL SESSION
JULY 4, 1861

It is with regret I search and cannot find, in your not very short letter, any declaration or intimation that you entertain any desire for the preservation of the Federal Union.

LETTER TO GOVERNOR BERIAH MAGOFFIN OF KENTUCKY
AUGUST 24, 1861

One strong nation promises more durable peace and a more extensive, valuable and reliable commerce than can the same nation broken into hostile fragments.

ANNUAL MESSAGE TO CONGRESS
DECEMBER 3, 1861

Broken eggs cannot be mended; but Louisiana has nothing to do now but to take her place in the Union as it was, barring the already broken eggs. The sooner she does so, the smaller will be the amount of that which will be past mending. This government cannot much longer play a game in which it stakes all and its enemies stake nothing. Those enemies must understand that they cannot experiment for ten years trying to destroy the government, and if they fail still come back into the Union unhurt. If they expect in any contingency to ever have the Union as it was, I join with the writer in saying, "Now is the time."

LETTER TO AUGUST BELMONT
JULY 31, 1862

I never did ask more, nor ever was willing to accept less, than for all the states and the people thereof to take and hold their places and their rights in the Union under the Constitution of the United States. For this alone have I felt authorized to struggle; and I seek neither more nor less now.

LETTER TO JOHN A. MCCLERNAND
JANUARY 8, 1863

The purpose of the people within the loyal states to maintain the integrity of the Union was never more firm nor more nearly unanimous than now. . . . It is an unanswerable argument to this effect, that no candidate for any office whatever, high or low, has ventured to seek votes on the avowal that he was for giving up the Union. . . . On the distinct issue of Union or no Union, the politicians have shown their instinctive knowledge that there is no diversity among the people.

ANNUAL MESSAGE TO CONGRESS
DECEMBER 6, 1864

## Usury

It seems as though we are never to have an end to this baneful and corroding system.

COMMUNICATIONS TO THE PEOPLE OF
SANGAMON COUNTY, ILLINOIS
MARCH 9, 1832

## Variety

Dished up in as many varieties as a French cook can produce soups from potatoes.

SPEECH AT SPRINGFIELD, ILLINOIS
JULY 17, 1858

## Verses

### MY CHILDHOOD HOME I SEE AGAIN

My childhood home I see again,
　And gladden with the view;
And still as mem'ries crowd my brain,
　There's sadness in it too.

O memory! thou midway world
　'Twixt Earth and Paradise,
Where things decayed, and loved ones lost
　In dreamy shadows rise.

And freed from all that's gross or vile,
　Seem hallowed, pure, and bright,
Like scenes in some enchanted isle,
　All bathed in liquid light.

As distant mountains please the eye,
  When twilight chases day—
As bugle tones, that, passing by,
  In distance die away—

As leaving some grand waterfall
  We ling'ring list its roar,
So memory will hallow all
  We've known, but know no more.

Now twenty years have passed away,
  Since here I bid farewell
To woods, and fields, and scenes of play
  And schoolmates loved so well.

Where many were, how few remain
  Of old familiar things!
But seeing these to mind again
  The lost and absent brings.

The friends I left that parting day—
  How changed, as time has sped!
Young childhood grown, strong manhood gray,
  And half of all are dead.

I hear the lone survivors tell
  How nought from death could save,
Till every sound appears a knell,
  And every spot a grave.

I range the fields with pensive tread,
  And pace the hollow rooms;
And feel (companions of the dead)
  I'm living in the tombs.

And here's an object more of dread
  Than ought the grave contains—
A human-form, with reason fled,
  While wretched life remains,

Poor Matthew! Once of genius bright—
  A fortune-favored child—
Now locked for aye, in mental night,
  A haggard madman wild.

Poor Matthew! I have ne'er forgot
  When first with maddened will,
Yourself you maimed, your father fought,
  And mother strove to kill;

And terror spread, and neighbours ran,
  Your dang'rous strength to bind;
And soon, a howling crazy man,
  Your limbs were fast confined.

How then you writhed and shrieked aloud,
  Your bones and sinews bared;
And fiendish on the gaping crowd,
  With burning eyeballs glared.

And begged, and swore, and wept, and prayed,
  With maniac laughter joined—
How fearful are the signs displayed,
  By pangs that kill the mind!

And when at length, tho' drear and long,
  Time soothed your fiercer woes—
How plaintively your mournful song,
  Upon the still night rose.

I've heard it oft, as if I dreamed,
  Far-distant, sweet, and lone;
The funeral dirge it ever seemed
  Of reason dead and gone.

To drink its strains, I've stole away,
  All silently and still,
Ere yet the rising god of day
  Had streaked the eastern hill.

Air held his breath; the trees all still
    Seemed sorr'wing angels round.
Their swelling tears in dewdrops fell
    Upon the list'ning ground.

But this is past, and nought remains
    That raised you o'er the brute.
Your mad'ning shrieks and soothing strains
    Are like forever mute.

Now fare thee well: more thou the cause
    Than subject now of woe.
All mental pangs, but time's kind laws,
    Hast lost the power to know.

O death! Thou awe-inspiring prince,
    That keepst the world in fear;
Why dost thou tear more blest ones hence,
    And leave him ling'ring here?*

And now away to seek some scene
    Less painful than the last—
With less of horror mingled in
    The present and the past.

The very spot where grew the bread
    That formed my bones, I see.
How strange, old field, on thee to tread,
    And feel I'm part of thee!

FEBRUARY 1846 (?)

### THE BEAR HUNT

A wild-bear chace, didst never see?
    Then hast thou lived in vain.
Thy richest bump of glorious glee,
    Lies desert in thy brain.

* This stanza does not appear in the original manuscript. It apparently was written for a letter to Andrew Johnston, September 6, 1846, in which Lincoln quoted twelve other stanzas of the work.

When first my father settled here,
  'Twas then the frontier line:
The panther's scream, filled night with fear
  And bears preyed on the swine.

But wo for Bruin's short lived fun,
  When rose the squealing cry;
Now man and horse, with dog and gun,
  For vengeance, at him fly.

A sound of danger strikes his ear;
  He gives the breeze a snuff:
Away he bounds, with little fear,
  And seeks the tangled *rough.*

On press his foes, and reach the ground,
  Where's left his half munched meal;
The dogs, in circles, scent around,
  And find his fresh made trail.

With instant cry, away they dash,
  And men as fast pursue;
O'er logs they leap, through water splash,
  And shout the brisk halloo.

Now to elude the eager pack,
  Bear shuns the open ground;
Through matted vines, he shapes his track
  And runs it, round and round.

The tall fleet cur, with deep-mouthed voice,
  Now speeds him, as the wind;
While half-grown pup, and short-legged fice,
  Are yelping far behind.

And fresh recruits are dropping in
  To join the merry *corps:*
With yelp and yell,—a minged din—
  The woods are in a roar.

And round, and round the chace now goes,
   The world's alive with fun;
Nick Carter's horse, his rider throws,
   And more, Hill drops his gun.

Now sorely pressed, bear glances back,
   And lolls his tired tongue;
When as, to force him from his track,
   An ambush on him sprung.

Across the glade he sweeps for flight,
   And fully is in view.
The dogs, new-fired, by the sight,
   Their cry, and speed, renew.

The foremost ones, now reach his rear,
   He turns, they dash away;
And circling now, the wrathful bear,
   They have him full at bay.

At top of speed, the horse-men come,
   All screaming in a row.
"Whoop! Take him Tiger. Seize him Drum."
   Bang,—bang—the rifles go.

And furious now, the dogs he tears,
   And crushes in his ire.
Wheels right and left, and upward rears,
   With eyes of burning fire.

But leaden death is at his heart,
   Vain all the strength he plies.
And, spouting blood from every part,
   He reels, and sinks, and dies.

And now a dinsome clamor rose,
   'Bout who should have his skin;
Who first draws blood, each hunter knows,
   This prize must always win.

But who did this, and how to trace
  What's true from what's a lie,
Like lawyers, in a murder case
  They stoutly *argufy*.

Aforesaid fice, of blustering mood,
  Behind, and quite forgot,
Just now emerging from the wood,
  Arrives upon the spot.

With grinning teeth, and up-turned hair—
  Brim full of spunk and wrath,
He growls, and seizes on dead bear,
  And shakes for life and death.

And swells as if his skin would tear,
  And growls and shakes again;
And swears, as plain as dog can swear,
  That he has won the skin.

Conceited whelp! we laugh at thee—
  Nor mind, that not a few
Of pompous, two-legged dogs there be,
  Conceited quite as you.

SEPTEMBER 6, 1846 (?)

You are young, and I am older;
  You are hopeful, I am not—
Enjoy life, ere it grow colder—
  Pluck the roses ere they rot.

Teach your beau to heed the lay—
  That sunshine soon is lost in shade—
That *now's* as good as any day—
  To take thee, Rosa, ere she fade.

INSCRIPTION IN THE AUTOGRAPH ALBUM OF ROSA HAGGARD
SEPTEMBER 28, 1858

A sweet plaintive song did I hear,
And I fancied that she was the singer—
May emotions as pure as that song set astir
Be the worst that the future shall bring her.

TO LINNIE HAGGARD
SEPTEMBER 30, 1858

## Veterans

In the dispensing of patronage towards the men who, by fighting our battles, bear the chief burden of saving our country, my conclusion is that, other claims and qualifications being equal, they have the better right; and this is especially applicable to the disabled soldier and the deceased soldier's family.

LETTER TO MONTGOMERY BLAIR
JULY 24, 1863

We never should, and I am sure never shall, be niggard of gratitude and benefaction to the soldiers who have endured toil, privations and wounds that the nation may live.

LETTER TO MRS. HUTTER, THE MISSES LAGER AND
MISS CLAGHORN
AUGUST 10, 1863

## Victory

*Wise councils* may *accelerate* or *mistakes delay* it, but sooner or later the victory is *sure* to come.

"A HOUSE DIVIDED" SPEECH, SPRINGFIELD, ILLINOIS
JUNE 16, 1858

# War

Military glory—that attractive rainbow that rises in showers of blood, that serpent's eye that charms to destroy.

SPEECH IN HOUSE OF REPRESENTATIVES
JANUARY 12, 1848

The provision of the Constitution giving the war-making power to Congress was dictated, as I understand it, by the following reasons. Kings had always been involved and impoverishing their people in wars, pretending generally, if not always, that the good of the people was the object. This our Convention understood to be the most oppressive of all kingly oppressions; and they resolved to so frame the Constitution that *no one man* should hold the power of bringing this oppression upon us.

LETTER TO WILLIAM H. HERNDON
FEBRUARY 15, 1848

If one people will make war upon another, it is a necessity . . . to unite and co-operate for defense.

FRAGMENT
JULY 1854 (?)

I sincerely wish war was an easier and pleasanter business than it is; but it does not admit of holy days.

LETTER TO THOMAS H. CLAY
OCTOBER 8, 1862

A measure made expedient by a war is no precedent for times of peace.

OPINION ON ADMISSION OF WEST VIRGINIA INTO THE UNION
DECEMBER 31, 1862

Actual war coming, blood grows hot, and blood is spilled. Thought is forced from old channels into confusion. Deception breeds and thrives. Confidence dies and universal suspicion reigns. Each man feels an impulse to kill his neighbor, lest he be first killed by him. Revenge and retaliation follow. . . . But this is not all. Every foul bird comes aboard and every dirty reptile rises up. These add crime to confusion. Strong measures deemed indispensable but harsh at best, such men make worse by maladministration. Murders for old grudges, and murders for self, proceed under any cloak that will best cover for the occasion.

LETTER TO CHARLES D. DRAKE AND OTHERS
OCTOBER 5, 1863

## Washington, George

To add brightness to the sun or glory to the name of Washington is alike impossible.

ADDRESS TO WASHINGTON TEMPERANCE SOCIETY,
SPRINGFIELD, ILLINOIS
FEBRUARY 22, 1842

Washington is the mightiest name of earth—*long since* mightiest in the cause of civil liberty; *still* mightiest in moral reformation.

ADDRESS TO WASHINGTON TEMPERANCE SOCIETY,
SPRINGFIELD, ILLINOIS
FEBRUARY 22, 1842

## Whiskers

As to the whiskers, having never worn any, do you not think people would call it a piece of silly affection if I were to begin it now?

LETTER TO GRACE BEDELL
OCTOBER 19, 1860

## Wind

The wind is an *untamed* and *unharnessed* force, and quite possibly one of the greatest discoveries hereafter to be made will be the taming and harnessing of the wind.

FIRST LECTURE ON DISCOVERIES AND INVENTIONS,
BLOOMINGTON, ILLINOIS
APRIL 6, 1858

## Women

I want in all cases to do right, and most particularly so in all cases with women.

LETTER TO MARY S. OWENS
AUGUST 16, 1837

Others have been made fools of by the girls; but this can never be with truth said of me. I most emphatically, in this instance, made a fool of myself.

LETTER TO MRS. ORVILLE H. BROWNING
APRIL 1, 1838

The truth is I have never corresponded much with ladies; and hence I postpone writing letters to them as a business which I do not understand.

LETTER TO MRS. M. J. GREEN
SEPTEMBER 22, 1860

I appear before you to bid you farewell—to see you, and to allow you all to see me. At the same time I acknowledge, ladies, that I think I have the best of the bargain in the sight.

REMARKS AT UTICA, NEW YORK
FEBRUARY 18, 1861

Today, Mrs. Major Paul . . . calls and urges the appointment of her husband as Brigadier General.* She is a saucy woman and I am afraid she will keep tormenting till I may have to do it.

MEMORANDUM ON APPOINTMENT OF GABRIEL R. PAUL

AUGUST 23, 1862

I have never studied the art of paying compliments to women; but I must say that if all that has been said by orators and poets since the creation of the world in praise of woman were applied to the women of America, it would not do them justice for their conduct during this war. . . . God bless the women of America!

REMARKS AT SANITARY FAIR, WASHINGTON, D.C.

MARCH 18, 1864

I know not how much is within the legal power of the government in this case; but it is certainly true in equity that the laboring women in our employment should be paid at least as much as they were at the beginning of the war.

LETTER TO EDWIN M. STANTON

JULY 27, 1864

This lady would be appointed Chaplain of the First Wisconsin Heavy Artillery, only that she is a woman. The President has not legally anything to do with such a question, but has no objection to her appointment.

COMMUNICATION TO EDWIN M. STANTON

NOVEMBER 10, 1864

## Work

Half finished work generally proves to be labor lost.

COMMUNICATION TO THE PEOPLE OF

SANGAMON COUNTY, ILLINOIS

MARCH 9, 1832

* Major Paul was appointed Brigadier General September 5, 1862.

You are destitute because you have *idled* away all your time. Your thousand pretenses for not getting along better are all nonsense—they deceive nobody but yourself. *Go to work* is the only cure for your case.

LETTER TO JOHN D. JOHNSTON
NOVEMBER 4, 1851

If you intend to go to work, there is no better place than right where you are; if you do not intend to go to work, you cannot get along anywhere.

LETTER TO JOHN D. JOHNSTON
NOVEMBER 4, 1851

Every man is proud of what he does well; and no man is proud of what he does *not* do well. With the former, his heart is in his work and he will do twice as much of it with less fatigue. The latter performs a little imperfectly, looks at it in disgust, turns from it, and imagines himself exceedingly tired.

SPEECH AT MILWAUKEE, WISCONSIN
SEPTEMBER 30, 1859

The lady—bearer of this—says she has two sons who want to work. Set them at it, if possible. Wanting to work is so rare a merit that it should be encouraged.

LETTER TO GEORGE D. RAMSAY
OCTOBER 17, 1861

This man wants to *work*—so uncommon a want that I think it ought to be gratified.

MEMORANDUM ON UNIDENTIFIED MAN
ADDRESSED TO "HEADS OF DEPARTMENTS AND BUREAUS"
JANUARY 23, 1862

I am always for the man who wishes to work.

RECOMMENDATION FOR UNIDENTIFIED MAN
AUGUST 15, 1864

## World's Fairs

The first of all inventions of which we have any direct account—*the fig-leaf apron*— . . . was a joint operation, Eve having shared with Adam in the getting up of the apron. And, indeed, judging from the fact that sewing has come down to our times as "woman's work" it is very probable she took the leading part; he, perhaps, doing no more than to stand by and thread the needle. That proceeding may be reckoned as the mother of all "sewing societies"; and the first and most perfect "world's fair," all inventions and all inventors then in the world being on the spot.

SECOND LECTURE ON DISCOVERIES AND INVENTIONS,
JACKSONVILLE, ILLINOIS
FEBRUARY 11, 1859

## Youth

The United States don't need the services of boys who disobey their parents.

LETTER TO GIDEON WELLES
NO DATE

Go it while you're young!

LETTER TO WILLIAM H. HERNDON
JULY 11, 1848

We have all heard of Young America. He is the most *current* youth of the age. Some think him conceited and arrogant; but has he not reason to entertain a rather extensive opinion of himself? Is he not the inventor and owner of the *present* and the sole hope of the future? . . . As Plato had for the immortality of the soul, so Young America has "a pleasing hope—a fond desire—a longing after" territory. He has a great passion—a perfect rage—

for the *"new"*; particularly new men for office, and the new earth mentioned in the Revelations, in which, being no more sea, there must be about three times as much land as in the present. He is a great friend of humanity; and his desire for land is not selfish, but merely an impulse to extend the area of freedom. He is very anxious to fight for the liberation of enslaved nations and colonies, provided, always, they *have* land and have *not* any liking for his interference. As to those who have no land, and would be glad of help from any quarter, he considers *they* can afford to wait a few hundred years longer. In knowledge he is particularly rich. He knows all that can possibly be known; inclines to believe in spiritual rappings, and is the unquestioned inventor of *"Manifest Destiny."* His horror is for all that is old, particularly "Old Fogy"; and if there be anything old which he can endure, it is only old whiskey and old tobacco.

SECOND LECTURE ON DISCOVERIES AND INVENTIONS,
JACKSONVILLE, ILLINOIS
FEBRUARY 11, 1859

# INDEX

Ability, confidence in my own, 62
Acquiescence, continuing the government is, 171
Act, unconstitutional, not a law, 147
Action, unanimity of, 171
Administration fails, if the war fails, 220
Advancement, chances of personal, 154
  in a society of equals, 103
Advice of a friend, 210
Amalgamation, indiscriminate, of the white and black races, 176
  only perfect preventive of, 176
Ambitious, within reasonable bounds, 13
Americans, all, are brothers, 18
Anarchy, secession is the essence of, 250
Animal, with a thorn in its vitals, 41
Anti-slavery, I am naturally, 232
Anxious, while I am, 137
Apple of gold, 151
Armies, all the, of Asia, Europe and Africa, 6
Army, save the, at all events, 37
Aspiration of men is to enjoy equality, 253
Assertion without knowing whether it is true, 2
Authority, public purpose to maintain, 209

Babel, the tower of, 67
Ballot, the appeal from the, to the bullet, 207

appeal from the, to the sword, 32
Ballots, peaceful, not bloody bullets, 254
Bargain, if you made a bad, 172
Battle, fight this, on principle, 234
Bible, burn the last copy of the, 1
Black man getting rich, 20
Blackberries, Major Generalships, not as plenty as, 12
Bloodshed, there needs to be no, 27
Books, the same in all places, 149
Burdens, cheerfully borne, 33

Cabbages, sprouting out, 205
Cage, why build a, 184
Campaign, little trappings of the, 213
Candidate, I would not be a, again, 212
Candles, blazed like tallow, 274
Capital, connection between, and labor, 143
  is only the fruit of labor, 144
Cause, doing what I can for the, 217
  if you would win a man to your, 248
Chance, you have another, in four years, 229
Character, weight of his, 2
Charity for all, 35
Chase, with the catching end the pleasures of the, 281
Chestnut, prove a horse, to be a chestnut horse, 169
Citizen, harsh feelings toward any, 18

Government, cannot have free, without elections, 83
cannot make men, 14
duty it owes the people, 16
has endured half slave and half free, 292
hazard all for the sake of destroying the, 31
I do not believe this, can endure permanently, 266
in support of, 10
interfere with slaves or slavery, 262
must be perpetuated, 231
must not undertake to run the churches, 22
of the people, 121
rests in public opinion, 239
right to rise up and shake the existing, 247
sustained, by all the churches, 23
tariff is to the, what a meal is to the family, 284
we must discard all, 139
worthy object of any good, 143
Governments, based on the denial of equal rights, 98
Great Britain, abolition of the slave trade by, 274
effecting our separation from, 54
people of, 7
we constantly condemn, 260
Grip, hold on with a bulldog, 129
Guerrillas, expel, 23

Habeas corpus might be suspended, 26
Habits of our whole species, 143
Harm, there is but little, I can do, 228
Haste, make, slowly, 21
Hearts, it is upon the brave, 10
History, repeal all past, 134
Hogs, no difference between, and Negroes, 186
Home, my childhood, 173
Honest, resolve to be, at all events, 149
Honors, I claim no insensibility to political, 6

never professed an indifference to, 154
pretending no indifference to earthly, 57
Hope, free labor has the inspiration of, 268
is gone, I will not say that all, 28
pure slavery has no, 268
ray of, is blown out in darkness, 188
Horn, sound your own, 181
Horse, prove a horse chestnut to be a chestnut, 169
Horses, swap, when crossing streams, 214
House divided against itself, 75
responsibility of pulling the, down, 75
Humanity, that immortal emblem of, 57
Hypocrisy, base alloy of, 99

Impedimenta, expanding and piling up of, 38
Independence, the maintenance of national, 127
Indifferent, the people are not, 224
Industry, encouragement to, 20
Injury, brood over the attempted, 2
Injustice, slavery is founded on, 255
Innocent, fall victims to the ravages of mob rule, 180
injure some who are, 104
Institutions, aim at the elevation of men, 25
free, in support of, 10
Insurrection, to suppress an, my duty, 29
Integrity, maintain its territorial, against its own domestics foes, 59
Intemperance, demon of, 168

Jealousy never did help any man, 283
Jewel, fair play is a, 108
Judge, I am a very indifferent, 14
I cannot pretend to be a, 14
I must myself be the, 19
Judgment, I have acted according to my best, 231

Morals, established maxim in, 2
one lesson in, 2
Motive to do otherwise, 133
Motives, easy and common to
ascribe, 51
Negroes, like other people, act
upon, 190
voluntary weighing of, 77
Murder, if I cannot rightfully, 106
Mutiny in the army, 130

Names, undistinguished mass of, 16
Napoleon's bulletins, bombastic and
hollow as, 18
Nation, conceived in liberty, 121
consist of its territory, its people,
and its laws, 225
lose the, yet preserve the Constitution, 49
Necessity, bow to, 265
Negro cannot be a citizen, 78
is not our equal in color, 102
oppressed condition of the, 25
power to make, a citizen, 24
woman for a slave, 177
Negroes, without making either
slaves or wives of, 177
Nomination, I shall accept the, 221

Oath, break my, 35
Offensive, placing one's self on the,
3
Office, an anxiety for, 213
I dislike to make changes in, 8
Officer, dismissed on suspicion of
disloyalty, 170
Opinion, differences of, 202
Opportunity, your golden, 40
Oppressions, most oppressive of all
kingly, 305
Outsiders, interference of, 140

Pains to be endured, 134
Parades, bombastic, 68
Parents, boys who disobey their,
310
Party man, bound as a, 220
Passion, recant whatever we may
have said in, 170
Patient man, I am a, 245
Patronage, in the dispensing of, 304

Paymasters, speculating, 10
Peace, more durable, 296
preservation of, 127
Penitentiaries, effectual, in prevent-
ing the crimes, 51
People, confidence and devotion of,
239
naturally divide into parties, 215
trust the, 81
People's business in their hands, 58
Perfection, aim as nearly as possible
at, 19
Perjury, witnesses may commit, 105
Perpetuity, law of all national gov-
ernments, 295
Picture, made for the apple, 151
Pigeon, boiling the shadow of a, 223
Pleasure, we have no, if we have
no friends, 117
Pleasures to be enjoyed, 134
Political questions, different views
on, 27
Politician, most distinguished, 141
Politics, do not mix, with your
profession, 13
in considering military merit, 12
Possession of the fairest portion of
the earth, 6
Poverty, those who toil up from,
116
Power, beware of surrendering a
political, 116
the political, 82
Powers of governments, 253
Prejudice, I have no, 258
they excite, 59
vote without fear or, 254
Presidency, I do not think myself
fit for the, 155
President, fail to elect a, 25
nobody has ever expected me to
be, 154
twice made of him, 141
Press, tight rein on the, 21
Pretense, I make no such hypocritical, 5
Principle, fought for the, 112
maintaining a, 69
Proficiency in industrial arts, 139
Property, rights of, 218
Public interest, dangerous to the, 22